ROMANTIC READERS AND
TRANSATLANTIC TRAVEL

Ashgate Series in Nineteenth-Century Transatlantic Studies

Series Editors: Kevin Hutchings and Julia M. Wright

Focusing on the long nineteenth century (ca. 1750–1900), this series offers a forum for the publication of scholarly work investigating the literary, historical, artistic, and philosophical foundations of transatlantic culture. A new and burgeoning field of interdisciplinary investigation, transatlantic scholarship contextualizes its objects of study in relation to exchanges, interactions, and negotiations that occurred between and among authors and other artists hailing from both sides of the Atlantic. As a result, transatlantic research calls into question established disciplinary boundaries that have long functioned to segregate various national or cultural literatures and art forms, challenging as well the traditional academic emphasis upon periodization and canonization. By examining representations dealing with such topics as travel and exploration, migration and diaspora, slavery, aboriginal culture, revolution, colonialism and anti-colonial resistance, the series will offer new insights into the hybrid or intercultural basis of transatlantic identity, politics, and aesthetics.

The editors invite English language studies focusing on any area of the long nineteenth century, including (but not limited to) innovative works spanning transatlantic Romantic and Victorian contexts. Manuscripts focusing on European, African, US American, Canadian, Caribbean, Central and South American, and Indigenous literature, art, and culture are welcome. We will consider proposals for monographs, collaborative books, and edited collections.

Romantic Readers and Transatlantic Travel

Expeditions and Tours in North America, 1760–1840

ROBIN JARVIS

University of the West of England, UK

ASHGATE

Published by
Ashgate Publishing Limited
Wey Court East
Union Road
Farnham
Surrey, GU9 7PT
England

Ashgate Publishing Company
Suite 420
101 Cherry Street
Burlington
VT 05401-4405
USA

www.ashgate.com

British Library Cataloguing in Publication Data
Jarvis, Robin, 1956–
   Romantic readers and transatlantic travel : expeditions and tours in North America, 1760–1840. – (Ashgate series in nineteenth-century transatlantic studies)
   1. North America – Description and travel – Sources. 2. North America – Foreign public opinion, British – History – 18th century. 3. North America – Foreign public opinion, British – History – 19th century. 4. North America – In literature. 5. Public opinion – Great Britain – History – 18th century. 6. Public opinion – Great Britain – History – 19th century.
   I. Title II. Series
   820.9'327'09033-dc23

Library of Congress Cataloging-in-Publication Data
Jarvis, Robin, 1956-
   Romantic readers and transatlantic travel: expeditions and tours in North America, 1760–1840 / by Robin Jarvis.
      p. cm. — (Ashgate series in nineteenth-century transatlantic studies)
   Includes bibliographical references and index.
   ISBN 978-0-7546-6860-2 (hardcover: alk. paper) — ISBN 978-0-7546-9517-2 (ebook)
   1. English literature—19th century—History and criticism. 2. Travelers' writings, English—History and criticism. 3. North America—Description and travel. I. Title.
   PR788.T72J37 2012
   820.9'355—dc23

                                                                    2012010834

ISBN: 9780754668602 (hbk)
ISBN: 9780754695172 (ebk)

MIX
Paper from responsible sources
FSC
www.fsc.org
FSC® C018575

Printed and bound in Great Britain by the MPG Books Group, UK.

In loving memory of my father
KENNETH JAMES JARVIS
1922-2012

Contents

List of Illustrations

Acknowledgements

It is a pleasure to acknowledge the support provided by the School of Humanities, Languages, and Social Sciences at the University of the West of England (UWE), and by the Arts and Humanities Research Council, who together funded a year's research leave and allowed me to complete this project in a timely and enjoyable manner.

Colleagues at UWE who have helped in various, equally indispensable, ways include Gill Ballinger, Bill Greenslade, Peter Rawlings, and Kerry Sinanan. I am grateful to them all.

Ann Donahue at Ashgate – prompt, efficient, and accommodating beyond reasonable expectations – has shown how fruitful transatlantic relationships can be. I am grateful for her faith in my initial proposal and for her help throughout the writing process.

I have also been fortunate in my dealings with librarians and other staff at various institutions along the way. I would particularly like to offer thanks to Nicholas Cooper in the St Matthias Library at UWE, Colin Harris at the Bodleian, Stuart Malcolm at the National Library of Scotland, Graham Sheriff at the Beinecke, Gayle Richardson at the Huntington Library, Jeff Cowton and Alex Black at The Wordsworth Trust, and Gudrun Miller at the Tate.

David Allan, Heather Jackson, and William St Clair have been generous and patient in their replies to unsolicited emails, and I have benefited from their advice, just as I have drawn inspiration from their published work.

As ever, my greatest personal debt is to Carol Jarvis, whose love and support have kept me going throughout.

Robin Jarvis
University of the West of England

Introduction

The bicentenary of the French Revolution in 1789 fixated Romantic studies for ten to fifteen years, so that the only material and imaginative relations that appeared to matter were those defined by the English Channel. However, the rise of transatlantic Romanticism, in deflecting scholarly attention to connections and exchanges across a much larger expanse of water, has begun to complicate further what was already a deeply fractured and heavily contested narrative of this rich period in British literary history. As the editors of an anthology that marks its establishment as a field argue, whereas literatures have traditionally been studied as single-nation stories, the 'international community of thought and feeling we now call Romanticism' (Newman 9) is best appreciated on a much larger canvas, with a particular focus on the interdependencies, mutual awarenesses, and influences among Britain, the United States, and Canada during the late eighteenth and early nineteenth centuries. In an excellent programmatic overview of the field, Joel Pace suggests that transatlantic Romanticism is best served by a diversity of approaches, and that research should not be limited 'to authors, works, and objects that cross the Atlantic,' but might also embrace people 'aware of distant lands (that border the Atlantic) but removed from personal contact' (238). The present book, which examines the reception of travel books on the United States, Canada, and the Arctic archipelago by British readers, the vast majority of whom never made a transatlantic crossing, is written in the spirit of that manifesto.

How and why did people read travel literature in the Romantic period, and to what extent did different classes or communities of readers read in different ways? How, in particular, did readers respond to the copious literature relating to North America produced by explorers, travellers, emigrants, and tourists, and how should we contextualize these responses with respect to the broader contours of British society and culture and to the unstable ground of transatlantic relations? Did writers of poetry and prose fiction, who made plentiful use of travel literature, read the latter any differently to other consumers? In general, what does the British reception of North American travel narratives tell us about the imagining of America in the period that witnessed, according to one historian, the birth of the 'special relationship' (Johnson 41–3)? Answering these and related questions should add to our knowledge of travel literature, at a formative time in the evolution of that genre, contribute to the history of reading (most studies of literary reception to date have been preoccupied with the major literary genres of poetry, fiction, and drama), and shed new light on the growth of transatlantic interests and perspectives during a particularly turbulent period in Anglo-American relations.

The travel books I am concerned with in the chapters that follow are exclusively those that publishers, booksellers, and the reading public of the Romantic era understood as falling within the category of 'voyages and travels.' Essentially, this means factual accounts of real travels, whatever the precise form or style adopted (narrative or journal, for example).[1] Of course, the boundary between fictional and true travels had been a fluid one for centuries – a situation that Swift, for example, had humorously exploited in *Gulliver's Travels*, which places imaginary lands in more or less real geographic locations. Nevertheless, Enlightenment science and the complementary imperatives of imperial and epistemological expansion demanded a clearer separation of travel fiction and travel fact, and 'voyages and travels' as a classification became firmly aligned with the latter. It is the reception of these kinds of books that I intend to explore, rather than the many other contemporary forms of writing that incorporated travel themes or travel experiences. Byron's *Childe Harold's Pilgrimage* is in part a record of the author's wanderings on the Continent, but it is not travel writing as the early nineteenth-century literary marketplace construed the term. I am interested in poets and novelists only insofar as they were avid readers of factual travel writing, and drew on it in demonstrable ways in their creative output; this will be the main focus of Chapter 4, which will consider several major writers as 'end-users' of documentary travels.

I have already made clear that I am interpreting 'transatlantic travel' to refer to travel to and within North America. The modern concept of transatlanticism betokens, of course, a much larger and more complex circuit involving movements and exchanges (of people and ideas) among the Americas, Europe, and Africa. My own narrower application of the term to specific reading relations between Britain, the United States, and Canada is governed by practical more than theoretical or ideological considerations. The empirical challenges of the project – to gather scarce records of private reading experiences of the travel genre in the Romantic period, as well as to survey a vast corpus of formal reviews in the periodical press – were formidable enough without further broadening the geographical frame or attempting to assimilate other national readerships and cultures. When British readers in the late eighteenth and early nineteenth centuries invoked the 'transatlantic,' it was invariably with reference to North America – unsurprisingly in view of the two countries' closely interwoven histories. Assessing readers' responses to these particular textual American imports – examining, that is, how they sifted, sorted, interpreted, and evaluated the relentless flow of information and images from the United States and Canada – may seem like a parochial reduction of transatlanticism to modern eyes, but it is a relatively manageable form of scholarly labour and reflects the preoccupations of the historical readers I have studied.

---

[1]   I am, of course, aware of the complexity of modern debates on the generic status of travel writing, which most critics recognize as an unstable, hybrid category. Jan Borm argues that while travel writing or travel literature are best seen as collections of diverse writings, the 'travel book' or 'travelogue' can be more narrowly defined as 'any narrative characterized by a non-fiction dominant that relates (almost always) in the first person a journey or journeys that the reader supposes to have taken place in reality while assuming or presupposing that author, narrator and principal character are but one or identical' (17). This definition, inevitably a hostage to fortune, in fact profiles reasonably well the travel writing I am concerned with in this study.

Studying readers, the so-called 'missing link' of book history (Finkelstein 100), is no straightforward task. Although the 'return of the reader' has been a major feature of the critical scene for more than twenty years,[2] she or he has returned in a bewildering variety of forms. Roger Chartier, in a book published in 1994, argues that a serious student of reading ought to pay attention to both 'texts in their discursive and material forms' (as part of a broadly sociological approach to readers as consumers of print products) and 'readings, understood as concrete practices and as procedures of interpretation' (2). In actuality, as scholarly interest in readers and reading has grown, two major fields of enquiry have developed on parallel lines, never meeting and rarely communicating. One is theory-driven and largely resistant to contextualisation or empirical specification; the other is unashamedly empirical and takes pride in its committed historicism.

On the one hand, Anglo-American reader-response criticism and theory, which came into prominence in the 1970s and was neatly packaged and summarized in Jane Tompkins's 1980 essay collection, typically invokes an abstract or ideal reader whose operations are programmed by the text itself, and it makes little acknowledgement of ways in which those operations vary under specific social and historical circumstances. Stanley Fish uses the analogy of transformational grammar to talk of readers who perform these operations as 'informed readers' possessing both linguistic and, more importantly, literary 'competence.' 'Each of us,' Fish declares, 'if we are sufficiently responsible and self-conscious, can, in the course of employing the method, become the informed reader and therefore be a more reliable reporter of his experience' ('Literature' 49). It is not clear how one knows when one is sufficiently informed and responsible, or at what point one's readings graduate to reliability. In Fish's early criticism, the New Critics' artefactual notion of the text as a structure of words and formal devices, built to last, may have yielded to a focus on the temporal structure of the reader's experience, but the reader in question comes across as a sophisticated and scholarly navel-gazer attending too minutely to his or her cognitive journey through a line of blank verse to bother about how readers at other times and in other places might have done things differently.

Wolfgang Iser, perhaps the name most closely associated with reader-response theory, rejects Fish's informed reader because the concept departs from its linguistic base and strays into an inaccessible subjective domain; he also finds Michael Riffaterre's 'superreader' and Erwin Wolff's 'intended reader' unsatisfactory as heuristic devices. Neither is he very interested in what he calls the more traditional categories of the '"real" reader, known to us by his documented reactions,' and the 'hypothetical reader,' subdivided into the 'ideal reader' and 'contemporary reader' (27). Iser seems to concede a limited value to the 'real reader' in studying the 'history of responses,' while pointing out that in the absence of documented responses one is forced to reconstruct a hypothetical contemporary reader, on the

---

[2]   As discussed in Elizabeth Freund's *The Return of the Reader: Reader-Response Criticism* (London: Methuen, 1987).

basis either of social and historical context or of 'what can be gleaned from the literary works themselves' (28). The ideal reader, on the other hand, is dismissed as a figment of the critic's imagination, worthless chiefly because of the inability of any such creature 'to realize in full the meaning potential of the fictional text,' irrespective of historical circumstances (29). To crush any speculation that he has exhausted all possible types of reader, Iser then produces his own, preferred concept: the 'implied reader.' This he defines as 'a textual structure anticipating the presence of a recipient without necessarily defining him' (34), a curious formulation that sounds a long way from any reader one might bump into in the library or bookshop. What it represents is Iser's effort to acknowledge the variability of interpretation of a text over time, and the freedom readers enjoy to 'actualize' the potential of a text in ways personal to themselves, but at the same time to insist that those varied actualizations, produced in diverse historical circumstances, are nonetheless 'prestructured' by the text itself. The real reader can fulfil the role of the implied reader in different ways, but 'the structure of the text *allows* for different ways of fulfillment' (37).

Iser's theory has been criticized by Marxists and poststructuralists, but it does at least make some kind of sense when applied to the complex, multi-perspectival eighteenth- and nineteenth-century novels he favours in his case studies. In relation to the less verbally sophisticated world of Romantic-era travel literature, however, its applicability is less obvious: is it really appropriate or productive to speak of the travel reader as 'a network of response-inviting structures' (34)? It is interesting, though, how often Iser relies upon travel metaphors to describe the reading experience: he states, for example, that 'As the reader passes through the various perspectives offered by the text and relates the different views and patterns to one another he sets the work in motion, and so sets himself in motion too' (21). My aim in this book is to find out as much as possible about the 'real readers' (of travel literature) that Iser marginalizes in favour of his transcendental alternative, but there is an element of freedom – a sense of active reception – in this notion of a travelling reader that is worth holding onto.

In the hands of Hans Robert Jauss, reception theory presents itself as more clearly historically oriented than with Iser or Fish, in that he conceives of literature as a 'dialogue between work and public' in which literary works display different faces to readers in successive periods. His seminal essay, 'Literary History as a Challenge to Literary Theory,' argues that readers assimilate a new work by comparing it with other works with which they are familiar, in a continuous process of horizon setting and horizon changing; reconstructing the contemporary horizon of expectations 'enables us to find the questions to which the text originally answered and thereby to discover how the reader of that day viewed and understood the work' (*Towards* 68, 74). Unlike Iser, Jauss sees the different interpretations of a work produced by successive generations of readers as building upon each other: individual responses do not 'reciprocally falsify each other' but coalesce in an 'enrichment of understanding,' and 'testify to the historically progressive concretization of meaning' (185, 187).

From the point of view of my own interest in the reception of travel writing, Jauss's approach is less helpful than at first appears. He applies the influential concept of a horizon of expectations chiefly to the intraliterary framework of genre and literary tradition within which new literary texts are said to stake out their meaning: his focus is on measuring 'aesthetic distance,' the degree of discrepancy between dominant tastes and conventions and the mould-breaking newcomer.[3] By contrast, Romantic-era travel literature rarely strives for aesthetic distinction or seeks to challenge its readers' preconceptions purely in terms of their customary associations with the genre. If it presumes to 'revise' its predecessors, it invariably does so in order to correct errors, fill in gaps in existing knowledge, or supply more accurate observations, and will aim to present its own version of 'reality' in a way that carries conviction. Its stylistic protocols place no emphasis on originality but instead prioritize plain, matter-of-fact, reportorial language, shorn of rhetorical ornament. The extent to which its contemporary readers shared these biases (or whether, alternatively, they valued those rare works of travel that genuinely challenged their expectations of the genre) cannot be determined purely through formal analysis of the texts themselves; instead, contrary to Jauss's cheerful disregard of empirical testimony, it is imperative to recover and respect such records of 'actual reception' as diligent research can bring to light.

The reader postulated by reader-response and reception theories therefore seems too abstract, supercompetent, or genre-limited to be of much use for a study of travel literature and its audience. There exists, however, a very different tradition of reader-oriented research – namely, the large and impressive body of interdisciplinary work produced under the umbrella of book history. Once again, very little of this work is directly related to the literature of travel and exploration; in addition, much of the really influential research has been focused on the national literatures of France and Germany, countries where the cultural and political circumstances were (and are) very different to those in Britain. This does not, of course, render such contributions worthless, but it does mean that applying their insights to the British literary marketplace can only be done with caution. As a broad field of research, history of the book has become such a jungle of ancillary disciplines that, as Robert Darnton has wittily observed, the average critic or scholar is tempted simply 'to retire to a rare book room and count watermarks' (*Kiss* 110); but even in the sub-area of book history concerned with the history of reading, the number of discrete topics and approaches is daunting. In Darnton's view, a great deal of effort has gone into excavating the 'external history of reading,' or answering 'the "who," "what," "where," and "when" questions' (*Kiss* 157), but the 'whys' and 'hows' are more elusive. It is nearly thirty years since he wrote this essay, but the observation probably still stands up. Researching the more straightforward (albeit time- and labour-consuming) 'external' questions has produced a wealth of information about many factors bearing on the size and

---

[3]   In this respect, Jauss is, ironically, as James L. Machor has observed, 'More concerned with production than with response' (ix).

composition of historical readerships, including print runs, pricing, sales figures, distribution networks, subscription lists, different types of libraries and book clubs and their contents, memberships, and lending practices, and so on. Important as these studies are, they invariably seem remote from the experience of actual readers. In terms of those more challenging 'why' and 'how' questions, one is battling against the intrinsic ephemerality of reading – a practice that, as Chartier states, 'only rarely leaves traces, that is scattered in an infinity of singular acts, and that easily shakes off all constraints' (1–2). The student of Romantic-era reading practices usually has to make do with sweeping generalizations about trends and transformations: a 'reading revolution' that replaced 'intensive' with 'extensive' reading, a shift from public, collective reading experiences to a more solitary, private activity, and a related development from oralization to silent, visual reading.[4] But what of individual readers and their reading experiences?

In the most weighty and iconoclastic modern study of the 'reading nation' in this period, the sheer difficulty of gathering the fugitive records of individual reading experiences, as well as the imponderable question of how to contextualize and interpret them, leads William St Clair to dismiss their relevance to a meaningful history of reading. Such 'micro evidence,' St Clair argues, may be completely unrepresentative of the majority of readers and needs to be compared with the macro evidence of a systematic economic analysis if it is to be used at all. 'To help to understand and trace the possible effects of reading on mentalities,' he insists, 'we need to trace historic reading' (42), by which he means the books that were most frequently reproduced and most widely available at the time, not those that have come to be synonymous with the period as far as modern literary criticism is concerned.

With the aid of extensive research into publishers' and printers' archives, book trade catalogues, and the records of libraries and book clubs, and by assembling detailed information on print runs, prices, and sales, this is what St Clair has tried to establish. The 'layering of readership by time,' by which readers in different socioeconomic groups 'read different texts at intervals of different lengths from the time they were first written' (40), is one of the most prominent features of his survey. Of fundamental importance to his analysis is the legal ruling of 1774 that abolished perpetual copyright: before the term of copyright was successively extended in 1808, 1814, and 1842, there came into existence what St Clair calls a 'copyright window,' during which cheap, smaller-format editions and anthologies of many classic British writers, along with cheap reprints of selected works in other genres, such as conduct manuals and didactic literature, came within direct reach of a much larger segment of the population as the 'minimum price of access' fell to a quarter of its previous level (116). St Clair calls this newly enfranchised

---

[4]   In recent years, all these alleged developments have been re-examined, and the general narrative has been qualified, complicated, and, almost certainly, brought closer to reality. It now seems likely that intensive and extensive reading habits complemented each other during the Romantic period, and that reading was at times a gregarious and sociable pleasure, at others a more self-absorbed pursuit.

body of work the 'old canon,' and crucially it was literature with an essentially conservative ethos, dominated by imagery of rural England, patriotic sentiments, domestic affections, traditional Christian morality, and natural religion: in the hands of people inducted to the book-buying community for the first time, it 'offered a Counter-Enlightenment to readers who knew nothing of the Enlightenment' (134).

Well outside the homely environs of this old canon, it is worth noting, were the handsomely produced and expensive new works of travel and exploration, vehicles of the Enlightenment *par excellence*, that earned a comfortable profit for publishers at the top end of the market. High prices, small sales, restricted access is the relentless logic of St Clair's argument: the reading public may have been expanding, but, with its notions of 'abroad' shaped chiefly by works like *Robinson Crusoe* and *Gulliver's Travels*, its mental horizons in a crucial sense were not. St Clair's thesis is that the old canon 'reached far more deeply into the reading nation than any texts actually written during the period' (138), helping to constitute and reinforce an 'official mainstream ideology' (269) that all readers would have recognized, if not embraced, and against which the more heterodox Romantic literature that modern readers value would have had to define itself. Although St Clair denies wishing to imply that such an ideology 'was always assented to or practised even by those to whom it most appealed' (269), almost despite himself he conveys the impression that a conservative, introverted, pietistic atmosphere hung over the Romantic period like the darkness of an Arctic winter, against which the occasional rebelliousness of a Byron or Shelley appeared as no more than temporary phosphorescence. What seems overlooked in this account, despite St Clair's occasional allusions to 'readerly autonomy' (5) and the possibility of 'reading against the grain' (373), is precisely a convincing sense of diverse readers having diverse reading experiences – reading sceptically or disapprovingly in some cases, perhaps lazily or inattentively in others, but just as likely to be reading *actively* as passively.

The attraction of reader-response theory is precisely that it features an active reader, who makes meanings out of texts, although the reader in question is at best idealized (taken out of history, shorn of social and gender identity) and at worst a mere doppelgänger of the critic; furthermore, his or her creative freedom is often less real than at first appears (individual customers navigating their own way around the supermarket aisles is a fair analogy). History of the book, by contrast, is empirical in approach, but its centre of gravity lies in macro rather than micro analysis, and it seems more comfortable speaking of communities or constituencies of readers than of individuals and their reading experiences. One valuable aspect of book history, though, is its attention to the material history of texts and its interest in books as physical artefacts rather than disembodied sequences of words. In studying the 'voyages and travels' genre in the Romantic period, it is impossible to ignore what Jerome McGann calls the 'bibliographical codes' (78) of the luxurious quarto volumes in which such narratives frequently first appeared, or deny D. F. McKenzie's claim that 'the material forms of books, the non-verbal elements of the typographic notations within them, the very disposition of space itself, have an expressive function in conveying meaning' (31). If the surging output of travel and exploration literature in this period encouraged readers, in St Clair's words, to take 'all geography and all history into their consciousness,' so that 'there was nothing in the world which the British did not feel was partly their own' (233–4), the high prices and production values of such books conveyed the message that this expanded consciousness was the preserve of a tiny elite. I shall argue that this imaginative apartheid was by no means as absolute as the economic analysis would imply, but there is no doubt that accessing these textual 'realms of gold' (to borrow Keats's phrase) was a lot easier for some readers than for the majority.

In his much-cited essay, 'First Steps toward a History of Reading,' Robert Darnton summarizes five approaches to those difficult 'how' and 'why' questions concerning historical readers. These approaches are:

1. Researching the assumptions underlying reading in the past, through representations of reading in documents of various types;
2. Studying how reading was learned, whether in schools or elsewhere;
3. Studying autobiographical accounts of actual reading experiences, in published or unpublished forms;
4. Addressing the problem through literary theory, as in reader-response criticism; and
5. Analytical bibliography, or studying books as physical objects.[5]

In the chapters that follow, I employ a mix of these approaches, although my methodology is fundamentally empirical, and I lean towards the third of Darnton's lines of enquiry. I believe it is important to find out what 'real readers' had to say about travel literature, and this kind of research has never been attempted in a systematic or thoroughgoing way. Chapter 1 focuses, accordingly, on the recovery of personal accounts of reading experiences of American travels from a variety of sources. Here I lay the groundwork for a comparison of private and public responses, and I consider class and gender factors. I show that readings of North American travels ranged widely between purely recreational encounters and more reflective or interrogative modes of engagement and that private readers' responses typically had very little overt political content. Although the readers I quote manifest certain assumptions or dispositions that clearly link them to the textual orientation of professional reviewers, I argue that the distinctive element in the archive of private reading experiences is an emphasis on the pleasures of imaginative transport.

In Chapter 2, which concentrates on the United States, I make the case for taking periodical reviews seriously as evidence of contemporary reception, and I highlight their importance in disseminating awareness of the latest travels and explorations. Although the format and style of Romantic-era reviews – whether the modestly sized, quotation-heavy reviews typical of eighteenth-century journals, or the expansive, opinionated articles pioneered by the new quarterlies – tend

---

[5]   See Darnton, *Kiss* 171–85.

to attract patronizing comment from modern critics, I argue that their approach to travel writing was in some ways very congenial to the reading mentalities of the period and that the practice of generous excerpting, in particular, served this genre particularly well. As opposed to the common assumption of a pervasive anti-Americanism in the press at this time, I try to show that professional readers generally did not share the petty-minded nationalistic bias of most British travellers; and while there were particular times, and particular issues (notably emigration), that served to politicize reviews and polarize attitudes, in the main reviewers worked to well-established literary and aesthetic criteria and shadowed their readers' presumed curiosity about the transatlantic continent and its inhabitants.

Chapter 3 shifts the focus to British North America, a loose and somewhat anachronistic designation which covers not only the established colonies of Upper and Lower Canada but also the vast territories to the north and west that were steadily opened up by fur traders, along with the Arctic coastline and archipelago. I show that the reception of travels and explorations in these parts of North America worked a very different repertoire of topics to that which I unpacked in the previous chapter: in one extended case study, for example, I discuss the reasons for the extraordinary prominence of natural history in representations of Canada, and the impact that this had on readers. As with travels in the United States, reader responses were, on the face of it, predominantly curiosity-driven, but could be overtaken by issues in the public realm that aroused strong collective passions. In the reception of Arctic exploration narratives, in particular, the intense delights of mental transport got closely entwined with patriotic self-esteem and a proud sense of national destiny. With particular reference to two major fur traders' narratives, I also highlight in this chapter the dissonance between historic reading experiences and modern postcolonial critiques, thus emphasizing the need to assess Romantic readers' responses and judgements within their contemporary horizon of expectations.

Finally, in Chapter 4 I take up the more specialized topic of how Romantic poets and novelists read, interpreted, and recycled American travels. There were, I argue, clear affinities between the interests of these literary end-users and those of the professional and recreational readers surveyed in previous chapters. In other ways, though, the six poets on whom I focus varied greatly in their reading strategies, from ruthless filtering or highly selective attention at one extreme, to equally active, yet reflective and constructive forms of engagement, at the other. In this chapter, I highlight the prominent role in certain poems of the prose footnote cross-referencing poetic images with quotations from factual travel accounts. I thus introduce another distinctive form of evidence (of reading experiences) alongside the public and private sources studied in earlier chapters. In this way, I hope to strengthen my response to the call made by James Raven, Helen Small, and Naomi Tadmor for a variable methodology capable of reconstructing (plausibly) 'not just what materials people read in the past, but how they read them, why they read them and, wherever possible, what it meant to them' (15).

In that same essay, Raven and his co-authors make clear the special significance of the fugitive records of individual acts of reading to this larger enterprise: elusive as it is, such evidence shows that reading 'can be highly individualistic – culturally conditioned, certainly, but not in any easy sense reducible to a cultural norm' (15). This is a crucial point to bear in mind given the trajectory of modern criticism of travel writing over the past twenty to thirty years. Since the revival of interest in the genre, the agenda has to a large extent been set by feminist criticism, on the one hand (there have been major advances in republication and anthologization of early women's travel writing, as well as significant studies of female travellers and related gender-oriented criticism), and postcolonial studies, on the other. The latter field has been strongly drawn to travel literature for the obvious reason of the prominence within it of encounters and relationships between developed and undeveloped cultures and their official or unofficial representatives. The tone was set by Edward Said's seminal critique of Orientalism as 'a Western style for dominating, restructuring, and having authority over the Orient' that came to the fore in the late eighteenth century, and in the service of which travel books had an important role in promoting a 'textual attitude' towards 'relatively unknown and threatening' peoples and places, often creating 'not only knowledge but also the very reality they appear to describe' (3, 93–4).

Even more influential, perhaps, because of its sophisticated close readings of travel texts from the eighteenth and nineteenth centuries, has been Mary Louise Pratt's *Imperial Eyes* (1992), which looks at how 'travel and exploration writing *produced* "the rest of the world" for European readerships at particular points in Europe's expansionist trajectory' (5), thereby implicating its sedentary readers in the profit and guilt of that enterprise. Pratt is especially illuminating about travel writings on Africa and South America, not least about the representational strategies they deploy to mask the disparate ways in which they exert discursive authority. However, the cumulative effect of her readings is to construct an omnipotent, monolithic 'text of Euroimperialism' (2), and her inattention to the readers of travel literature means that the latter cannot help but appear as helpless associates in the project of colonial expansion and exploitation. I have sympathy with Steve Clark's critique of Pratt, notably his argument that she glosses over the 'ramshackle' and precarious nature of much early colonial activity, and that her Foucauldian power thesis erases not only countless variations in the practice of empire but also the distinctions between different elements within European societies (where the material benefits of empire were anything but evenly distributed) and different communities of readers. Clark concedes that postcolonial criticism, with its sweeping denunciations of travel writing as a toxic residue of Western hegemony, has been largely responsible for raising the genre's profile on bookshelves and syllabuses and making it interesting for a new generation of critics – 'usually,' he notes, 'as a kind of love that dare not speak its name' (3). This is more than a wickedly ironic aside: it begs serious questions of why so much critical energy has been invested in what is often no more than a 'ritual indictment' of the values and purportedly malign influence of a genre that the critics themselves clearly find abhorrent.

Clark urges that Pratt's (virtually non-existent) 'reception argument' should be 'pinned down far more closely (particularly the class and gender of audiences)'

(8), although it is not his business to pursue this brief himself. It is, however, part of what I am trying to do in this book, in the specific context of travel writings on North America. I want to challenge the assumption, latent in much criticism, that the historical reader of travel literature was a passive and unquestioning recipient of whatever retrograde ideas and values our enlightened twenty-first-century outlook detects and deplores in the stories told by that generation of travellers. Jonathan Rose has aptly dubbed such an approach the 'receptive fallacy' – that is, affecting 'to discern the influence of a text on an audience simply by examining the text' ('How Historians' 209). Michel de Certeau, in a well-known essay from *The Practice of Everyday Life*, makes a similar point, rejecting the notion that consuming books means '"becoming similar to" what one absorbs' (166). Interestingly, de Certeau reaches for the metaphor of travel to express the 'silent, transgressive, ironic or poetic activity' (172) of ordinary readers: whereas writers, he suggests, can be viewed as pioneers, settlers establishing textual property out of the wilderness of language, readers are latter-day travellers, moving 'across lands belonging to someone else, like nomads poaching their way across fields they did not write' (174). I find the idea of Romantic readers poaching their way across the wilderness of North American travel texts, discovering their own pleasures, and placing their own emphases more appealing than the model of uncritical consumers seeing the world through the imperial eyes of untouchable authors.

I want to begin my enquiry, therefore, by introducing my own 'ramshackle' assembly of individual Romantic readers' responses to travel texts, drawing on evidence wherever it can be found, in autobiographies, diaries, letters, journals, commonplace books, reading notes, marginalia, and so on. These sources all require careful handling, since none can be taken to present totally unmediated personal testimony, and considerations of purpose and potential audience always need to be borne in mind. Nevertheless, I endorse the view expressed by Heather Jackson, whose painstaking studies of books with manuscript notes have been an inspiration for this project, that empirical study of this nature, or on this scale, is far from pointless. As Jackson says, the sources we have, or can gather through laborious research, are real, and we should not avoid dealing with them: although they cannot guarantee us 'the ever-elusive holy grail of the historian of reading, the mental experience of the individual reader' (251), they can edge us closer to that goal. In a defence of manuscript study, Darnton writes of the importance of manuscripts in complicating the tidy pictures we have formed of the past, keeping the kaleidoscope turning with the addition of new ingredients – not under any epistemological delusion that we can 'get back' to what really happened, but always with the hope that we can 'deepen, freshen, and rethink' our understanding of events ('Seven Bad Reasons' 38). In the same spirit, the scarce records of individual reading experiences from two centuries ago point to 'a world of messiness, strewn with inconsistencies, overgrown with contradictions' – a world, however, that rings true – through which the literary scholar, like Darnton's historian, must hack his or her way, pursuing, in his elegant phrase, the 'scent of vanished humanity' (42).

Chapter 1
Reading North America

The subject of this book is the impact on British readers in the late eighteenth and early nineteenth centuries of travel and exploration literature produced about North America. In this chapter, I begin my enquiry by gathering and scrutinizing evidence of public interest in the 'transatlantic continent,' and records of private reading experiences of North American travels, from a heterogeneous array of letters, diaries, and other autobiographical sources. The underlying premise of this investigation is that in the Romantic period a keen appetite for knowledge of foreign places and peoples was fed to a very large extent by the literary genre known to contemporary readers as 'voyages and travels.' That the reading public, most of whom were armchair travellers or whose expeditions were limited to Britain or a well-trodden western European itinerary, should take a particular interest in books about North America should be no surprise given the close historical ties, the uneasy and sometimes fractious political relationship, and the mesmerizing spectacle of apparently unstoppable growth on the other side of the Atlantic. Before delving into the primary material, it might be worth providing a brief overview of this most turbulent period in Anglo-American relations.

1776 and all that

Huge changes did, indeed, take place in North America during the years covered by this study. The population of the United States grew from around three and a half million at the end of the War of Independence (as compared with a British population of nearly ten million) to more than seventeen million in 1840, at which point its human resources began to outstrip those of the mother country. Territorially its growth was just as impressive: between 1783, when it took possession of the entire territory east of the Mississippi and south of the Great Lakes, and 1840 the United States doubled in size by means of the Louisiana Purchase[1] and the acquisition of Florida. As for British North America, there were no more than 350,000 European settlers (over half of them of French descent) inhabiting what remained of Britain's transatlantic colonies at the end of the eighteenth century, but this figure was approaching two million by 1840. Most of

---

[1]   The Louisiana Purchase, covering all or part of fourteen modern American states, increased the size of the United States by a million square miles, all for what now seems a paltry $15 million. Napoleon, faced with renewing the war against Great Britain after the Peace of Amiens and discouraged by his failure to suppress the slave rebellion in Haiti, decided it was politically expedient to sell a vast territory he would be unable to occupy or defend.

the population continued to reside in the St Lawrence and Great Lakes basin, but British territorial possessions were vast, comprising 'Rupert's Land,' the private landholding of the Hudson's Bay Company, and the wilderness further west which explorers and fur traders steadily penetrated, helping to define the boundaries of the future Canadian nation-state.

Politically and economically the changes were equally dramatic. The Seven Years' War, in which France and Austria fought an alliance of Britain and Prussia in both Europe and the colonies, saw France driven out of North America completely, permanently altering the balance of power. The assimilation into the British Empire of large numbers of Catholic French speakers, and the need to effect some kind of *rapprochement* with existing French laws and institutions, created formidable problems. Between 1763 and 1774 Quebec lacked any kind of representative assembly because the British government could not decide what form of governance to institute. The Quebec Act of 1774 then controversially recognized the Catholic Church, maintained French civil law, and effectively consolidated the existing elite, whilst implementing tight executive control via the Governor and an appointed Council. In 1791 a Constitutional Act divided Quebec into Lower and Upper Canada (the latter comprising present-day southern Ontario), Upper Canada to be ruled by British law and Lower Canada retaining the French system; limited democracy was introduced with a House of Assembly in both provinces. Despite the concessions to their institutions and culture, French Canadians remained suspicious that the new imperial power was bent on Anglicizing them, and this was certainly William Pitt's ultimate intention, but the outbreak of war with France gave him more pressing things to worry about. The result was that from 1763 to 1815 and beyond, British North America was, in the words of Peter Marshall, 'governed largely by default' (392), and in fact the next major constitutional change was the 1840 Act of Union that merged Upper and Lower Canada into a single political entity.

The central event interrupting this muddled history was, of course, the American Revolution. Parliament's attempt to tax the colonies to make them pay part of the cost of their own defence, and the fundamental questions this raised about principles of governance, in particular the relationship between the imperial centre and colonial peoples that had become used to managing their own affairs, created a volatile situation which resulted in the rebellion of the Thirteen Colonies (only Quebec, Nova Scotia, Newfoundland, and St John's Island stayed loyal), seven years of armed struggle, and the declaration and ultimately recognition of American independence. The associated adoption of an ideology of universal human rights meant that Americans endowed these developments with, Howard Temperley suggests,' a significance quite out of proportion to their [then] position in the world and the wrongs they had endured' (Temperley 10). The political legacy was soon evident in the French Revolution, which was to divert Britain's attention from the trauma of a defeat compared by some (in terms of the blow to national self-esteem) to the United States' failure in Vietnam nearly two hundred years later.[2]

The post-war settlement was favourable to the United States, which secured an unexpectedly large territorial expanse in return for agreeing to settle pre-Revolutionary debts and compensate Loyalists whose property had been seized during the conflict. These undertakings were problematic because at this stage the United States was no more than a loose confederation of states whose future cohesion and sustainability was in some doubt – indeed, the likely break-up of the union was a constant theme in the British press for several decades. It was for this reason, among others, that Britain initially (and controversially) continued to occupy a number of forts on what had become American soil. However, the implementation in 1788 of a new Constitution, which created a strong central government with tax-raising powers, and the establishment of a national currency, put the infant republic on a firmer footing, and most outstanding issues between the two countries were resolved by Jay's Treaty in 1794. This included progress on, but not final resolution of, the thorny question of trading relations. Whereas the United States had looked on independence as an opportunity to escape from the mercantilist system that had shackled its commerce, a hostile House of Commons saw no need to give the rebellious colonists a helping hand and passed a new Navigation Act that 'specifically denied the ships of the United States access to trade with Britain or her overseas territories' (Conway 344). Although Jay's Treaty made concessions to the United States in this area and stimulated trade in the short term, the passage to a fully free-trade environment remained a long and turbulent one.

Even before Jay's Treaty was negotiated, Britain had gone to war with revolutionary France, a generation-long conflict which would cause immense collateral damage to Anglo-American relations. France had supported the American colonies in the War of Independence, so it was no surprise that the United States initially welcomed a Revolution that it saw as the legitimate offspring of its own struggle. But just as the tide of British opinion turned in response to the September Massacres, the execution of Louis XVI and the inauguration of the Terror, so the progress of the Revolution highlighted divisions in the United States cabinet, pitting a more radical, Francophile Jeffersonian faction against Alexander Hamilton's Federalist grouping, which admired the British political system. To begin with, President Washington was determined to maintain neutrality, resisting French overtures aimed at calling in debts from its erstwhile ally, but this became more difficult once Britain started seizing American vessels trading with ports in the French Caribbean. As Howard Temperley observes, this ushered in 'a wrangle over maritime rights that was to bedevil Anglo-American relations throughout the nineteenth century and beyond' (25). The picture was further complicated when France, angered at the Americans' apparent ingratitude, began seizing their

---

[2]   Linda Colley, for one, sees merit in the analogy between these two 'David and Goliath' conflicts (153–4).

vessels herself, and it was France with whom the United States first engaged in open hostilities. With this dispute seemingly resolved by the time Jefferson took up residence in the White House, it was the Americans' relationship with Britain that became the next casualty of European affairs. Britain's economic sanctions against France, sharpened by the notorious Orders in Council of November 1807 and mirrored by French actions,[3] had a devastating impact on neutral shipping; Britain compounded its offence, in American eyes, by its high-handed policy of boarding American vessels and 'impressing' into military service anyone its officers claimed was a British deserter. In retaliation, America's own economic sanctions unfortunately punished herself more than her enemy, and a series of miscalculations and misunderstandings of similar magnitude led eventually to the War of 1812 – a 'confused and inconsequential affair ... with neither side able to sustain an advantage': although both sides scored successes – the British captured Washington and torched the White House, the Americans enjoyed a famous victory at New Orleans – the Treaty of Ghent 'offered no shift in the balance of forces in the New World' (Evans 85). Perhaps the most remarkable aspect of the contest was the inability of American forces, drawing on a population many times larger, to overcome the determined opposition of French Canadians and Loyalist refugees when they sought to take what seemed an ideal opportunity to seize the remainder of the continent.

The War of 1812 poisoned relations between the two antagonists for many years, but trade continued, as it always does: Britain went on importing most of its raw cotton from the United States to fuel the Lancashire mills, for example, while the United States went on importing large quantities of British manufactured goods. Gradually the old mercantilist system was dismantled, and the principles of free trade took root, although it was not until 1846 that the Corn Laws were repealed, allowing American wheat to flood the British market. The United States' early industrial development, meanwhile, benefited from British finance and intellectual capital. As its population and economy boomed, it began the relentless process of westward expansion that so astonished European visitors and commentators in the British press. The Monroe Doctrine of 1823 forbade any intervention by European powers in the affairs of the Americas (North and South), while 'Manifest Destiny' was a familiar concept, recognized and debated by British observers, well before the phrase itself entered the lexicon in 1845. By the 1840s, with American

---

[3]   Napoleon's Berlin Decree (1806) announced a blockade of the British Isles and prohibited the import of British goods into European countries under French control. The Orders in Council responded by blockading all ports from which British goods were excluded and imposing transit duties on any neutral vessels that wished to trade with those ports. Napoleon's retaliatory Milan Decree declared that neutral vessels sailing from a British port or submitting to the British regulations were liable to seizure. As Donald Hickey explains, 'If American ships complied with the French decrees, they were subject to seizure by the British; and if they submitted to the British decrees, they could be seized by the French'; in practice, more than 900 ships were seized by the warring nations and their allies between 1807 and 1812 (Hickey 18–19).

annexation of Texas following the latter's rebellion against Mexican rule, the capture of California and New Mexico (including present-day Nevada and Utah) from Mexico, and all outstanding boundary issues between the United States and British territory settled, there was nothing to stop the United States spreading its wings from one ocean to another – something its more celebratory twentieth-century historians still liked to call a 'natural process' (Nevins 189).

Natural, that is, except in the eyes of Native Americans who stood in the way of this remorseless expansion. Although Native groups fought on both sides in the Seven Years' War, they were not included in negotiations leading to the Treaty of Paris, and 'their homelands were parcelled out to European powers as if North America were an empty frontier ripe for exploitation' (Conrad 245). It was a betrayal repeated many times in the years that followed. During the War of Independence, indigenous peoples, who prior to 1763 had striven to keep the balance of power between rival European nations, struggled to maintain their favoured position of neutrality, and many groups enlisted with one side or the other. The peace treaty signed in 1783, however, ignored their claims in its transfer of all territory south of the Great Lakes to the United States: as Daniel Richter notes, 'Britain's Native American allies reacted with disbelief, as they confronted a victorious republic eager to claim their lands by what it deemed a right of conquest' (368). Although one reason behind Britain's refusal to relinquish its forts on American soil was to try to secure a better deal for those allies, Jay's Treaty again made no mention of them, and the Battle of Fallen Timbers in August 1794 and the ensuing Treaty of Greenville effectively gave the United States possession of the entire Ohio territory. In the War of 1812, Britain once again made use of Native allies, and once again the Treaty of Ghent (1814) abandoned them to their fate.

One casualty of the war was the Shawnee leader Tecumseh, who had mobilized a confederacy of Native peoples to oppose colonial expansion and reject white culture in general, and whose rebellion essentially continued into the War of 1812. 'Tecumseh's War,' like that of the Ottawa leader Pontiac, another pioneer of multi-tribal Nativist resistance, in 1763–66, was unsuccessful, however important a cultural icon he later became. After 1815 there was little serious prospect of aboriginal peoples on either side of the border withstanding the ever-growing demand for land or holding back the tide of white settlement, much of which took place without reference to formal diplomacy in any case. Ravaged by war, European diseases, and alcoholism from contact with Europeans (despite periods of amicable coexistence and trading relations), indigenous populations continued to decline – victims of violent suppression, enforced relocation, and one-sided, ineffectual, or misunderstood treaties and land deals. With no significant military role to play in support of either European power, they became a problem chiefly for bureaucrats: in the United States, the Indian Removal Act of 1830 paved the way for the involuntary migration of tens of thousands of Native Americans to land in the West, while in Canada indigenous peoples were isolated in reserves and bought off with annual gifts and permissive rights. Everywhere, 'Native policy was constrained by racial biases – at best, well-meaning but condescending; at worst, exploitative, fraudulent, and negligent' (Conrad 498).

If Romantic readers were fascinated, as they undoubtedly were, by representations of American 'Indians,'[4] whether in the reports of explorers and travellers or in more stylized literary genres, then travellers' accounts of another notoriously subjugated ethnic group — African slaves — were more commonly an occasion for political point-scoring and self-serving moral outrage. The British periodical press, across the ideological spectrum, teemed with readers' horrified responses to descriptions of inhuman slave auctions, brutal punishments of runaways, and the corrupting effect of the institution on slave-owners, their wives, and children. Commentators lost no opportunity to highlight the contradiction between the continuance of slavery and the United States' self-promotion as a nation founded on political and civil liberty – while denying the equivalence (if they took note of it at all) of the persistence of slavery in Britain's own West Indian possessions. Both countries in fact formally withdrew from the Atlantic slave trade at the same time, in 1807–08, although American-registered ships exploited a lack of enforcement to continue an illicit trade, while the internal U.S. traffic was unaffected. The British, for their part, continued to trade in, and consume, slave-produced commodities such as tobacco, sugar, and cotton after 1807. In particular, the importation of ever-increasing quantities of American cotton to supply the Lancashire textile industry fuelled the demand for land in the Deep South and created labour shortages, thus giving 'a powerful boost both to the traffic in slaves [from areas where the slave population was growing] and to the development of the southern plantation system' (Temperley 35). But in a more general way, as David Richardson notes (citing Malachy Postlethwayt), 'Britain's trading empire in America rested on an African foundation' (462). After the final emancipation of slaves in her overseas territories in 1833, Britain was even more evangelical in exercising her moral authority on this issue, and British abolitionists cooperated energetically with their transatlantic counterparts to address the iniquities of American slavery, much to the annoyance of a powerful Congressional lobby and southern opinion more widely.

In brief and simplified terms, this is the context in which British readers in the late eighteenth and early nineteenth centuries were reading and making sense of travel writing on North America. In the more formal judgements that were produced for educated audiences in the periodical press, aspects of this history are often addressed directly, frequently in more detail than I have attempted here. In the more fugitive reactions of private readers, such matters are more likely to be in the background but are part of the matrix of general knowledge and cultural references that shaped and informed their responses. It is now time to focus on the travel books themselves that fuelled the transatlantic obsessions of Romantic readers.

---

[4]   Terminology for the indigenous peoples of North America is a vexed issue. Aware that no term is acceptable to everyone, I use 'Native Americans' and 'First Nations,' which have particular currency in the United States and Canada respectively. I also employ the simpler form 'nations,' which is not only cognate with the latter term but was commonly used in the eighteenth century. I speak of 'Indians,' a term ubiquitous in Romantic discourse, only where it seems necessary to reflect contemporary usage.

Travel writing and Americo-mania

The popularity of travel literature among readers in the Romantic period has often been remarked upon, and is not hard to evidence, at least on the basis of talk *about* books in contemporary periodicals and other written sources. The anonymous editor of Carl Moritz's *Travels ... in England* wrote in 1795 that a 'passion ... for voyages and travels' was one of 'the most distinguishing features in the literary history of our age,' such books ranking second only to novels in terms of numbers published (Moritz 3). A contributor to the *Monthly Review* made the same point in 1805, asserting that 'Next to novels, voyages and travels constitute the most fashionable kind of reading' (51: 419), which is misleading only insofar as 'fashionable' implies a short-lived phenomenon, whereas the travel genre maintained its appeal throughout the period. One explanation for this is provided by an 1808 article in the magazine *La Belle Assemblée*, itself aimed at 'the first circles of fashion' but a more substantial publication than its title suggests. The author finds it unsurprising that 'travels should crowd upon travels, to satisfy the thirst after information' about foreign countries, even those that have been visited and described 'twenty times before': the pace of change in modern societies is such that travellers' accounts rapidly become obsolete, and this branch of literature is therefore as 'inexhaustibly teeming' as the manners of the nations that it portrays (3 supp.: 38).

This reviewer is introducing a book of travels dealing not with some European country affected by war or revolution but with Canada. In fact, the alterations visible on both sides of the border in North America after an interval of just a few years were a frequent source of comment in the periodical press. Of course, not every country or region *had* been visited twenty times before, and the 'thirst after information' was satisfied by narratives of exploration and discovery from every continental arena. In the eighteenth and early nineteenth centuries, European knowledge of the rest of the world increased enormously, as travellers broke new ground in central Asia, India, China, South America, western and central Africa, Australasia, and elsewhere. Whether for reasons of science, religion, diplomacy, or trade, if not outright colonial expansion, Britain's role in this activity, and in the accompanying production of discourse, was a key one: as Roy Bridges summarizes, 'Britain's ever closer engagement with the wider world meant that larger and larger numbers of travellers and explorers made journeys to report upon it,' invariably 'with some concern for perceived British interests' (55, 57). The accounts of James Cook's three voyages in the 1760s and 1770s – which disproved the existence of a vast '*terra incognita*' in the southern ocean, discovered numerous Pacific islands, and charted the east coast of Australia, the entire coast of New Zealand and much of the northwest coast of America – were an early benchmark for the new era of scientific travel, with knowledge of Cook's exploits penetrating all levels of the reading public through cut-price republications, abridgements, and periodical reviews. G. R. Crone and R. A. Skelton observe that Cook's voyages 'gave a stimulus to public interest in exploration comparable to that of Dampier's writings seventy years earlier,' and helped breathe new life into the established publishing genre of multivolume 'general collections' of voyages and travels, which started for the first time to include condensed and edited accounts of new expeditions along with all the old material (118). As Shef Rogers notes, surviving records show that such collections could be 'quite lucrative' for publishers (786), underlining their popularity with the book-buying public. It was developments like this, along with extensive coverage – including generous excerpts – in the periodicals, ever-improving access via circulating libraries, subscription libraries, and book clubs,[5] and the prolific exploitation of real-life travel stories by poets and novelists, that make it no exaggeration for Nigel Leask to declare that 'travel writing permeated all levels of eighteenth- and nineteenth-century literary culture' (12).

There is thus a broader context for the Romantic reader's fascination with North American travels, which is my particular focus in this study. But America certainly contributed to the general enthusiasm for travel literature, not least because of the shared history of colonization, transatlantic emigration, geopolitical conflict, Revolution, and Independence. North American travels were of different kinds, encompassing narratives of true exploration, tours of already settled parts of the continent, and literature predominantly in the form of advice to emigrants. The primary bibliography in Jane Mesick's standard work, *The English Traveller in America, 1785–1835* contains seventy-seven items, and there are numerous omissions, most notably the many narratives of Arctic explorers who participated in a renewed quest for the fabled Northwest Passage (which I shall discuss in Chapter 3). By definition Mesick's list also excludes many translations of travels by other European nationals, whose readily available works further fuelled British interest in this part of the world. This diverse body of literature, uneven in quality and formulaic as it often was, provided rich scope for Romantic readers to expand their knowledge and exercise their imaginations. On one side, this fuelled what the *Eclectic Review* called 'Americo-mania,' with readers absorbed in the competition of successive travellers to ascertain 'which part of the land of freedom was the freest, which prairie was the most paradisiacal' (22: 79). At the other extreme, it strengthened some pretty ugly national pride and prejudice, confirming readers in their ethnocentric self-esteem in contradistinction to their distaste for American manners and morals. It is my aim, in this chapter and the chapters that follow, to reveal some of the complexity of that history of reader response, examining the reception of American travels at both formal and less formal levels and observing such patterns as may exist among particular communities of readers. I begin, as stated in my opening paragraph, with the testimony of private individuals.

---

[5]   Paul Kaufman's analysis of books borrowed from the Bristol Library Society between 1773 and 1784 shows the broad category of 'History, Antiquities and Geography' (which included works of travel) well in the lead with 6121 borrowings of 283 titles ('Some Reading Trends'). His separate study of book sales to book clubs in southwest England reveals a 'pattern of dominant interests' in which foreign travel and topography holds second place to contemporary politics ('Glimpses of Reading' 72).

Readers at work

Scarce and elusive the records of individual readers may be, but there is little doubt that America was a subject of considerable interest and the focus of much discussion among Romantic-era readers. The editors of leading periodicals, many of which gave considerable prominence to American travels and American topics generally, did not misjudge their readers in this respect. Lucy Aikin – member of a prominent Dissenting family and author of numerous histories and biographies – spoke for herself and for many others in her social circle in a letter to the New England Unitarian theologian, William Ellery Channing, in 1827: 'The state of America is a peculiarly interesting subject to many of my friends, and one on which it is difficult here to gain authentic information: we want to hear ... how this great experiment turns out' (Le Breton 426). Her aunt, the poet and essayist Anna Barbauld, whose poem *Eighteen Hundred and Eleven* offers a peculiarly forceful vision of how the experiment would turn out, was, not surprisingly, equally fascinated by America; indeed, in 1793 her nephew (whom she had adopted) had to dispel the rumour that she intended to emigrate there.[6] Writing to a female acquaintance in 1818, she talked up the importance of transatlantic affairs compared to the limited horizons of classical literature: 'What is the whole field of ancient history, which knew no sea but the Mediterranean, to the vast continent of America, with its fresh and opening glories!' (Oliver 303).

Barbauld's enthusiasm was shared with the playwright and country story writer, Mary Mitford, epitome of the downwardly mobile middle classes, whose literary earnings only partially offset her father's spectacular financial improvidence.[7] Swayed, perhaps, by the popularity of her work in the United States, Mitford wrote to her father in 1814 that 'If all trades fail I shall set up for a poetess in America,' adding 'You know I have always longed to see it' (L'Estrange 1: 263). The fact that her financially strained and provincial existence meant that she never satisfied that longing did not prevent her writing children's books with American settings for the American market – drawing, no doubt, on the enthusiasm for travel literature evinced by her letters. A prolific and lively correspondent, she frequently shared her thoughts on her reading and did not adopt the patronizing tone towards American culture common to many of her compatriots: she preferred Fenimore Cooper to Scott, for instance, and an essay by the same 'Dr Channing of Boston' familiar to Lucy Aikin led her to comment (in a letter to the painter Benjamin Robert Haydon) on 'How wonderfully America is rising in the scale of intellect' (L'Estrange 2: 227). Mitford and the Aikins came from very different social milieus, but the interests expressed in comments like these, shared with their

---

[6]   Charles Rochemont Aikin wrote to her in March, 1793: 'Many people here have got a strange notion that my father and mother and family are going to migrate to America. I have been obliged to contradict it several times' (Rodgers 216).

[7]   'But for her father, she would have been rich,' according to her entry in the *DNB* (Garrett).

friends and acquaintances, contradict the myth of a pervasive anti-Americanism in British culture, and give a flavour – exactly how representative it is difficult to say – of the conversations that were taking place in different subsets of what we would now dismissively call the 'chattering classes.'

As these examples show, women were certainly included in the audience for travel literature, even if they were not the target readers. It is a commonplace that, although women were thoroughly immersed in print culture in the Romantic period, there was considerable anxiety, especially in the middle classes, about their activity as readers, which was in consequence constrained by self-censorship or by what their parents or husbands or peer groups thought was appropriate. Much of this anxiety was centred, of course, on the novel. Margaret Beetham has usefully summarized the case against this revolutionary genre, which was thought to distract women from household duties, arouse undesirable feelings, and encourage the misperception of romantic fantasy for reality; she highlights the view – which gathered strength as the nineteenth century progressed – that women should read not for personal development but to further their role as guardians of the home ('Women'). This is, presumably, the main point of a print depicting a circulating library published in 1804 (Figure 1.1). The woman talking to the librarian is interested only in fiction dealing with romantic love, as the accompanying prose monologue makes clear. It is a fair assumption that the two other women share her obsession, given that the shelves devoted to novels and romances behind the librarian are virtually bare. By contrast, the shelves of 'voyages & travels' (top right) are conspicuously full. At first sight, this seems to contradict all the testimony relating to the popularity of this genre among Romantic readers, including the patrons of circulating libraries – at which, Shef Rogers observes, 'travel narratives were in demand and heavily borrowed' (787). However, the artist's main object is clearly to satirize the contemporary cult of sentimental fiction in the context of conservative anxieties over women's reading habits, and in order to press home the attack it is evidently necessary to exaggerate the extent to which travel literature, as with other books in the catalogue offering what the caption calls 'mental pleasures,' has been sidelined by the seductive appeal of the novel.

It was in line with this growing orthodoxy on the perils of women's reading that, as Jacqueline Pearson has shown, an implicit division of texts along gender lines came into play: 'Genres which emphasised "imagination" were gendered as feminine [and therefore demanded careful oversight by male superiors], those requiring "severe application" as masculine. In effect this means the gendering of novels, romances, and some lyric poems as feminine, while men read "better books," epic, satire, classical literature, history and science' (19). Where travel literature might be thought to reside in relation to this classification is unclear. Given the devotion of most travellers to accurate observation and the accumulation of knowledge, it might be assumed that the genre had a masculine profile; yet, simply by virtue of its ability to abstract readers mentally from their habitual environs, it also had the potential to appeal to the imagination. In fact, as Pearson herself argues, voyages and travels were considered fit reading for women, and

Fig. 1.1   *The Circulating Library*. Hand-coloured etching, London, 1804. © Trustees
of the British Museum.

she provides several fictional examples in which such reading 'labels a virtuous female character' (55). The fact that 'wonder' was the main passion aroused by travel writing (as opposed to anything more dangerous), and its ability to inspire pride in one's country's achievements, were apparently key points in its favour.

Nevertheless, as Pearson also points out, approval of travel books was in some ways surprising, since they offered the prospect of irresponsible escapism (as with Jane Austen's Fanny Price) and at times – as, notoriously, with Cook's adventures in Polynesia – contained material that was morally outrageous. So it seems that two important qualifications need to be made. Firstly, whatever the official or unofficial gendered assumptions surrounding reading, women's actual reading practices did not observe such clear boundaries; secondly, women in this period were sometimes 'economical with the truth' about the reading they had done, even in private journals and letters, and did not always keep records of 'purely recreational reading' in any case (Pearson 13).

My own research certainly confirms that women read and enjoyed travel writing, although the evidence is not as plentiful as one might hope given the energy that women invested in letter- and journal-writing, and references are often frustratingly brief. Confident and socially nonconformist women like Mary Shelley and Claire Clairmont had no qualms about recording every book they read: Clairmont, for instance, notes on 10 June 1819 that she is reading William Cobbett's *Year's Residence in the United States of America* and Morris Birkbeck's *Notes on a Journey in America*, two books both controversial for different reasons.[8] She says nothing about her reactions to them, however. Sometimes, in trawling the archive for relevant reading experiences, one is pathetically grateful for such sparse information as that furnished by Mary Berry (1763–1852), daughter of a gentleman of modest independent income, who attracted the romantic attentions of the ageing Horace Walpole and later became a significant player in the literary marketplace herself. Berry made numerous trips to the Continent over the course of a long life, but never ventured further afield, filling the void in her knowledge with travel books. In the spring of 1808, she combined her editorial labours on what she called her 'French letters'[9] with a reading of Thomas Ashe's *Travels in America* (about which much more in Chapter 2). In her diary, Berry criticizes the 'abominable' style of Ashe's narrative (she had this in common with most of his reviewers), but finds them 'very entertaining' nonetheless: 'the wonderful country he describes makes every account of it, which one sees and feels is written on the spot, very interesting' (Berry 2: 347).

---

[8]   Cobbett's 'year's residence' was occasioned by his fear of imprisonment in the wake of government alarm at the popularity of his cheap radical weekly, the *Political Register*. Birkbeck's *Notes*, at the eye of a storm over American emigration, will be a main focus of the next chapter.

[9]   *Letters of the Marquis Du Deffand to the Hon. Horace Walpole, afterwards Earl of Oxford, from 1766 to 1780. To which are added Letters of Madame Du Deffand to Voltaire from 1759 to 1775* (1810).

This elementary pleasure in being imaginatively transported to a remote and otherwise unknowable country is a recurrent theme in more personal accounts of reading travel narratives, but far less noticeable in the formal responses found in periodical reviews. Perhaps just as valuable from the point of view of a history of reading is the mere evidence that Berry read this travel book in its entirety, over a two-week period. Sometimes one gets the impression that Romantic readers read these long and often (to modern eyes) very pedestrian works selectively, homing in on the more colourful passages – indeed, the Sheffield cutler, Joseph Hunter, studied by Stephen Colclough, admits to doing just that, as well as to 'plundering' works for their illustrations and to abandoning a travel book completely if he was not sufficiently 'entertained' (Colclough 114). Mary Berry, however, was more patient with Ashe, beginning the first volume on 21 April, continuing her reading most evenings, and eventually finishing the book on 6 May. The fact that it seems to have helped her wind down after more demanding occupations ('finished the evening with Ashe's Travels') indicates that she considered travel literature 'light' reading.

Special mention should be made here of the diaries of Anna Larpent (1758–1832), wife to the inspector of plays in the Lord Chamberlain's office, whose voluminous diaries, preserved in the Huntington Library, demonstrate her significant contribution to this official process. The diaries, which begin in earnest in 1790 and conclude in 1830, also provide a detailed and intimate record of the wider reading of an intelligent, independent-minded woman of the upper middle classes. A devout Anglican, Larpent's diary entries always give priority to her devotional reading, but they also give full play to her other interests, which ranged over history, politics, fiction, biography, and – notably – travel literature. Between 1790 and 1830 Larpent read just about every significant work in the genre, including those relating to North America, and used her diary to take notes on her reading and register her opinions, some of them extremely caustic. I shall draw on her observations in several places in this study. Here it is worth noting two representative examples of her travel reading. As with Berry, it is possible to track Larpent's progress through a travel book over several days or weeks. She begins Isaac Weld's (recently published) *Travels through the States of North America and the Provinces of Upper and Lower Canada* on 15 November 1799 and finishes it on 29 November. Long passages in her diary amount to a very able synopsis of the work, interspersed with occasional evaluative remarks; she ends by saying that Weld is an 'observing impartial Traveller,' and that his *Travels* are 'very interesting very entertaining,' containing 'much information given in an animated spirited manner.' In this instance, her judgement conforms perfectly to the 'official' criteria for travel literature, which, as I shall discuss in Chapter 2, demanded that such works purvey both 'amusement' and 'instruction.'

More enthusiastic-seeming, perhaps, is Larpent's response to William Bartram's *Travels through North and South Carolina* (1791), in her entry for 13 January 1793 (Figure 1.2):

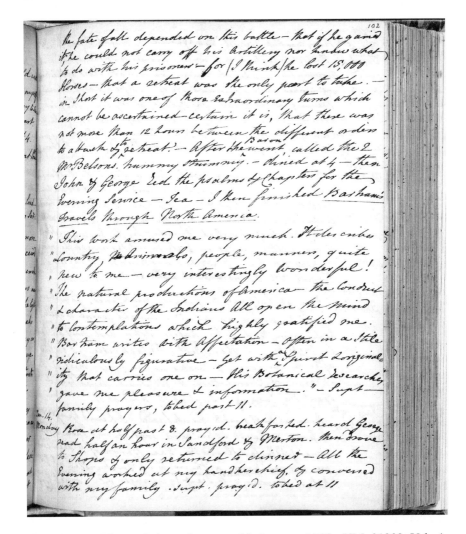

Fig. 1.2   Diary of Anna Larpent, 13 January 1793; HM 31202 Vol. 1.
            Reproduced by permission of The Huntington Library, San Marino,
            California.

This work amused me very much. It describes a Country, animals, people,
manners, quite new to me – very interestingly wonderful! The natural productions
of America – the conduct & character of the Indians all open the mind to
contemplations which highly gratified me. Bartram writes with affectation –
often in a stile ridiculously figurative – yet with a spirit & originality that carries
one on – His Botanical researches gave me pleasure & information.

The combined informality and opinionatedness of these remarks is very striking:
although Larpent, in common with other contemporary diarists, may not have

regarded her diary as a completely private document, the honesty and authenticity of what she called her 'Self Conversation' (31 December 1797) is compelling. If she is shaping her utterance towards a potential audience, it must be a small and intimate one. At the same time, her comments on Bartram's 'very interestingly wonderful' work show the same biases – the delight in entertaining novelties, the eager absorption of information on traditionally 'masculine' subjects – as public discourse on travel writing, suggesting that the kind of reader projected by periodical reviews is a fairly good approximation of at least some 'real' readers.

As already mentioned, the potential of voyages and travels for fostering national pride was a key factor in establishment approval of travel literature for 'vulnerable' categories of reader. In her *Hints Towards Forming the Character of a Young Princess*, published by Cadell and Davies (a leading publisher of travel literature), Hannah More wrote that the genre was 'a very necessary class of books' for educative purposes, and that travels would be 'peculiarly suited to the royal pupil; especially those which have been undertaken, greatly to his honour, by command of his present Majesty' (More 2: 143). That such sentiments were not restricted to compliant royal princesses is nicely illustrated in the correspondence of the well-connected writer and salonnière, Hester Piozzi. The elderly Piozzi, writing to a youthful admirer, William Conway, on 13 February 1820, declares that it is the 'Fate of our intrepid Discoverers' that interests her more than any other 'public and political events.' This certainly gives William Parry's first voyage in search of the Northwest Passage a high importance alongside the death of George III, the forthcoming general election, and the aftermath of the Peterloo massacre; Piozzi acknowledges that 'No great Benefit will indeed accrue to us, save Honour and Glory' from Parry's accomplishments (which did not, as she mistakenly assumes, solve 'all our Geographical Problems'), but insists it is 'a pleasant Thing for Loyal Hearts to hear of a new Reign beginning with so magnificent a Disclosure of National Spirit and Greatness' (*Letters* 368–9). Here is another example of a highly educated upper-middle-class woman, whose own travel experiences were limited to Continental visits in the mould of the Grand Tour, taking a keen – and patriotic – interest in North American exploration. Not all readers' hearts were so loyal, of course: there is an amusing entry in William Beckford's commonplace book on 'Mr Barrow's national covetousness' (Barrow, as Second Secretary of the Admiralty, was the official promoter of Parry's voyage), noting that he 'scarcely ever meets with a convenient Bay or a pretty Island which he does not long to transfer to the English' (12r).

Piozzi's long-running fascination with the Arctic voyages of John Ross and Parry, as recorded in her letters between 1818 and her death in 1821, offers evidence of other readerly expectations and habits consistent with the standards articulated in formal reviews – namely, the fixation on natural and human 'curiosities' and the desire to separate fact and fantasy in travellers' tales. Piozzi had inside knowledge of these expeditions and their leaders because, during her final retirement in Bath, her physician was Dr Charles Parry, the explorer's brother. Following Ross's aborted voyage in 1818 (on which William Parry was second-in command),

Piozzi enjoyed a private viewing of various 'Arctic Rareties' at Dr Parry's house, including a phial of 'Red Snow' that appeared to amuse her particularly[10] and some Inuit clothing (*Letters* 241). By April 1819 she had evidently read Ross's *Voyage of Discovery*, which she says 'would have been very entertaining had we not anticipated the whole in conversation at Charles Parry's, who permitted me to see his Bottle of Red Snow and Greenlanders Jacket, with drawings of those wild Creatures the new found Nation teems with' (259). Red snow, circular rainbows, black swans – Piozzi cannot stop mentioning these curiosities in her correspondence, and Parry's ground-breaking voyage of 1819–20 brought forth more: among all the novelties produced by the first British ship to overwinter in the Arctic Ocean, the 'most curious circumstance' for Piozzi was the story of how an officer's Irish setter 'attracted the Attentions of a She Wolf on Melville Island' and eventually abandoned the ship for her and her 'rough-haired Family' (478). Piozzi did not live to see the publication of Parry's *Journal of a Voyage for the Discovery of a North-West Passage*, which contained an account of this incident, but she must either have read all or part of it in manuscript or been familiarized with its contents via conversation with his brother.

At the same time that she relished 'curiosities' of this type, Piozzi had no wish to be bamboozled by fictitious phenomena. The rational, empirical travel narrative had had difficulty separating itself from the ancient tradition of the imaginary voyage, and *Robinson Crusoe* and *Gulliver's Travels* remained the most popular and easily accessible travel texts throughout the Romantic period, but Piozzi plainly wanted to keep the two genres apart. 'Truth is Native of no Clime hitherto discovered,' she asserted, but she wanted British explorers to be more reliable (and less credulous) than the primitive 'creatures' they encountered: it was for people like the Inuit, who mistook the masts of the *Isabella* and *Archer* for male and female giants, to be seduced by 'false Wonders' (241). After whalers had returned in consecutive years with reports of retreating ice in Baffin Bay, signalling the end of what is now called the 'Little Ice Age' and reinvigorating the quest for the Northwest Passage, Piozzi was quick to realize the significance: 'The Ice Field attached to our Ultima Thule[11] ... is now said to be mere Newspaper Story,' to which her response is: 'Oh do tell me Some *Truths* for we live in Fabulous Times' (186).

Piozzi's hankering for truth rather than travel 'fables' was shared by most contemporary readers. Her own published journal of a Continental tour[12] was praised by Anna Seward, in correspondence with one Mrs Knowles, for

---

[10]   According to Ross's account of the expedition, further analysis revealed the 'snow' to consist of seeds of a 'vegetable substance,' and the red colouring to be a 'minute fungus' (*Voyage* 1: 192).

[11]   'Thule' was in classical literature an island located somewhere north of the known world; by early modern times it was associated with Iceland, and by extension the name 'Ultima Thule' was – as in Piozzi's letter – applied to Greenland.

[12]   *Observations and Reflections made in the Course of a Journey through France, Italy, and Germany* (1789).

overcoming the limitations of a 'perpetual vulgarism of style' and presenting a detailed, objective description of the places she visited: 'If you would like to know the soil of the clime, the scenery, the disposition, the manners, the habits of the cities of Rome, Naples, Genoa, Venice, Bologna, etc. just as familiarly as you know all these things at Rugely, Birmingham, and Lichfield, you must shut yourself up for a few days with those volumes' (Seward 387–8). In the same spirit, and aware of the hyperbolic treatment Niagara Falls (already an established tourist attraction) had received from other travellers, Thomas Moore wrote to his mother in 1804 disapproving of her 'contempt for matter-of-fact description' and picking out the account in Weld's *Travels* as 'the most accurate I have seen' (*Letters* 1: 77). Fanny Trollope was unimpressed by Basil Hall's *Travels in North America* (1829), taking the view that he 'would have done quite enough service to the cause he intends to support if he had painted things exactly as they are, without seeking to give his own eternal orange-tawny colour to every object' (L'Estrange 1: 220). Since she was shortly to publish her own *Domestic Manners of the Americans* it might be argued that she had an ulterior motive for disparaging Hall's work in public, but this is unlikely to have been a significant factor in correspondence with a close friend. When it finally appeared, *Domestic Manners* drew mixed responses: Henry Crabb Robinson records a conversation with Thomas Hamilton, who thought that she had given 'an honest but one-sided account of American manners as seen from a peculiar point of view' (Robinson 1: 430), whereas an American correspondent of Mary Mitford's acknowledged that Trollope had told some 'disagreeable truths' about the 'crude state of society,' but considered that she had 'for the most part caricatured till the resemblance is lost' (L'Estrange 1: 240–241). In all these examples the essential criteria of honesty and empirical reliability are the same; the reference to 'a peculiar point of view' is a limited modification of a standard that is intolerant of interpretive bias and has little time for the subjectivity of the individual traveller. Similarly, readers wanted to indulge their curiosity, but they wanted their curiosities to be well-attested singularities of the unfamiliar landscapes and peoples 'discovered' by travellers and explorers, not the misshapen offspring of a perverse sensibility that cast its own false light on every object it encountered.

A good example of the enduring taste for natural 'wonders' can be found in the commonplace book of Warren Dawson, a fellow of the Society of Antiquaries and of the Royal Society of Edinburgh. Dawson includes in his album a long passage concerning an 'extraordinary cavern' recently discovered near Watertown in the State of New York, as described by a traveller who had descended into it. This was almost certainly copied (verbatim) from the *New Monthly Magazine*, although its original source was a local American publication and versions of it appeared in many British periodicals, including the Royal Society's own *Philosophical Journal*. Included in a general section entitled 'Foreign Varieties' and subtitled 'Geology,' the *New Monthly*'s item contains details of different chambers within the cavern system and of the rock formations found therein, and evidently appealed to a man of Dawson's scientific interests. It is an indication, furthermore, of what

one reader, and perhaps others like him, found most 'entertaining' or noteworthy
in contemporary travel accounts.

Dawson was not alone in using his commonplace book to make extracts
of interesting facts about foreign countries, including North America: travel
literature was not the most popular source of material for these albums, but it
certainly impacted on the anthologizing habits of some readers. As Stephen
Colclough has recently discussed, these manuscript compilations of extracts, for
which 'commonplace book' is a somewhat misleading generic term, represent the
continuation within an industrializing print culture of a form of notetaking with
its roots in early modern times. Originally designed as a pedagogic tool in which
readers would assemble 'a store of borrowed similes, metaphors, and maxims,'
organized under prescribed headings, 'that they could use in their everyday lives'
(31), by the late eighteenth century, commonplace books were more diverse
and individual productions (indexes were self-generated, emerging out of one's
reading). According to Colclough, they consisted 'mainly of transcripts from
contemporary poets, with perhaps a few concise extracts from novels or travel
writing, and some short prose aphorisms, often taken from Blair, Paley and other
widely available moral writers' (123–4).

As far as travel literature is concerned, 'perhaps' is indeed the operative word.
In my own limited sampling of commonplace books, I have come across very
few entries drawing on the genre. William St Clair, who has amassed a large
private collection of these volumes, comments in correspondence with the
present author that they contain 'very little excerpting of prose travel literature,'
although there is 'more of what might be called travel literature in verse' (of
which Byron would offer the best-known examples),[13] and some compilers are
fond of inserting cuttings (or their own copies) of engravings from travel books.
St Clair notes that his collection is heavily weighted towards female compilers,
and he suggests that 'if we had more commonplace books by men ... there would
be more prose extracts – and a more utilitarian aim in excerpting.' Dawson's
album certainly provides support for this theory, displaying a preference for hard-
edged prose over moral sententiae and purple passages of sentimental verse.
More immediately to my purpose, it offers an intriguing glimpse of a (male)
Romantic reader taking an interest in North America (there is another entry
headed 'Contest with America,' reacting to papers concerning the build-up to the
War of Independence and regretting the 'deplorable waste of Lives') and valuing
the reports of American travellers chiefly for the new knowledge they generate
about that part of the world. The commonplace book of William Beckford, Gothic
novelist and eccentric aesthete, is another case in point, consisting largely of
extracts from reviews, including many reviews of travel books. Beckford, too,
shows an interest in American politics, transcribing (for example) a description of
the War of Independence as 'a struggle between Imbecility – viz. that which was

---

[13]   I am very grateful to Mr St Clair for taking the time to reply to my enquiries on this
subject.

personal to the Members of the British Cabinet & that which was natural to an Infant State under an Executive without authority' (9r).

By contrast with St Clair's findings, a recent study by David Allan (evidently trawling different archives or bookshops) declares that the importance of travel and topographical literature to Georgian readers 'is emphatically confirmed by surviving commonplace books' (238). He examines several such books compiled by both men and women that show their delight in being mentally transported to unfamiliar places and sometimes dangerous situations by the latest travel accounts, as well as their liking for 'triangulating between the text in hand and other known information' (240). Interestingly, he also provides examples of albums that were used to record the owner's own travel experiences, and he finds little difference between male and female commonplace books in terms of the textual strategies they employ – 'the predictable result of their going to the same places as well as being exposed to identical reading and thus being subjected to largely the same textual promptings in structuring and responding to the experience' (248). Allan contends that the interweaving of personal impressions with the commonplacing of published travel texts ensured that travel became an important arena for self-fashioning against 'an external frame of reference' (252). In this way, readers became more than passive consumers of prior travellers' experiences; even the mere process of selection and transcription, it might be argued, implies a creative response, involving the application of independent critical judgement.

The features of private responses to North American travels that I have summarized so far (I accept that there is no such thing as a 'pure' personal response – all textual accounts of reading are a codification of cognitive and emotional processes that lie beyond historical scrutiny) cohere reasonably well with the kinds of opinions expressed in published reviews, which will be the main focus of the next two chapters. However, there are also qualities that emerge occasionally in private responses that are not so apparent in the formal archive. Most notably, these relate to the emotional and imaginative pleasures of reading. It is frustrating for the historian of reading that allusions to reading travel books in letters and diaries are invariably brief, highly generalized, and annoyingly bland: very often, as with Mary Berry's remarks on Thomas Ashe quoted above, a book will be described as 'very interesting' or 'entertaining' without further elaboration. Even Caroline Lamb's confession that she was 'enchanted' with George Lyon's *Private Journal* of his part in Parry's first Arctic voyage (Smiles 2: 145) raises the thermometer of enjoyment only slightly without telling us exactly what she found so absorbing. Nevertheless, this vocabulary of delight does, at the very least, demonstrate that the well-documented popularity of travel literature with the book-buying and book-borrowing public had its roots in pleasure – whether that be a narrative pleasure, or the pleasures of novelty, or the pleasures of emotional engagement with the protagonists (the Arctic voyages seem to have been particularly enthralling in this respect) – and not just satisfaction at imbibing the latest advances in geographical knowledge (an impression formal reviews sometimes convey). Occasionally one comes across language signifying a more acute or unusual form of pleasure taken from works in the travel genre. There is a memorable example among Coleridge's copious marginalia. In a copy of William Bartram's *Travels through North and South Carolina* that he gave to Sara Hutchinson, now preserved in the Wordsworth Museum at Dove Cottage, Coleridge wrote the following note on the flyleaf, below the presentation inscription:

> This is not a Book of Travels, properly speaking; but a series of poems, chiefly descriptive, *occasioned* by the Objects, which the Traveller observed. – It is a *delicious* Book; & like all *delicious* Things, you must take but a *little* of it at a time. Was it not about this time of the year, that I read to you parts of the "Introduction" of this Book, when William and Dorothy had gone out to walk? – I remember the evening well, but not what time of the year it was. (Figure 1.3; *Marginalia* 1: 227)

It is striking to hear a book of American travels being described as 'delicious,' as though it is some kind of rich confectionery to be savoured in small quantities – and perhaps such an adjective could only be applied to a work like Bartram's, which employs highly rhetorical prose in places, as Coleridge implies (most books about America would inspire more banal dietary metaphors). At the same time, this copy of Bartram is, as Heather Jackson observes, intended as a 'poignant souvenir' and functions within a context of intimate personal relations: when Sara sees the book, Coleridge wants her 'to remember an evening they spent alone together and to cherish the memory just as he does' (174). Bartram is therefore something of a guilty pleasure, and it is undecidable how much of his deliciousness is a property of the text and how much is superadded by those personal associations.

It is remarkable how seldom the pleasure taken from travel writing is ascribed to the personality of the traveller. Received ideas about Romantic travel, which owe their force largely to the cultural impact of certain travel-related poems and novels, such as Byron's *Childe Harold* or Germaine de Staël's *Corinne*, seemingly have little relevance to nonfiction ('factual') travel writing of the period, and North America is no different in this regard. Lady Dacre's response to Fanny Kemble's *Journal of a Residence in America* (1835), as conveyed in a letter to John Murray, is perhaps an honourable exception:

> One sees her *own self*, with her peculiarities, her great qualities and her faults, in every page. That little nostril tucking up more than its fellow is before me in all the sarcastic flings and droll passages. I hear her deep melodious voice in her descriptions of the sea, with her particular pronunciation of the first vowel. (Smiles 2: 402–3)

At the same time, the fact that Dacre is clearly well acquainted with its author must explain a good deal of this highly personalized and almost alarmingly phonocentric reading of the *Journal*, and readers less familiar with the behaviour of Kemble's nostrils would presumably have had a different experience of the work. Charles Lamb, however, had certainly never met J. Hector St John de Crèvecoeur, and judging from his comments on *Letters from an American Farmer* would have

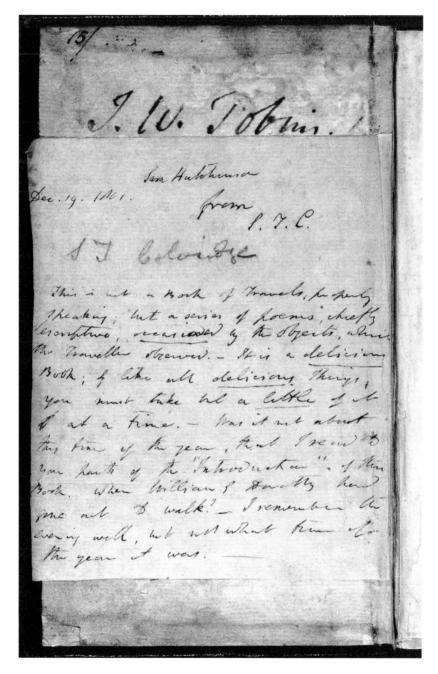

Fig. 1.3   MS note by Coleridge, on a flyleaf in William Bartram's *Travels* (1791). Dove Cottage, The Wordsworth Trust.

been happy to keep it that way. His response, contained in a letter to Hazlitt, is supremely *ad hominem*, not merely denouncing the book by reference to its author but actually *identifying* book and author, seeing the book *as a person*:

> Why should a book be pleasant to one, that if it were made into a man (the binding a coat, the leaves a shirt with a frill, the &c. &c. make out the rest of the metamorphosis yourself, I have no time ...) if the said book were a man & not a book, would be odious? A wretched purse-proud American Farmer with no virtue but industry & its ostentatious concomitant charity, no ideas but of clearing land & setting the poor to work (damn him for that if I was a lousy Beggar happy in the Sun) calling Ladies young Women & praising them for decent mirth & needle work & possibilities of being notable mothers ... (*Letters* 2: 198)

Lamb contrasts Crèvecoeur with James Bruce, a 'fine dashing fellow' who 'intrigues with Empresses & gets into Harams of Black Women, & was himself descended from Kings of Scotland' (199), and whose *Travels to Discover the Source of the Nile* was evidently a textual embodiment of these same virtues. If one is to take Lamb's comments at all seriously, the implication is that any pleasure one derives from a travel book (or indeed any book) is the outcome of a single, crass personification: the tale *is* the teller, and if the teller is not someone one could comfortably socialize with, then the tale must be ostracized. The Letters are a 'stupid uninteresting Book' because Crèvecoeur is no gentleman ('no virtue but industry'), is distastefully materialistic ('purse-proud,' like all Americans), and is guilty of vulgarity ('calling Ladies young Women'). One could not enjoy such a man's company, so one cannot enjoy his book.

It is tempting to linger over thought-provoking comments such as Coleridge's and Lamb's, but arguably these are the exceptional responses of exceptional men, rather than the 'ordinary reader' who constitutes the elusive quarry of book historians. This is not to reject outright what are now conventional assumptions regarding Romantic travel literature. Casey Blanton writes that by the end of the eighteenth century there was a marked emphasis on 'the effects of people and places on the narrator' rather than objective descriptions, and that travel writing had become as much 'a matter of self-discovery' as 'a record of the discovery of others' (15). Chloe Chard agrees that the 'Romantic view of travel,' which emerged at the end of the eighteenth century, posited travel as 'a form of personal adventure, holding out the promise of a discovery or realization of the self through the exploration of the other' (11), while Charles L. Batten identifies in the same period a 'growing shift in the direction of what would once have been considered excessively egotistical autobiography' (78). Roger Cardinal argues that under the aegis of Romanticism journeys became a powerful trope for 'aesthetic and psychic exploration' (135), and James Buzard sees it as Byron's special achievement to have made travel into 'an opportunity for self-staging' through the sheer force of his literary persona (128).

These (and other) scholars are not mistaken in observing the same or similar developments in literary history. However, I would argue firstly that, as the Buzard quote suggests, much of the 'Romantic view of travel' is predicated on characters, motifs, and plotlines in more 'literary' genres such as poetry and the novel. Secondly, insofar as nonfiction voyages and travels reflected a growing interest in travel as self-exploration or self-discovery, this was chiefly the preserve of a small minority of genuinely pioneering works – works that turned out to have a significant influence on the evolution of the genre but which were not representative of the general run of travel books in the period. Moreover, these 'Romantic' works faced an uncertain reception by readers who expected a harder currency in works of travel and were liable to be intolerant of excessive 'self-staging' by travellers. Wollstonecraft was clearly aware of this when she used the 'Advertisement' to her Scandinavian *Letters* to justify putting so much emphasis on her 'mind and feelings,' adding coyly that she tried to 'correct this fault, if it be one' (62); so was William Beckford when, in the 1830s, he finally published *Dreams,Waking Thoughts and Incidents*, his long-suppressed Continental travel diary, as *Italy, with Sketches of Spain and Portugal*: as Brian Fothergill notes, severe editing ensured that the incidents remained, but that 'many of the dreams and waking thoughts were banished' (329). Although there is counter-evidence of readers captivated by displays of sensibility, in the main consumers demanded more self-restraint from practitioners of a genre that came under constant suspicion with regard to its empirical creditworthiness. This was as much the case at the end of the period as it was at the beginning: the narrator of Sterne's *Sentimental Journey* (1768) criticizes (in the guise of the learned Smelfungus) Smollett's *Travels through France and Italy* for being nothing but an account of his 'miserable feelings' (52), and a not dissimilar note is struck by Anna Larpent, in her diary entry for 4 December 1829, when she dismisses Augustus Granville's *St Petersburgh* for being 'a sort of twaddle emanating from one point self & what self does = & what is done to self.'

   Although there is little doubt, therefore, that the personality of the author began increasingly to colour travel writing towards the end of the eighteenth century and on into the nineteenth (especially in post-Sternean sentimental tours, usually with a domestic or European focus), the readerly horizon of expectations was slow to adapt, and it is likely that the more remote or unfamiliar the geographical subject-matter of a travel book was, the more keenly readers were interested in facts, observations, and external realities rather than psychic self-exploration. North America definitely fell into the category of a little-known part of the world, albeit rapidly opening up to European explorers and settlers, about which the 'ordinary reader' was curious and hungry for information. Of course, that latter creature is every bit as much an ideal phantom as, for example, the 'hard-working families' ritually invoked by past and present British governments in defence of their policies: it makes just as little sense to talk of what the 'ordinary reader' made of Bartram's *Travels* (for instance) as it does to pontificate about what 'hard-working families' expect their taxes to be spent on. Nevertheless, it can only be helpful to spread the net as widely as possible and gather whatever evidence one can of readers who were not themselves, as Lamb and Coleridge were, significant players in the literary world.

In fact, some of the most striking testimony to the pleasure of the travel text in the Romantic period comes from working-class readers. Again, it must be conceded that such testimony emanates from that tiny elite of highly motivated, aspirational working-class people who eventually put pen to paper to tell their stories; but this does not mean that their experiences are devalued. Undoubtedly there are reasons why working-class autobiographers (many of whose narratives were never published, only to be recovered by twentieth-century scholars) might select and filter historical 'facts' to put the most positive gloss on their rise from obscurity (when Wordsworth performs the same operation in *The Prelude*, it is called a 'rememorialization' and commended for its poetic artistry). It may well be that artisans who wrote about their reading habits and experiences read other, less savoury material as well as those kinds of literature they admitted to; but if individuals make a point of mentioning their experience of travel literature – a genre that, while not unrespectable, would not confer real kudos on the consumer – I see no reason to doubt them.

David Vincent, co-author of the important bibliographical study, *The Autobiography of the Working Class*, concludes on the basis of extensive research that – contrary to what one might assume about more utilitarian motives – in the Romantic period and beyond 'The exercise of the imagination was the greatest and most persistent incentive for gaining a command of the tools of literacy, and their first and most satisfying application,' because through it 'events and emotions are given shape and value, and alternative visions of hope or despair are called into being' (*Literacy* 226). While chapbooks, with their 'heady brew of drama, fantasy and morality' (61), provided the most easily accessible means of fulfilling these yearnings, Vincent observes that labouring-class readers (mostly self-taught) were capable of gaining access to 'a surprisingly wide body of literature' (208), whether through pooling resources with like-minded individuals, or through more structured book clubs and reading societies, or by more informal and opportunistic means. Although the 'layering of readership by time' of which William St Clair speaks – or, as Vincent puts it, the inability of the majority 'to read in the same literary moment as the well-educated' (*Rise* 119) – must have been the reality for many, new novels and poetry were not completely out of reach; nor, for really committed and resourceful readers, were books – like travel literature – that were certainly far too expensive to be bought. In fact, voyages and travels have a direct relevance to a broad transition Vincent describes, whereby movement in all its senses became the essence of rising mass literacy:

> Literacy was a means of making connection with other ideas and knowledge over space and time. Its application altered the user's relationship with the immediate and local discourses sustained by oral modes of communication. Reading and writing promoted motionless mobility. The association between education and physical migration was not only inconsistent but also of limited significance. The key journeys were made in the mind. (*Rise* 99)

(An associated development, according to Vincent, was the rapid growth of the the postal and railway networks in the nineteenth century, both of which loosened people's ties to 'the physical and mental surroundings into which they had been born' [102].) Travel literature, when the poor and self-educated could get hold of it, was a powerful means of encouraging this motionless mobility, of opening mental horizons and eroding the encrustation of local customs and beliefs. Vincent cites the example of Alexander Somerville, a farm worker, who was introduced to poetry by a fellow worker and became an admirer of Burns, but whose outlook changed when he acquired a copy of George Anson's *Voyage around the World* (1748): 'everything gave way to admit the new knowledge of the earth's geography, and the charms of human adventure which I found in those voyages. I had read nothing of the kind before, and knew nothing of foreign countries' (Somerville 45). Interestingly, Somerville describes reading aloud from this book to his fellow workers ('they all brought their dinners afield, so that they might remain under the shadow of the trees and hear me read' [47]), so there is a vivid picture of this illiterate rural community collectively undertaking 'journeys ... in the mind.'

Similar enthusiasms are recorded in the life stories of men such as Francis Place, Robert Owen, Thomas Spence and Ebenezer Elliott.[14] Imaginative transport was not restricted to working-class readers – Maria Edgeworth, for example, was delighted by Chateauvieux's *Travels in Italy* (1748) and was 'sure of its *transporting* my aunt' (286), while Mary Mitford was enthralled by 'the singular mixture of romantic adventure and historical truth' in James Bruce's *Travels* (1790) and was 'never ... so carried away by a man in my life' (L'Estrange 1: 342) – but seems to have been of particular importance to this social group. Thomas Cooper, the shoemaker-turned-journalist and later prominent Chartist and religious lecturer, considered himself entirely self-educated although he spent several years at a free school employing the monitorial system. From his earliest years his happiest hours were spent alone with books, and by one means or another – circulating library, mutual improvement society, private collection, personal magnetism – seems to have been able to get hold of virtually any type of publication, including the latest works of Byron in his years of fame. Cooper too talks of books having the ability 'to transport me, at times, out of the vulgar world of circumstances in which I lived bodily' (64). Although this phrase is applied specifically to his reading of Shakespeare, among the other 'miscellaneous reading' he undertook in the 1810s and 1820s were works with transatlantic (albeit not North American) subjects such as Francis Head's *Rough Notes Taken during Some Rapid Journeys across the Pampas and among the Andes* (1826), William Bullock's *Six Months' Residence and Travels in Mexico* (1824), and 'many other volumes of travels' (65). He also had access to major reviews such as the *Edinburgh*, the *Quarterly*, and the *Eclectic*, which gave him further opportunities to satisfy this interest in travel literature via the long, synoptic reviews they contained. It is a shame that Cooper lost the journal that he 'kept so strictly' in this period, along with 'all written

---

[14] See Cruse 150–166 for examples.

records of my reading' (63), because one gets the impression that this working-class autobiographer, more than most, might have given us invaluable insight into the reading experiences of a self-taught man from a humble background.

The most pertinent piece of evidence from this constituency of readers relates to Thomas Carter, a tailor, who attended his own mother's dame school, followed by a Dissenting school between the ages of nine and thirteen, but like Cooper was largely self-educated and driven by the desire for self- improvement. During his early apprenticeship with a woollen-draper he had the use of his master's library; travel literature was an early enthusiasm, and North America seems from the first to have been his particular interest:

> About this time I read also the narratives of some eminent navigators and travellers; among the former were those of Cook, Perouse, and Bougainville; of the latter I chiefly remember those of Bruce, Le Vaillant, and Weld. Mr Weld's narrative so deeply interested me, as to have well nigh been the occasion of my emigrating to either the United States or to Canada. The desire of seeing these countries which was excited thereby remained with me for some years; it was the cause of my reading several works descriptive of North America and the condition of its inhabitants. (115–6)

Carter moved to London for a while in the hope of 'getting into society of an intellectual character' (117), but was disappointed in this and returned home for a while until fear of conscription into the local militia led him back to the capital. During his time in London he continued to read books relating to America – he mentions Smith's *Travels in Canada and the United States* (which I have not been able to identify) and Richard Parkinson's *Tour in America* (1805) – and to daydream about emigrating. He took a serious enough interest in the United States to arbitrate heated discussions among his fellow workmen about the War of 1812, always viewing the conflict himself with 'unmitigated regret' (182). By the 1820s Carter had set up in business on his own account; in spare moments he still indulged his passion for travel writing, including Parry's *Journal* of his first Arctic voyage, but he notes that 'henceforth when I say that I have read any book, it will only mean I gave it a hasty perusal, for I had no time for close reading' (211–2). It is ironic that, in the face of modern scholars who all but deny the possibility of an artisan like Carter getting hold of such an expensive book, he not only does so (by borrowing) but gives Parry's sumptuous quarto no more than a 'hasty perusal.' Perhaps the superb illustrations were sufficient to feed his imagination. The idea of mental transport or 'motionless mobility' seems to have been absolutely fundamental to Carter's interest in the travel genre, and perhaps, in the distressed economic circumstances of the 1810s of which he writes, there were others who shared his enthusiasm, along with his transatlantic daydreams, but who never told their stories.[15] My response to Carter supports the argument put forward by

---

[15] For many working-class people in this period, of course, the United States became more than a daydream, as I shall explore in more detail in Chapter 2. The vast majority has left no record; but among the intriguing exceptions is Dublin-born John Binns, quondam

Jonathan Rose (drawing mostly on later nineteenth-century sources), that travel literature was popular with working-class readers not because it gave free rein to their petty-imperialist fantasies of conquest and domination but because it filled the void in contemporary geography teaching and satisfied a craving for adventure. America, in particular, Rose suggests, fascinated the working class (in contrast to the elite segment of the reading public) 'because it promised ... a measure of freedom and affluence that the latter was not prepared to grant' (*Intellectual* 353).

There is evidence, therefore, that imaginative transport was a key element in the mental experience of travel literature for Romantic readers, especially those who lived more circumscribed lives, whose formal education was poor, and who had few opportunities for real-life travel. However, there were readers who responded in different ways, or performed different mental operations on the same kinds of texts. It is here that Heather Jackson's work on marginalia is of particular interest. Marginal notes are a uniquely intimate form of engagement with a text, as valuable for the historian of reading as they are difficult to hunt down, and they get us as close to the individual reading experience as anything can (even though one cannot assume they are a form of self-communion, as the example of Coleridge's note in Bartram vividly demonstrates). Jackson observes that progressive educational theory of the period encouraged readers to make notes in the books they read[16] – defining topics, commenting on beauties and defects, creating an index in the absence of one, and so on – and that it was natural for readers to keep up these well-ingrained habits of annotation. Jackson identifies three basic practices: 'extracting' or making copies of passages (either onto the flyleaves of the same book, or into a book on a similar subject, or into a book dedicated to the purpose, as in the commonplace tradition), 'linking' or making connections with other texts, and 'supplementing, which meant adding material of one's own, 'usually in a spirit of collaboration' (120). Marginalia could have a very personal dimension, with readers 'identifying passages especially relevant to themselves' (196), or even a sociable aspect if the book was circulating among readers who were, in this way, talking to each other. Notes might be inserted with an implied intention to contribute to the ever-growing store of knowledge on a particular subject, but they could also represent a form of 'unofficial criticism that shows not only how a particular reader responded to a particular book, but also

---

soap-boiler and plumber's assistant, who later became politically active as a member of the London Corresponding Society and whose involvement in Irish revolutionary politics led to his prosecution for high treason. In 1801 he emigrated to the United States, where he pursued a career as a political journalist. Binns describes having read 'thousands of volumes' in early life, which 'filled my mind with information and knowledge of various kinds' (19), but he provides few details. It was Joseph Priestley and Thomas Cooper who urged him to write his autobiography, so perhaps Binns was familiar with Cooper's *Some Information Concerning America*; but it would be interesting to know what else, if anything, Binns had read about America before taking the momentous decision to emigrate.

[16]   Unlike today, of course, when such a practice is seen as tantamount to vandalism, and students can face disciplinary action if found guilty of 'defacing' library books.

how that reader was accustomed to talk about books in congenial company' (196). The more critical type of annotation is characteristic of the summary judgements that are often written at the front or the back of a book, by means of which 'the reader emerges from a phase of pupillage to assert him- or herself, putting the text in its place' (259). Jackson writes suggestively of how annotation assists the process of 'self-definition,' achieved through reading either with, or against, the grain of the text. Although finding manuscript notes in works of travel literature is a difficult and time-consuming enterprise, and a transatlantic focus narrows the field to an almost impossible degree, Jackson's analysis offers a helpful framework for thinking about Romantic responses to the genre, not only in the form of marginalia but also in other sources – such as letters and diaries – upon which I have drawn.

Jackson herself discusses one instance of annotations to a travel book about North America – the notes Wordsworth made in his copy (now in the British Library) of John Davis's *Travels of Four Years and a Half in the United States of America* (1803), first brought to critical attention in an article by Carolyn Moss. Four of Wordsworth's five notes comprise cross-references to poetry: one to John Suckling, one to Shakespeare, and two to Horace. Jackson is surely right in suggesting that Wordsworth read this book 'recreationally and idly' (and probably very selectively, since four of the notes appear in the same short section of the book), and in her conclusion: 'Wordsworth's mind was so stocked with poetry that even a book of travels led him to think automatically of literary parallels' (263). A comparable example of this 'linking' mentality appears in a Rhodes House Library copy of Samuel Hearne's *Journey ... to the Northern Ocean*. It is, in fact, the only annotation in the book,[17] and appears at the point where Hearne describes the custom among the Chipewyan Indians 'for the men to wrestle for any women to whom they are attached,' and states how 'unpleasant' it was for him to witness such tussles, with 'the object of the contest sitting in pensive silence watching her fate' (Hearne 67–8). Against the latter passage, on page 106 of the Rhodes House copy, the anonymous owner/reader has inserted in the margin an abbreviated allusion: 'v. Soph. Trach. Line 1–50.' The reference is to Sophocles' *Trachiniae*, the first fifty lines of which are the lament of Deianira, wife of Heracles: she tells of Heracles joining in combat with her suitor, the river-god Achelous, then consigning her to marital unhappiness since he is rarely at home. The essence of the comparison is, of course, two men (loosely speaking) fighting over a woman; the striking thing is the dissimilarity of the two textual worlds. As Jackson says, making links to other texts (thus creating idiosyncratic networks within the knowledge derived from books) was a favourite reading practice of the period; in this example, the tone of

---

[17]   There is no ownership inscription in this copy of Hearne, nor have I been able to ascertain when or how it came into the possession of the Bodleian (from where it was transferred to Rhodes House Library in the 1920s). It is impossible to say for sure that the annotation was not made at a much later date, but everything I have discovered about the circulation and relatively short shelf life of travel books in the Romantic period suggests that it is more likely to have been the work of a contemporary or near-contemporary reader.

the allusion is hard to gauge, but the cross-referencing of sexual customs among 'uncivilized' native people in North America with events from a play by one of the greatest classical tragedians suggests an amused, ironic response – perhaps another instance of the uncomplicated, 'recreational' reading of travel literature.

A similar delight in incongruity is evident in a journal entry made by Hester Piozzi on 1 December 1778. She has been describing some of the improbable remedies deployed by acquaintances, such as Lord Tamworth taking 'Neville Hott Water' for a dislocated hip, and this prompts an allusion to Jonathan Carver's just-published *Travels Through the Interior Parts of North America*, 'where the Writer (who for other Observations deserves Attention if not Respect) tells me the Indians possess some Herbs which are admirable in the Cure of <u>Fractured Bones</u>' (*Thraliana* 347). Here the intention is obviously to mock her associates by comparing their gullibility to the superstitious medicine of 'savages,' which many of her contemporaries would take as proof of innate inferiority. This is perhaps an example of the 'supplementing' approach to texts, or more specifically the preference for relating texts to one's personal circumstances and experience via comment and aside. Of more viscerally opinionated comments, there are fine examples in the correspondence of Mary Mitford. She urges Barbara Hofland to read Henry Fearon's *Sketches of America* (1818) because he 'gives good reasons for old prejudices': 'Nothing is more agreeable than to find one's preconceived notions of a place or people confirmed by a good matter-of-fact knock-me-down authority, like Mr. Fearon ... Every America-hater should read Mr. Fearon' (Mitford 1: 41). John Ross's *Voyage of Discovery* receives equally energetic but contrasting treatment: 'He a discoverer, forsooth! All that he did was to go about christening rocks, capes, bays, and mountains after all the great men, dead and living, whom he thought to gain by, and then to come home and write a huge quarto about nothing' (Mitford 1: 68). The interest of such utterances is that they illustrate how readers responded to travel books when they were not overly concerned with harvesting information from them, or weighing up their accuracy and fairness, or assessing their curiosity-value; in their extreme informality they convey an impression of how contemporary readers talked about such literature among people with whom they felt completely comfortable, as opposed to when they composed reactions for the public arena.

A more carefully judicial form of commentary – and a classic example of 'supplementary' note-making – can be found in one of Coleridge's annotations to a copy of Hearne's *Journey* now residing in the Houghton Library at Harvard. Coleridge was fascinated by Hearne's lengthy description of the 'Northern Indians,' but did not take it all on trust:

> The most doubtful part of this excellent work is that (p. 344, 345) respecting the utter irreligion of the Northern C. Indians. An instance of speculative Religion occurs in the very page preceding, 343 – as respectable a cosmogony, as that of the E. Indians, and the allegory more intelligible. I should suspect strongly, that Matonnabee [Hearne's native guide] represented his own *Fort-esprit* rather than gave the true account of his fellow countrymen. Hearn should have questioned the old men, and the women. (*Marginalia* 2: 986–7)

Here Coleridge is, as Jackson observes in relation to other marginalia, following his own recommended practice of 'genial' reading, by which he meant 'reading as far as possible in the same spirit as that in which the work had been composed' (Jackson 269); at the same time, he is concerned to supplement and correct Hearne's account not on the basis of superior knowledge but through close attention to Hearne's own text. Whereas the approach of many readers and reviewers of the period was to treat the ethnographical portions of travel narratives as material suitable only for a shallow or prurient curiosity, and to mock in particular the examples provided of native peoples' 'superstitious' beliefs and rituals, Coleridge in 'genial' mode is willing not only to contest the irreligious character of the 'Northern Indians' but also to argue that different individuals or groups within the population as a whole might have a different religious outlook. On the one hand, the fact that Coleridge fastened on this passage in Hearne to enter a debate with the author is representative of the keen interest that British readers of the period took in accounts of North American 'Indians,' but on the other hand the note itself is exceptional for the open-minded and inquiring spirit in which it is written.

At the other extreme from Coleridge's practice of genial reading are the annotations and reading notes of the novelist, antiquarian, and aesthete, William Beckford. A prolific note-taker, Beckford's standard practice was to make his notes in serial fashion on the flyleaves of a book – anything from a few words to two or three sentences, neatly written with an accompanying page reference. The books in which he made such notes are disseminated worldwide in private and institutional collections, and no catalogue exists. Beckford also kept separate albums of reading notes (the Bodleian has a good collection), and his commonplace book (mentioned above) offers an additional window on his reading, including extracts from book reviews that appealed to his sensibility. As one would expect from an author with his interests, travel literature is prominent in all these forms of manuscript, while Beckford's well-known Orientalist enthusiasms did not prevent him from keeping up with publications on North America.

Beckford gives the impression of grazing on travel books, picking out interesting observations or entertaining anecdotes in a fairly random manner. Sometimes his manner of presentation is neutral (though his selection of passages always implies a point of view), but his characteristic style of annotation is lightly ironic summary: he likes to have intellectual fun, either at the author's expense or at the expense of people described by the author. In his copy of Bartram's *Travels*, now in the Beinecke Library, his notes mainly focus on the author's botanical explorations, the size and splendour of American trees and flowers evidently impressing him. (Although best known as a collector and a patron of the fine arts, Beckford was a lover of the countryside and his enthusiasm for natural history is well documented in his letters and travel diaries.) However, he also homes in on the celebrated description of an alligator feeding frenzy, and the phrase 'a tremendous scene' indicates genuine excitement (the word 'tremendous' occurs in Bartram's text, but here it seems to be a summative comment on Beckford's part). In annotating his copy of Thomas Ashe's *Travels*, also in the Beinecke, Beckford is far more satirical. He notes various natural curiosities, certain scenes exemplary of the sublime and beautiful in American nature, and a few episodes featuring quaint characters or local communities – all more or less in sympathy with the author. However, Ashe's claim to have found genuine paintings by Van Dyke and Corregio in a 'small frame house' in Cincinnati prompts the comment that the author is 'a better judge of Barrows [Indian earthworks] than of paintings,' and his observation that the numbers of Indians on the banks of the Ohio have declined from four million to two thousand in just forty years is damned by exclamation mark and a scornful 'Is this credible?' In his reading notes on Ross's *Voyage of Discovery*, Beckford's tone is consistently mocking, whether directed at the 'Arctic Highlanders' (Inuit) encountered by the expedition or the expedition's commander: his concluding remark is that 'Capt. Ross, a mighty good plain man, seems never to have entertained any sanguine expectations of discovering the N. W. Passage & to have resigned himself to the failure of his dull expedition with much placidity' (MS Beckford c.57, fol. 107). This is a remarkably succinct yet incisive judgement which mirrors public criticism of Ross's abortive voyage. Occasionally Beckford is so moved by something he reads that he drops the ironic mask and writes from the heart. William Faux's *Memorable Days in America* (1823) brought the iniquities of slavery uncomfortably to his attention, and Beckford (himself, of course, the son and heir of a Jamaican planter and slaveholder) made an anguished note that 'the atrocious barbarities practised by some Carolina planters on their Slaves are sufficient to make the most callous and unfeeling shudder' (MS Beckford c.55, fol. 75). A close study of Beckford's manuscript notes on American travel books reveals a playful, learned, and sophisticated reader, moving freely between a recreational interest in curiosities, a cheery contempt for exaggeration or insincerity, and deeper forms of emotional engagement.

The most expansive example of a 'supplementary' manuscript response to a North American travel book I have come across occurs in a British Library copy of Thomas Cooper's *Some Information Respecting America*. The anonymous owner has written a long summary note that extends over three pages at the start of the book. The note, which is too long to quote in its entirety, quotes statistics concerning the United States' rapid increase in population, annual imports and exports, and land clearance over a fifteen year period to argue for the high fertility of the land, and it implies a favourable comparison between the political and economic circumstances of the 'American farmer' – 'Owner of the soil on which he lives' – and his British counterpart. By glancing back to the state of development in England two hundred years before, the writer is almost certainly replying to contemporary adverse commentary on American culture and the poor prospects for emigrants,[18] and this leads into his or her concluding remarks:

---

[18] On internal evidence, the note was certainly written after 1805, since it refers to Richard Parkinson's *Tour in America*, which was published in that year; and probably before the first Reform Act in 1832, on the basis of an allusion to the corrupt British electoral process. Taking into account other data included in the note, such as the figure of 6 million provided for the population of the U.S.A., a date in the very early 1800s seems probable.

time, with industry has made England what she is, the great honour of the
Inhabitants: and time with Industry will give to the United States of America
all that [is?] [refined?] in Science & gratifying to rational man ... a Fren[chman]
accustomed to the culture of the vine, would make a b[ad] farmer in England:
& the English farmer would become a Bankrupt among the vines of France –
Hence [if we?] look into ourselves and examine the habits we have acq[uired]
we shall find that by going to reside in a foreign coun[try] the circumstances
change and the unhappiness or ill success we experience arises more from
ourselves than the defects of the Country which we adopt. – The description of
America which Mr Cooper has given is too highly coloured to be quite palatable
– he has overstrained the Subject to induce Englishmen to follow his Example &
[implicitly?] to believe all he says respecting his terrestrial paradise – Yet there
is much truth here [mixed?] with fiction.

The writer, drawing together his or her thoughts, perhaps for the annotator's own
benefit or perhaps for the edification of another likely or potential reader of the
book, here attempts to reach a balanced judgement on the merits of Cooper's book.
Whether this reader is aware of Cooper's ulterior motive for promoting emigration
to America (see Chapter 2) is not clear, but the lightly ironic 'terrestrial paradise,'
set against Cooper's neutral-sounding title (*Some Information ...*), implies a
sceptical attitude towards the author's motives; at the same time, the reference
to 'much truth' and the positive tone of the note as a whole suggests that there is
no knee-jerk anti-Americanism here and that the reader is determined to take a
reasonable, moderate view of this contentious contemporary issue.

Horace Walpole despised Hester Piozzi's style of annotating books, deploring
its general vulgarity, its 'colloquial smartness' and proximity to the speaking
voice (qtd. in Brownell 99). However, as a prolific annotator himself, it was very
much Piozzi's practice, rather than the principle, that he disliked, and, as Morris
Brownell insists, it is precisely the informality of her notes that makes Piozzi
valuable today, opening a window on 'the affective response of an eighteenth-
century reader' (100). Indeed, the special attraction of marginalia generally, from
the point of view of reception history, is the illusion they can generate of hearing
a dead reader speak. Brownell also suggests that for a woman writer like Piozzi,
whose literary career 'encountered many frustrations,' book annotation may have
seemed 'a kind of publication in limited editions of a single copy' (99). Piozzi, of
course, *had* a literary career; for other readers, perhaps, this form of piecemeal
authorship may well have been the nearest they ever got to publication. Whether
that was the case or not (and it obviously was not in the case of Beckford or
Coleridge), it is a mode of writing that raises intriguing questions about the textual
orientation of Romantic readers. Whether they were noting choice extracts or
copying them into another book, or cross-referencing one text with another in a
studious or merely frivolous manner, or supplementing a passage with ideas or
information of their own, they seem to have seen books as composite, divisible
entities with permeable boundaries, capable of being extended or, conversely,
broken up and enjoyed piece by piece. As Jackson observes, this plays havoc with

traditional notions of Romantic form as predicated on an analogy with living things, underscoring instead 'the commonsense assumption that books do not grow, but are made' (252). The annotated travel books I have examined are no different to any of the more diverse genres surveyed by Jackson. Indeed, in some ways travel literature seems exceptionally well suited to this reading mentality. By its very essence, travel, according to Eric Leed, imposes a 'logic of sequence, an order of change and transformation which serves and fosters a variety of longings' (22). By making notes of varying kinds in travel books, readers in this period were doing no more or less than insert themselves in that sequence, effecting further change and transformation – becoming, in a sense, an unbidden travelling companion, alert to different possibilities.

The miscellaneous reading experiences discussed in this chapter are drawn from varied sources: letters, diaries, autobiographies, reading notes, commonplace books, marginalia. They encompass a range of responses to the subject-matter of North America over a period in which, as my brief historical overview at the beginning of the chapter made clear, huge changes took place both on the continent itself and in its relationship – or what became the relationship of its constituent parts – to Great Britain. These responses include a hunger for knowledge of the infant United States and a strong interest in learning the 'facts' rather than trusting to 'travellers' tales' in the older, pejorative sense; an enjoyment of narrative incident and human drama contained in some travel books – the Arctic expeditions are a prime example – underpinned by the assurance that these events *really happened*; a keen curiosity about countries geographically and culturally so different from the reader's own, yet settled by people in the main so similar; the gratification of reinforced national self-esteem; a pleasure in being imaginatively transported out of one's habitual environment to somewhere new and exciting; a form of mental recreation, delighting in making associations with other texts, however remote in provenance or theme; a serious effort to wrestle with issues raised by the text. One thing that these heterogeneous responses have in common is that they are not noticeably driven by any partisan political agenda; in that they are clearly distinct from some of the formal reviews I shall be examining in the next chapter. It is not that questions of audience never arise: letters clearly have recipients, journals were often written with sympathetic readers in mind, and marginalia can be seen as a form of intellectual exchange within a culture of collective reading and ownership. But in these modes of communication the stakes are not so high, the pressures for conformity or dissimulation less intense, and it is not necessary to harbour illusions of complete transparency to believe that, nevertheless, in such fragmentary and unscripted utterances one is getting closer to the bone of the reading experience. The historical record is untidy, contradictory, and not nearly as substantial as one would like, but only by immersing oneself in such evidence can one begin to follow the mental footprints of Romantic readers and pick up the scent of their vanished humanity.

Chapter 2
'A Continent of Information':
America in the Periodical Press

All the evidence that one can gather, however patiently and painstakingly, from whatever sources, of private reading experiences of travel narratives as recorded or described by individual readers in the Romantic period, is dwarfed by the vast archive of published reviews produced by elite, professional, or semi-professional readers. The contemporary popularity of 'voyages and travels' is underlined by the seriousness of the attention, and the sheer column-inches, devoted to them by the weekly, monthly, and quarterly literary journals, especially those that maintained a selective reviewing policy. Some of the leading reviewers of the age, such as John Barrow, Francis Jeffrey, and Robert Southey, specialized in reviews of this genre. It seems senseless to ignore this prodigious and fascinating body of work in trying to assess the impact of North American travels on the reading public, whatever qualifications might need to be made regarding the value or legitimacy of formal reviews as evidence of contemporary reception. This chapter, based on a study of reviews of travel books in more than thirty Romantic-era periodicals, considers how these public responses articulated perceptions of, and attitudes to, America, and mediated debates that were central to the culture and politics of the time. My focus here will be on aspects of the period's enduring obsession with the newly independent United States, leaving Canada, the Northwest, and the Arctic to be treated separately in the next chapter.

Periodical reviews had an especially important role to play in disseminating awareness of the latest travel literature; for many readers they may well have been the nearest they got to the travel books themselves. In her recent study of the reading public's generation-long immersion in the vicarious thrills of British Arctic exploration, Janice Cavell argues that readers typically consumed accounts of these voyages – beginning after Waterloo, and culminating in the many expeditions sent in search of John Franklin's lost expedition of 1845–47 – not via the original published narratives but via the periodicals, which not only printed lengthy excerpts from the primary texts but also added supplementary materials such as extracts from the explorers' personal correspondence. The periodical coverage, initiated by long articles in the *Quarterly Review* from 1816 onwards and filtering down eventually to mass-market magazines like the *Mirror of Literature and Amusement* and the *Penny Magazine*, constituted a 'connected narrative,' an ongoing national epic that gripped the imagination of the late Romantic and early Victorian reading public. As Cavell points out, the reviews were 'available to a wider audience than the books themselves,' and given the generosity of their coverage 'even those who did not read the narratives in full could regard themselves as knowledgeable about the subject' (33). I think she makes a persuasive case, and one that I believe should be generalized with reference to travel books published throughout the Romantic period. These books were typically produced as luxurious quartos, often embellished with handsome maps or illustrations, in small print runs of around 750 copies, with only the more popular subsequently republished in slightly less pricey octavo editions. The £1, 10s charged for Isaac Weld's *Travels through North America* and the £1, 11s, 6d asked for Alexander Mackenzie's *Voyages from Montreal* – at a time when a reasonable income for an upper-middle-class person was £5 a week, and the highest-paid skilled workers earned around £1, 16s a week (St Clair 194–5) – were entirely unexceptional. At these prices, most potential readers were as likely to take a holiday in America as to purchase the latest transatlantic travel book.

I have already established in Chapter 1 that the readership of these expensive books was not necessarily limited to wealthy individual purchasers: subscription libraries, book clubs, and other facilities for shared access widened the potential audience. My own scrutiny of the unique borrowing records of the Bristol Library Society reveals that, for example, Mackenzie's *Voyages* was borrowed a total of thirty-four times between 1802 and 1807. (Of course, we do not know how many of these readers read the book from cover to cover; it is also likely that this library's members' well-attested preference for travel literature[1] yields an extreme multiplier for a work in this genre.) Even allowing, however, for single copies passing through many hands, it seems beyond doubt that the community of readers that had first-hand acquaintance with the latest travels and explorations via the original editions was small and socially exclusive. It is with this in mind that William St Clair observes that the explosion in travel writing between 1790 and 1820 led the reading elites of Britain to appropriate imaginatively 'the whole civilised and uncivilised world,' so that there was 'nothing which [they] did not feel was partly their own' (233–4), but that readers lower down the social scale, stuck with a selection of cheap, out-of-copyright literature purveying a homely blend of patriotism, natural religion and family values, had much more limited mental horizons.

Periodicals, however, had a significantly higher circulation than travel books, the leading journals selling between five and twelve thousand copies an issue. With monthly journals costing between one and two shillings and the weightier quarterlies selling for six shillings (Altick 319) they were more affordable than new books, and more importantly they benefited from a broad distribution network that saw them taken in by subscription libraries, book clubs, and literary societies, perused in reading rooms and coffeehouses, and otherwise passed from hand to hand. Southey may have exaggerated when he claimed in 1817 that the *Quarterly Review*'s print run was ten thousand, and that 'fifty times ten thousand read its contents' (Smiles 1: 204), but it seems reasonable to assume that large numbers of readers had regular access to that journal's long reviews of travel narratives.

---

[1]   See Kaufman, 'Some Reading Trends.'

Whatever the true size of the reading nation in this period – Burke's 1790 estimate of 80,000 (Altick 49) and Jeffrey's 1814 figure of more than 200,000 (St Clair 478) are equally unverifiable – it was the periodical press that did most to unite the diverse constituencies of readers of which it was actually composed. What this means is that knowledge of new travel literature was not necessarily restricted to the book-buying elite, but that for many readers reviews of such works stood in for the primary texts themselves: reviews were not adjuncts to a personal reading experience, as they later became and perhaps still are, but a substitute for it. This is of some importance in assessing the review as a mode of reading and in considering its legitimacy as evidence of reception.

It has long been a reflex attitude in reception studies to discount or diminish the value of reviews as indicators of how literary works were read in historically removed times. It can be alleged against them that they are unrepresentative in class and gender terms of the reading public as a whole; that they record the views of the most articulate and opinionated, rather than the 'average' reader; that their authenticity is bedevilled by systemic plagiarism among an overworked corps of hack writers, compounded by the anonymity that was an institutional requirement; and that they were written to appeal to specific audiences and were subject to commercial pressures and political and religious censorship, albeit often of a voluntary or self-regulated nature. For many scholars, it would seem, periodical reviews are valuable chiefly for helping us map the broad horizons of reception in a period, or for their insight into general cultural and institutional conflicts, rather than as examples of how individual works were read, interpreted, and evaluated. It is symptomatic, albeit understandable, that the pioneering *Reading Experience Database*, a project managed by the Open University and funded by the Arts and Humanities Research Council, does not include reviews among its allowable forms of evidence.

There has, of course, been a marked upsurge of interest in British periodical culture of the Romantic era in recent years. As recently as 2000, Mark Parker, in his study of selected late Romantic literary magazines, expressed the view that magazines and periodicals were still not taken seriously as 'an object of study in their own right,' pointing to the lack of an 'existing conceptual framework' for such analysis or even 'a reliable description of the materials' (1–3); he also noted with some irritation the tendency for literary critics to draw on these sources merely to show how contemporary readers failed to appreciate the quality of some now-canonical poet or novelist. A swathe of books published in the intervening years has made Parker's annoyance look somewhat outdated. The historicist essays gathered in Kim Wheatley's *Romantic Periodicals and Print Culture* take pride in decentring canonical Romantic literature within the larger conversations that took place in the pages of the journals. William Christie and Jonathan Cutmore have contributed major new studies of the *Edinburgh Review* and *Quarterly Review*, respectively, adding substantially to our understanding of these major publications and the culture wars in which they were implicated. Focusing on the literary magazines of the late Romantic period, David Stewart has examined their negotiation of the troubled boundary between high and low cultures, while David Higgins has explored their role in shaping and disseminating conceptions of literary genius. Andrew Franta has shown how the growth of the periodical press (and the associated 'regime of publicity') affected the practice and theory of poetry, while Karen Fang has mapped subtle connections between late Romantic authors, periodicals, and imperialism. Mark Schoenfield's engrossing study complicates traditional assumptions regarding anonymous, corporate authorship by analysing the ways in which periodicals and individual writers 'developed, confronted and inhabited competing models of identity' (3), while in perhaps the most ambitious modern reassessment to date, Alex Benchimol dissects the competing critical discourses of liberal bourgeois and radical plebeian public spheres, as exemplified in key periodical projects in Scotland and England.

Timely and important as these new studies have been (and the above is by no means a complete summary), from the perspective of a student of reception history the situation has in some ways not changed very much. While the output of what Cutmore calls this 'renewed scholarly commitment to explore the cultural impact of early nineteenth-century periodicals' (*Conservatism* 1) is impressive, the overwhelming thrust of recent criticism has been at the larger discursive and ideological functions of the periodical press, along with the participation of major authors in the wider, politicized intellectual networks that the public journals afforded. There has been much less interest in the reviewing practice of individual periodicals, in reviews as vehicles for disseminating knowledge to a literate public thirsty for information, or in reviews as evidence of the reception of individual works. As for works in a 'non-literary' genre like travel writing, with the exception of a single essay by Massimiliano Demato on the *Edinburgh Review*,[2] there has been no treatment proportional to the genre's prominence in the journals' tables of contents. William St Clair argues that the literary reviews, although 'generally believed to be influential, both on opinion and on sales,' are in fact 'a poor indicator both of commercial sales and of the reactions of readers' (189), and it would seem that most critics are disposed to follow his lead and look elsewhere for the 'reactions of readers.' By contrast, Stephen Colclough's close examination of the diary of Sheffield cutler, Joseph Hunter, finds that this reader, at least, often read reviews and works of various kinds 'in tandem,' and that his 'reading strategies were clearly influenced ... by the interpretative strategies of the periodical reviewers' (112–3), although he was not slavishly deferential to their authority.

Colclough's research offers a valuable corrective and prompts us to reconsider the relationship between reviewers and 'ordinary' readers. With that in mind, it is worth revisiting the objections to periodical reviews I summarized above. It is true

---

[2]   Demato's article is an excellent survey of the *Edinburgh*'s treatment of travel literature over the period of Jeffrey's editorship. The present author has built on it with a more concentrated account of the journal's reception of North American travels (Jarvis, 'Contesting').

that periodical writers were overwhelmingly – though not exclusively[3] – male, and mostly from what we would now think of as solidly middle-class backgrounds; but given that the entire literary archive of the period suffers from a similar class and gender bias this cannot be allowed to disqualify their use as sources. Moreover, as we have seen in Chapter 1, there is a thin vein of female testimony to compare and contrast with the voluminous records of male readers. While reviewers cannot be regarded as ordinary, or perhaps not even typical, readers, their responses, as Janice Cavell argues, 'must have had much in common with those of the general public' (34); more to the point, they knew the particular community of readers a particular journal was addressing and shaped their responses in relation to largely unspoken assumptions about that community's tastes, attitudes, and beliefs. This may appear to undermine the radical sincerity we like to associate with reader response; in fact, it merely acknowledges the dialogic nature of meaning-production and the 'socialization of texts' theorized by Jerome McGann[4] and renders reviewers untrustworthy only in opposition to an illusory authenticity ascribed to more informal and supposedly more spontaneous utterances. The traditional put-down that literary reviews were staffed by hacks cravenly puffing their publishers' own productions was convincingly rebutted many years ago by Derek Roper, who revealed it as an urban legend originating in self-serving propaganda disseminated by Smollett and perpetuated by lazy criticism: as Roper says, modern research on the authorship of periodicals has shown that most so-called 'hacks' were men of considerable learning, and given that the journals were sold to an educated public 'Systematic abuse of the kind so often described would ... have been self-detecting, self-defeating, and fatal to the sale of the Review' (31). Finally, while religious and political motives undoubtedly had a bearing on reviewing, these were as much the personal property of the authors as they were a corporate 'line' to which they tamely subscribed; moreover, ideological positions – for example, the *Eclectic*'s Dissenting bias as against the *Edinburgh*'s anticlericalism – were common knowledge, and readers could make allowance for them.

In his important study of Romantic-era reading audiences, Jon Klancher argues that the French Revolution fractured the ideal, aspirational social unity modelled by early eighteenth-century periodicals, which conveyed the promise of an egalitarian world of print insulated from the divided, hierarchical society outside; from this point onwards, he suggests, readerships had to be produced, defined, and maintained along ideological lines, and audiences learned 'their identity as audiences only by becoming aware of the pressure of other audiences, interpretatively and socially competing for position in cultural and social space' (38). However, this presumes an astonishing degree of dutiful conformity on the part of periodical writers and an equally implausible degree of passivity on the part of readers. In fact, even during the Revolutionary and Napoleonic period,

---

[3]   Mary Wollstonecraft's many contributions to the *Analytical Review* – I count twenty-seven reviews of travel books between 1788 and 1797 – are a well-known exception.

[4]   See McGann, *The Textual Condition*.

there seems to have been more freedom or manoeuvrability within the world of periodical publishing than is implied in this top-down model of discourse. Writers contributed articles to a range of journals without necessarily donning a different suit of beliefs, and if they were not unduly provoked by the politics of the book under review would not feel obliged to obtrude their own views, let alone ventriloquize those of the publication they were working for: as Alvin Sullivan says, there was 'considerable independence even in periodicals of opposing political persuasions' (xxii). By the same token, in their book clubs and library reading rooms readers perused a variety of periodicals, presumably without having to learn a new identity with each new magazine they picked up.[5] My main point here is that periodical writers were not robotic hirelings of a single publication or a monolithic ideology, and it makes sense to take them seriously as *readers*, because much of the time, despite the need to take account of religious and political sensitivities, the voice of an individual reader is still discernible in their reviews.

My discussion in this chapter therefore starts from the premise that reviews are rich and under-utilized texts, interesting as much for their patterns of approval and disapproval as for the flashes of personality that show through the pall of anonymity, restricted admittedly in terms of the social background of their authors, but intellectually and rhetorically diverse in ways that have yet to be satisfactorily described and analysed. With reference to voyages and travels, they were, in addition, important vehicles of dissemination and transmission. Before I turn to the particular themes and topoi of North American travels, I want to say something about the formal characteristics of these reviews and the publications in which they appeared. (Some of my remarks apply equally to reviews of different types of books, but I shall inflect this discussion throughout towards the specific subject-matter of travel.)

What, then, are the key attributes of reviews of travel books in this period? To begin with, the reviews differ widely in terms of length and format, although the differences are best thought of as a spectrum rather than as rigid categorical distinctions. At one end of the spectrum there are those reviews that consist exclusively or very largely of a series of long extracts from the work in question: the *Literary Magazine, or Monthly Epitome of British Literature* (1797–1806) and the *New Annual Register* (1780–1825) fit this description, while many articles in the *Gentleman's Magazine* (1731–1907) offer very little more than substantial excerpts. While it is customary to dismiss such reviews as lazy compilations produced by journeymen critics interested only in their pay cheque (reviewers were paid by the folio sheet, usually made up of several reviews, and received

---

[5]   Again, Stephen Colclough's study of Joseph Hunter's diary is an interesting case in point. Among the periodicals Hunter regularly accessed via local libraries were the *Oeconomist, Monthly Magazine, Analytical Review, Gentleman's Magazine*, and *Monthly Review* (99). Anna Larpent's diaries show that she browsed an even wider range of journals. On the basis of Klancher's argument, both readers must have suffered severe personality disorders.

their money regardless of how they filled the pages), I have suggested above that they had the merit of offering the reader a first-hand experience of expensive books they might otherwise find difficult to access. Further along the spectrum the proportions of editorial and quoted material alter in favour of the former; reviews are typically much longer, and in the case of journals like the *British Review* (1811–25), *Critical Review* (1756–1817), and *Eclectic Review* (1805–68) could be very substantial, although the bias is towards précis rather than analysis or evaluation. Derek Roper ably characterizes this form of review:

> For long works a favourite method was what might be called the 'guided tour,'
> in which the reviewer first gives a short statement of the scope and nature of the
> book and then works his way through it, summarising, quoting, and occasionally
> criticising. At the end comes an attempt to cast the balance of its merits and
> defects, or perhaps only a brief general verdict. (41–2)

I shall return to this neat description shortly. Finally, though, at the other end of the spectrum there are the long essay-like reviews pioneered by the *Edinburgh Review* (1802–1929) and subsequently imitated by the *Quarterly Review* (1809–1962) and others. These can engage closely with the book under review but are just as likely to use that book as the starting point for an independent examination of some topic connected with it. They are intellectually heavyweight pieces, often fiercely opinionated, and when their authors are unimpressed with a book they can be harshly judgemental. Quotation may not figure much at all: it is a quirky feature of reviewing in this period that the amount of quotation decreases in inverse proportion to the length of the article.

Long extracts, whatever ignoble purposes they may have served in some quarters, were especially suited to reviews of travel literature in that they allowed readers to immerse themselves fully in the texture of the work – to get a measure of the self-presentation of the traveller, experience the style of description or narration, or sample the observations of people, manners, and customs, in a way that was simply not possible via summary or critical commentary. Nevertheless, understanding a reviewer's excerpting strategy – why these particular passages have been chosen – is occasionally a challenge when studying periodical literature: sometimes there is a logic and consistency to the selection, at other times the impression is of randomly aggregated quotes. I shall take up this subject later in the chapter.

Is there anything else to say about this much-derided aspect of eighteenth-century and Romantic-era reviewing? It is worth remembering here the persistence throughout this period of the practice of copying passages from texts of different sorts into albums and commonplace books. As I observed in Chapter 1, travel books were not the most popular source material for commonplacing, but were certainly not excluded from such activity and may well have been more popular with male readers. Heather Jackson's study of marginalia suggests that readers' habits of annotation, encouraged by the progressive educational theory of the age, produced a specific textual orientation. Practices of extracting, linking, and supplementing, evident in marginal annotations as much as in album-making, resulted in

> a piecemeal approach to reading and composition, an attention to trees rather than to the forest. We observe readers of the period virtually taking a book apart for the sake of good bits they might be able to use themselves by attaching them to other books or by incorporating them in some sort of new writing. And that must mean that they came to their books looking out for short extractable passages. (120)

One of the most interesting findings in Stephen Colclough's study of Joseph Hunter's diary is precisely that some of the entries 'mimic the structure of reviews by including a summary of a text followed by an extract or discussion of a particular scene,' indicating that 'they were important in forming the way in which he approached texts and contributed to his sense of self as a reader' (113). In this light, there would have been nothing odd or contemptible about the mode of reviewing practised by a miscellany like the *Gentleman's Magazine* or weightier reviews like the *Eclectic* and *Critical*; rather, it was custom-made for readers' purposes and perfectly attuned to their mindset. Moreover, if readers of the period, as Jackson suggests, viewed books as provisional structures, 'built up from discrete parts and consequently susceptible of similarly piecemeal revision and improvement' (120), then maybe a longish review of a travel book, omitting all that was dull or repetitive in the narration but presenting a few choice episodes or descriptions, would have seemed to them a perfectly acceptable redaction of the original – perhaps even an improvement? Perhaps, too, this encouraged a piecemeal way of viewing the countries they were reading about – as a menagerie of quotable observations or commonplaces, a gallery of images, a cabinet of curiosities? If this was the way that readers were habituated to encounter foreign countries, it is hardly surprising that the latter could easily be reduced to stereotypes and clichés.

I am struck by the congruence between Roper's description of the eighteenth-century mode of reviewing and the subject-matter of the travel genre I am concerned with. A reviewer takes his readers on a 'guided tour' of a book in which an explorer or traveller guides his readers through a journey in which he was himself, invariably, 'guided' by settlers or indigenous people. Is there something about this apparently clumsy print genre that nevertheless resonates with the experience of travel? The often poorly motivated transition from one notable episode or 'extractable passage' to the next recalls Eric Leed's account of the mental effects of travel, notably the imposition of a logic of sequence or 'progressional ordering of reality.' Travellers in this period liked to believe they were acquiring new knowledge, amenable to systematic arrangement, but this is often in tension with the narrative form in which they cast their written account. The journey, according to Leed, 'gives rise to a structure of representation, the epic and journal form of one place, scene, thing after another' (73); on a much reduced scale, might not the periodical review preserve something of that 'structure of passage'? If 'motion resolves all orders of space ... into an experiential order of continuously evolving appearances,' connected only by the motions of the traveller, does this not chime rather well with a textual progress from one remarkable anecdote or descriptive event to the next, connected only by the motionless mobility of the reader? Perhaps the 'guided tour' method of reviewing found its 'objective correlative' in the travel genre?

Travel, Leed suggests, generates and satisfies contrary needs. In its linear progress through distinct phases of departure, passage, and arrival it 'fosters a variety of human longings: for motion and rest, liberty and confinement, indeterminacy and definition' (22). Curiously, Margaret Beetham has said something similar about the nineteenth-century periodical, identifying 'the particular balance of closure against open-ness' as 'the form's characteristic mode' (99). The periodical's open-ended character comes from the need to keep readers buying each new number as it appear (hence serializations, series of articles, constant self-referentiality, and so on), and from the freedom it offers readers to construct their own texts (by choosing which items they read, and in what order). Against this are the very periodicity of the journal, the regularities of its format, and its consistent tone of address. Readers, Beetham appears to suggest, find gratification in this oscillation between openness and closure. Perhaps the Romantic reader found additional pleasure in contrary facets of the vicarious experience of travel that periodical reviews afforded: in almost every issue, interesting snapshots of another set of travels in some remote corner of the world that would only ever be known through the medium of print; at the same time, reassurance in the familiarity of the journal's approach to its subject, in the consistency of its reading strategies, and in the fact that someone else had already beaten a track through the primary text and made it easier for those who followed.

Instruction and amusement

I have argued that periodical reviews were especially important in disseminating awareness of the latest travel and exploration literature. It seems clear that in devoting considerable space and serious attention to voyages and travels the journals were conscious of feeding a strong demand among their readers – not only for news of the genre in general but for information on American travels in particular. A review of Hearne's *Journey ... to the Northern Ocean* in John Murray's *English Review* in 1796 notes that the 'present taste for books of travels and voyages is stronger than that for any other species of composition or compilation,' attributing this popularity to the facility with which the genre ministers to two quite contrary readerly tendencies: 'an indolent wish to be amused without any great exertion of attention and intellection' and 'a preference to matter of fact before mere works of imagination.' The author considers that the combination of 'savoury entertainment' with the intrinsic interest belonging to the 'real aspect' of different peoples and places is crucial in broadening the appeal of travel literature beyond the 'learned and inquisitive' to 'the most part of readers in general' (28: 1). As with other kinds of writing, though, the value of the best works of travel is debased by many worthless imitators – the 'myriads of tourists, who dash forth, if not into new tracts, at least on the highways, where they endeavour to kick up a dust as well as the others' (28: 2).

The *English Review* was not alone in commenting on this trend. In its annual roundup of new publications for 1799, the *Monthly Magazine*, a recently established forum for the radical intelligentsia, confirmed the current popularity of travels, and American travels in particular. Responding favourably (and with admirable impartiality) to the *Tour* of La Rochefoucault-Liancourt, a prominent royalist émigré who spent three years in the United States, its reviewer commends the mix of 'authentic information' and 'personal anecdote and adventure'; he or she insists that, now the dust has settled in the years that have passed since Independence, British readers can rediscover their links with a country still seen at this stage as something of an estranged child, so 'every authentic account of the actual state of that rising people cannot fail of being received with eagerness' (8: 1046–7). The *Annual Review* typically began its yearly survey with a chapter on voyages and travels, its entries for 1803–06 comprising an impressive 22, 27, 14 and 22 titles. A general preface to the coverage for 1805 declares that such books are 'best calculated to excite a strong and general interest in the reading part of the community' – the entire spectrum from mere 'loungers' to the 'philosopher' searching for 'materials of useful contemplation.' America, the editor startlingly suggests, is a bigger unknown even than Africa to the domestic audience, and 'it is therefore with peculiar satisfaction, that we perceive an increasing curiosity concerning the transatlantic Continent' (4: 1). By 1824, the build-up of American travels, boosted most recently by Timothy Dwight's *Travels in New England, and New York*, was such that the *Eclectic Review* contemplated with awe a veritable 'continent of information' (2nd ser. 22: 79).

As these quotations may already have indicated, the criteria applied by professional readers, across the ideological spectrum, in evaluating travel literature were almost wearily predictable, amounting to little more than travel-inflected elaborations of the Horatian poetic dictum, *prodesse et delectare*. The *English Review*'s preference for factually informative travels enlivened by entertaining anecdote is echoed in the staunchly conservative and Anglican *British Critic*'s demand for 'amusement and instruction,' a demand it considers ill met by too many books of American travels full of 'dry detail of places seen, spaces passed, and posts established' (39: 118). An unusually full statement of criteria, accompanied by a typology of travel books, is supplied by the *British Review*, a journal founded on evangelical Christian principles which gave prominent attention to travel literature[6] and took a particular interest in North America. A review of Zebulon Pike's *Exploratory Travels through the Western Territories* (1811) begins dividing this proliferating genre ('more numerous perhaps than works in any other literary department') into six classes: travellers who have discovered countries 'before unknown to the European public'; those who deliver more accurate information

---

[6]   In its first ten years, 16 per cent of the works reviewed were travel books (Sullivan 73).

on countries 'before imperfectly known'; travels distinguished by the superior knowledge of the traveller; travels given importance by virtue of their specialist insights in some field (for example, Arthur Young's expertise in agriculture); travels notable for their 'originality or singularity, or for some uncommon circumstances relative to the author'; and the remainder, up to one half of the total, that are none of the above, and offer 'neither instruction nor amusement' (1: 175–6). Pike's travels, according to this reader, fall proudly into the first category; but I am interested more in the light shed by this classification on the contemporary horizon of expectations regarding travel writing. Only in a limited way in the fifth category is any allowance made for the author-traveller as, in Mary Wollstonecraft's famous words in the preface to her Scandinavian *Letters*, the 'little hero' of her or his tale (Wollstonecraft 62). Confirming my observations in Chapter 1, there is little sign here of that radical reorientation towards the subject-in-motion that has come to be synonymous with Romantic travel. Instead the relentless focus is on the new knowledge of places and peoples to be gained from the work in question, thus honouring the humanist and Enlightenment tradition of scientific or philosophical travel and its project of 'appropriating the world as information' (Leed 188). In formal statements concerning the genre, here as elsewhere, the personality, adventures, or interior, spiritual (rather than material) journey of the traveller[7] contributes at best a mere leavening of 'amusement' to the firm dough of 'instruction.'

The hierarchical nature of these mantra-like criteria brings with it a preference for a plain, simple and accessible style, a respect for accurate observation, a concern with the author's credentials, intolerance of any suspected reliance on other written sources, and aversion to any admixture of fact and fiction. William Priest, for example, is censured in the *Annual Review* for including 'a novel writer's story of an Indian' (1: 106) in what is otherwise a faithful account of *Travels in the United States of America* (1802). These anxieties of authenticity stem, of course, from post-Enlightenment travel writing's awkward self-differentiation from other genres such as the imaginary voyage and the travel novel, as well as from the viral proliferation of travel hoaxes in the eighteenth century, including fraudulent claims to have descended the Mississippi to its mouth and to have penetrated the Northwest Passage. As Percy Adams states in his classic study, 'the continent that gave birth to the great majority of untruths about topography was North America' (45).

Instruction and amusement can also be correlated with the ambiguities and ambivalences of 'curiosity' and its cognates – terms that circulate with contagious force in readings of American travels in this period. Nigel Leask and Barbara Benedict, in chronologically divergent but equally thought-provoking studies, have provided ample intellectual and historical context for this most ideologically loaded of concepts. Leask finds in Lord Kames's *Elements of Criticism* the grounds of a distinction between 'positive and negative, rational and vulgar, valences for

---

[7]   For this distinction, see Todorov.

"curiosity"' (28) that permeate travel writing of the late eighteenth and early nineteenth centuries: on the one hand, there is a genuine epistemological impulse that can lead to the creation of new intellectual structures; on the other, a superficial, acquisitive, prurient, or sensation-seeking pursuit of novelty. The former might be embraced by a polite and learned audience, leaving the latter the preserve of plebeian readers seeking short-term entertainment, but in the absence of institutional structures and full methodological rigour 'rational' curiosity is constantly in danger of collapsing into its 'vulgar' alter-ego, not least because strangeness and novelty are readily marketable in a consumer culture. Benedict too focuses on the potential of curiosity – or the collecting of curiosities – as a means of displaying wealth and power among the privileged elite, or as a form of cultural ambition among the aspirational classes beneath them. As she makes clear, the relationships enacted by curiosity are profoundly unequal: in the contest between 'the power to forge curiosity and the weakness of becoming one' (72) it is always preferable to practise the curious gaze rather than become its helpless or unwitting object. Throughout the seventeenth and eighteenth centuries, Benedict argues, travellers were active in bringing back, physically or discursively, natural or human wonders and curiosities to the centres of European civilization. In epistemological terms, this entailed detaching such objects from whatever frameworks or narratives might have given them meaning within their indigenous culture: 'travelers manufactured curiosity by concealing the purpose and context of the wonders they reported, thus making their information strange' (11) – and profitable. By extension, reading a travel narrative, for those without the means to travel, meant imaginatively appropriating curiosities they could neither see, nor collect, nor possess.

Although I would like to retain the possibility of a less sinister connotation for curiosity – something closer to Justin Stagl's definition of a '"superfluous" activity having no immediate utilitarian goal' (2) – these ideas are undoubtedly helpful in understanding the responses of professional readers to the scores of transatlantic travel books that appeared in this period. This is especially so given the very strong bias in the reviews towards the 'curious' appearance, dress, customs and beliefs of the Native peoples of North America. The approach varies, as indeed the approach of the books they are reviewing varies, from one of ethnological precision to one of vulgar anecdotalism, but there is no denying that in their fascination with 'Indians' the periodical reviews betray an insatiable mental appetite for human curiosities and assume such an appetite among their own readers.

The practical application of the criteria I have described can be observed by examining the contrasting reception accorded to two prominent travel books of the period (both now sunk in obscurity), Thomas Ashe's *Travels in America* (1808) and Isaac Weld's *Travels through the States of North America and the Provinces of Upper and Lower Canada* (1799).

In the little that is known of the life of Thomas Ashe,[8] a feckless yet resourceful army officer for whose career the term 'picaresque' might have been invented,

---

[8]   See Henderson's entry on Ashe in the *DNB*, and Herrick for more detail.

there is little to inspire confidence in the reliability of his account of a journey along the Ohio and Mississippi valleys. He was suspected or accused of seduction, embezzlement, theft, and blackmail; and he evidently had a romantic disregard for financial probity. Yet somehow he fell on his feet time and time again – serving on the front line in the war against France as a young man, later ingratiating himself with Jefferson and securing the editorship of the *National Intelligencer*. The authenticity of Ashe's *Travels* was called into question by an American, Charles Schultz, who had followed in Ashe's alleged footsteps, in a book published in 1810, but British reviewers had by this stage already savaged Ashe's claims.

The *Annual Review* began its discussion with a withering attack on the author's vanity, insinuating that his anonymous preface, which compares him favourably to giants of contemporary exploration such as James Cook and Mungo Park, was in fact his own work; it further challenged Ashe's integrity by suggesting that he had not actually passed through a region (the Kentucky Barrens) that he wrote about with such assurance, and knew 'no more about [it] than his printer's pressman' (7: 42). Even more devastating in its criticism was the *Eclectic Review*, perhaps the most formidable competitor to the *Edinburgh Review* at this time and a journal with a strong interest in America and American literature. The *Eclectic* launches its review with a barrage of ironic praise of Ashe's versatility and 'perpetual good fortune' (1st ser. 4: 791) as a traveller, the clear message being that much of the narrative is pure invention; and the journal impugns his use of sources by suggesting that it would be possible, with the aid of previous travellers' accounts, to 'form a very amusing book, extremely like Mr Ashe's, on a very narrow basis of original information, supplied by a trader's journal' (793). These two reviews confirm the absolute incommensurability of fact and fiction in the travel genre, in the eyes of its consumers, and the scorn and intolerance of these elite readers is symptomatic of a general vigilance towards malpractice and the constant suspicion of being imposed upon. Travel writing is viewed, ideally, as an artless, innocent genre, the unpremeditated, unadulterated record of personal experience; any sign of contrivance, or stylization, or working to a formula and the reviewers' knives leap from their sheaths. While the *Critical Review*, honouring the Horatian mantra, concludes, unusually, that Ashe provides 'no small share of information and amusement' (3rd ser. 17: 266), the *Eclectic* decides that the miscellaneousness of Ashe's book suggests someone more concerned with capturing readers than capturing the truth:

> exploits, philosophising speculations the most absurd and unscientific, topographical details, scandal, discoveries, abuse of the Americans, and anecdotes enforcing the author's warnings against emigrating to the anterior settlements, are all crowded together, as if with a solicitude to exhibit specimens of every kind of bait which the work affords... (1st ser. 4: 794)

Prominent among the varied contents of Ashe's *Travels* are his descriptions of numerous Indian mounds that he visits, and in some cases crudely excavates, as he pursues his course down the Ohio and the Mississippi, and which become the

occasion for 'philosophising speculations' about an antediluvian master-race that
once roamed the Midwest, much more polished and technologically advanced
than present-day indigenes. This theory keys in with another of his favourite
themes, borrowed from the French naturalist, the Comte de Buffon, namely the
inevitable degeneration of man and animal in the unpropitious environment of
North America; this in turn fuels his deep disgust with the 'vicious propensities
of the genuine American character' (Ashe 1: 42–3) that he sees steadily emerging
as the population expands. What is interesting is the uniform resistance put up
by professional readers to these elements of Ashe's work. The *Annual Review*
dismisses his partiality for Buffon's theories with the ironic compliment that it was
'infinitely to the credit of Mr Ashe that the stream of his own eloquence should
have remained unfrozen' (7: 35) after spending so long under American skies.
The broadly sympathetic *Critical Review* cannot help remarking that 'conjecture
furnishes no small part' of all Ashe's forays into Indian archaeology (3rd ser. 17:
255), while the *Eclectic* denounces the 'solemn absurdity' of his 'philosophical and
antiquarian deductions,' which it finds 'very amusing [which here subtly becomes
a pejorative term], unless the reader be more disposed to snarl at folly than to
laugh at it' (1st ser. 4: 798, 796). The *Edinburgh Review* shares the impatience
with Ashe's 'ravings' on Indian antiquities, which it notes have been 'described
before by far more sober and competent observers' (15: 452, 448), as well as
his 'unmeasured hatred of the Americans' (442): it prefers an environmentalist
explanation for what Ashe takes to be innate flaws, viewing American manners as
'those of a scattered and migratory, but speculating people,' which will improve
as the population 'becomes more dense, and more settled in its habits' (442). The
reception of Ashe's *Travels* – hardly a work of towering genius – militates against
assumptions of a pervasive anti-Americanism in the British periodical press at this
time[9] and shows that independent-minded readers were capable of resisting the
Anglocentric bile of some travel writers. It shows too how high the bar was set in
the desire for 'instruction': professional reviewers and the 'widening circle' of their
readers had a real thirst for knowledge of the United States, which it was largely
the responsibility of travel writers to supply, and they were not prepared to put up
with sloppy, prejudiced, or platitudinous writing in place of that empirical duty.

Almost a decade earlier, Isaac Weld's *Travels* had enjoyed a much more positive
reception than Ashe. Weld, an Irishman, crossed the Atlantic in 1795, at an early
stage in the Revolutionary wars when the 'storms ... gathering over his native
country' made it sensible to investigate the possibility of 'refuge in a foreign land.'
(1: iii). He spent more than two years in America, restricting his travels in the
United States to the eastern states of Pennsylvania, Delaware, Maryland, Virginia,

---

[9]   This was a decade before the so-called 'Battle of the Quarterlies' between British
and American periodicals, which mingled British paranoia over the rising tide of emigration
with American hypersensitivity over any trace of condescension from the other side of the
water. For a succinct account, see Allen 144–50. I have elaborated elsewhere on the broadly
pro-American stance of the *Edinburgh Review* (Jarvis, 'Contesting').

New Jersey, and New York (his travels in Canada will feature in Chapters 3 and 4). When he returned to Ireland, it was 'without a sigh, and without entertaining the slightest wish to revisit' the continent (2: 376). Clearly, he had taken against aspects of American life and of what he perceived as the American character, and his critical observations were resented by American commentators. By contrast, the *Travels* were in general well received in Britain, but it is by no means clear that this was owing to a shared hostility towards the United States.

It is true that emigration was a hot political issue in the 1790s, not least because America attracted many liberals and radicals as, in Michael Wiley's words, 'a space to refocus their displaced political, social, and religious energy after France failed to fulfil its early revolutionary promise' (57). Consequently most periodicals had an editorial stance on emigration, and some were keen to use Weld's observations as ammunition for their views: prominent among these were the *British Critic* and *New Annual Review*, both of which were anxious to counter the seduction of America, and especially the *Anti-Jacobin Review*, which openly expressed the hope that Weld's book would dissuade the 'superior orders' from emigration and prevent the 'lower orders' from being 'imposed upon' if they were 'made acquainted' with its contents (2: 53; a revealing indicator, as it happens, of the presumed readership of a travel book). Unsurprisingly, these periodicals, among others, highlighted Weld's more negative observations, including his unflattering portrait of the American character as defined by covetousness and 'impertinent curiosity' (Weld 1: 134).

However, reviewers did not focus obsessively on the emigration issue: most took a broader interest in Weld's travels and judged his narrative by the standard criteria. The *European Magazine* acknowledged that Weld had 'steered a middle course' between exaggerated praise and vicious misrepresentation of the United States (36: 175), and seemed to value this concern for accuracy and impartiality. The *Monthly Review* considered that Weld's style was sometimes 'inelegant and incorrect,' but more importantly his book fulfilled the requirement to provide both 'entertainment and instruction' in good measure (30: 207). The *British Critic*, delighted though it may have been with Weld's potential usefulness in enlightening would-be emigrants, had a broader respect for his 'plain, simple, and satisfactory' descriptions and 'careful and sober' observations,' and it was for these qualities that its reviewer thought his book would become a standard point of reference. These critical and ethical judgements appear to operate independently of ideological commitments; at least, this is the impression given by the space and attention bestowed on extracts that have little or no bearing on emigration. Reviewer after reviewer picked out the same passages from the *Travels* to engage their readers' interest: the description of Washington, the enlightened penal system in Philadelphia, Natural Bridge in Virginia, Niagara Falls, and the social life of Canadians during the long winter. Above all, most reviews gave pride of place to Weld's 'brief account' of the 'Indians,' despite the fact that this occupies only a small part of the second volume of the *Travels*. The same features of his sympathetic, albeit ethnographically imprecise portrait of Native Americans were repeatedly highlighted: their physical strength and stamina, their orienteering and hunting skills, their deep emotion masked by perfect self-command, their indifference to private property, their public-spiritedness, their capacity for merciless revenge and cruelty, and their resistance to Christian conversion. Whereas Weld himself had condemned American settlers on the frontier as 'far greater savages than the Indians themselves' (2: 217), only the *Monthly Review* chose to pick up this strand in his account, lamenting the violent depletion of 'all the tribes of that once virtuous and happy people' to 'a few wretched and wandering families' (30: 204–5). This concentrated focus upon the culture and mentality of Native Americans appears in the main benignly curiosity-driven, and presumably was the tip of a considerable iceberg of such curiosity among the wider readership that the reviewers were addressing. Put another way, the strong impression conveyed by a full immersion in reviews of a book like Weld's is that elite readers' reactions were relatively autonomous of the narrow political agendas sponsored by the journals they wrote for.

Transatlantic manners

Isaac Weld, as briefly noted in the previous section, had some pretty exceptionable things to say about American manners and customs, and about the American character. These themes, which were evidently of great interest to reviewers and readers generally, were prominent in periodical coverage and constituted an important strand in contemporary discourse on America. James Chandler, in his searching analysis of the cultural politics of *England in 1819*, states that the question of 'how to judge American manners' had achieved 'extraordinary currency' (445) in Britain by this date and suggests that the consensus was overwhelmingly 'against America' (446). In his study of the representation of Americans in Romantic-period British literature, Christopher Flynn adopts a broader historical perspective and sees a gradual shift from seeing Americans as transplanted Englishmen, and America as a place where Englishness could be regenerated,[10] to more negative constructions of a distinct national character, in which Americans metamorphose into 'a separate race ... in a unique evolutionary trajectory' (138). The context for both critics includes the manifest differences between the early 1790s, a period in which America held well-documented practical and symbolic appeal for radicals and Dissenters, and the post-Waterloo period in which relations with America were strained by the latter's pro-French stance during the conflict, trade disputes, the War of 1812, and the sharply rising curve of emigration. Broadly in agreement is Tilar Mazzeo, who shows how an Anglo-American identity, at best a fleeting possibility in the early 1790s, became an impossibility with mounting transatlantic tensions: English and American identities were increasingly seen as independent productions, with no transnational possibilities in between.

---

[10]   I here use the term 'English' because Flynn does, although English immigrants to the U.S. in this period were in fact outnumbered by Scottish and Irish.

While it would be rash to contend that nothing resembling these large-scale shifts (which are not, of course, identical) occurred, it is worth entering one or two qualifications. The idea of a separate – and rather ugly and unpalatable – American character appears much earlier in travellers' accounts than the critics cited above seem to imply: Weld, for instance, touring in the decade after Independence, saw the key differences as being those between German immigrants and the 'Americans,' defined as 'the descendents of the English, Scotch, Irish, and other nations, who from having lived in the country for many generations, and from having mingled together, now form one people, whose manners and habits are very much the same' (1: 123). Equally, it is possible to find writers emphasizing the Englishness of Americans, albeit in the somewhat questionable form of a defence of the American character (as though nothing intrinsically American could be so defended), very late in the Romantic period. Secondly, Washington Irving's famous complaint, in his 1819 sketch of 'English Writers on America,' that 'there is no people [that is, the Americans] concerning whom the great mass of the British public have less pure information, or entertain more numerous prejudices' (50), almost certainly overstated the case. A detailed study of British readers' responses to those 'writers on America' shows, on the contrary, that educated readers were well capable of detecting prejudice, rejecting bias, and making up their own minds about the American character.

One English radical attracted to the idea of America in the revolutionary euphoria of the early 1790s was Mary Wollstonecraft, who had an ill-fated relationship with the American topographical writer and land-jobber, Gilbert Imlay, and at one stage planned to emigrate with him to the United States. Wollstonecraft, who probably had an influence on Imlay's transatlantic novel *The Emigrants*, reviewed many travel books for the *Analytical Review*, the house journal of Joseph Johnson's circle of rational Dissent. She was predisposed to admire the *Nouveau Voyage dans les Etats-Unies* (1791) of Jacques-Pierre Brissot, a leading Girondin politician, and took pleasure in noting his observations on the purity of manners and morals in America, including the 'easy, unreserved behaviour of the women' (11: 38). A generation later, but in similar vein, Sydney Smith reviewed four books of American travels in the *Edinburgh Review* and judged that 'generally speaking ... their testimony is in favour of American manners' (31: 141), backing this up with lengthy quotations that foregrounded positive qualities of egalitarianism, hospitality, good humour, and courtesy. Smith was by no means a pro-American zealot, and this review in particular was the cause of much offence among American readers on account of its condescension towards the primitive state of American literature, but his remarks exemplify a willingness to accentuate the positive in representations of the American character that was not unusual in elite readers' responses.

Just as there were readers who were well disposed to America and glad to find positive reinforcement of their attitudes in the latest travels, so there were others who were all too ready to have negative preconceptions strengthened. The reception of Weld's *Travels* provides ample illustration of this trend. Weld, by no means the most hostile commentator on American manners, nevertheless provided an early and full anatomy of the American character of the kind that became routine in the narratives of British (and Irish) travellers: incivility, suspicion of strangers, impertinent curiosity, dogmatism, inordinate pride in their own constitution, restlessness, a spirit of dissatisfaction, materialism and greed – these are the hallmarks of the national character assassination that many travellers collaborated or colluded in manufacturing. The incivility that was so often remarked upon was seen by many, Weld included, as the curse of American notions of liberty and equality, and this was a theme that many reviewers chose to dwell on: the *Critical Review*, for example, selected two passages dealing with the 'prying disposition' of people in the street, the poor standard of accommodation in the inns, and the insolence of the staff, as adequate illustration of what Weld revealed of 'Trans-Atlantic manners' (2nd ser. 25: 396); while the *New London Review*, making the implicit explicit, brandished the same observations as proof that 'the stern pride of republicanism is incompatible with an interchange of social duties, and inimical to the soft polish of agreeable manners' (4: 373). It is not too much to say that bad manners were made the infallible sign of a misguided political system in this silent compact between travel writers and travel readers.

Nevertheless, reviewers were also prepared to challenge the perspectives offered by travellers. John Howison's *Sketches of Upper Canada* (1821), a tour narrative which strays into the United States, contains a number of scenes that are essentially low life burlesques, designed to hold ordinary citizens up to ridicule for their awkward manners and bizarre vernacular. As the reviewer at *Blackwood's* was well aware, such scenes carried a political subtext, in that 'the manners of the vulgar' were portrayed as 'brutalized to a horrible degree by [the] almost total absence of superior models' (10: 545) that imperilled an egalitarian society. (Although the review quotes a scene set in New York State, allegedly illustrating 'Yankee petulance,' it also shows a tendency to blur the distinction between American and Canadian culture.) While finding much to admire in Howison's sketches, this reader is keen to observe that the author is 'quite wrong if he thinks such vulgarity ... at all peculiar to transatlantic manners,' and that if he had 'visited Manchester, Paisley, Glasgow, and such towns, ere he sailed for Canada' (10: 544–5), he would probably have been more tolerant. The *Edinburgh Review* was equally forthright in dealing with the same author, pointing out the contradictions in his account of the 'manners and morals' of the inhabitants, declaring his least flattering comments 'overcharged,' and, with its typical environmentalist bias, insisting that such people would find the physical demands and potential rewards of their new lives a better 'school for reform' than the overcrowded cities they ha[d] come from (37: 264–5).

As a further example, take the reception of Charles Janson's *A Stranger in America* (1807), the testimony of a man who was equally unsuccessful in land speculation, trade, and the law during his thirteen years in the country. The *Monthly Review*, robust and independent-minded as always, was not alone among the periodicals in finding fault with Janson's invective against America. Answering Janson's familiar complaints about the incivility of the average American, its reviewer noted acerbically that 'if the Americans were deficient in civilities to him, he has amply repaid them in his own coin,' and refined its critique by underlining the inevitable friction between 'an English gentleman's habits' and 'the roughness and inurbanity of republican manners' (53: 53), the implication being that Janson was just as much to blame as his interlocutors. In their willingness to challenge attitudes and examine prejudices, Romantic reviewers often seem more open-minded than the travellers whose accounts they are evaluating; it is another useful reminder that educated readers in this period were not empty vessels into which ideas and beliefs, however unpalatable, could be unresistingly poured.

There is a significant intertextual dimension to travel narratives concerning North America. It is not always possible to determine whether travellers are describing something they (are claiming to) have observed themselves or whether it is something they have read or been told about during their stay; undoubtedly, there was a subculture of plagiarism, of unknowable extent, wherein writers borrowed material from other travellers' accounts or from other, anonymous, oral or written sources. This is probably part of the reason why the same anecdotes or observations supposedly exemplary of American manners turn up repeatedly in one publication after another. Of these, perhaps the most colourful, and a key element in the popular mythology of the United States in this period, is the peculiar mode of conflict resolution allegedly practised in the southern states. Both Weld and Ashe describe the practice of eye-gouging as the distinctive fighting technique of citizens of Virginia and Kentucky, although Weld's combatants also try to tear each other's testicles off, whereas Ashe's restrict themselves to removing noses and ears. Ashe claims to have actually witnessed a violent quarrel of this nature, whereas Weld vouches only for having seen men confined to their beds from injuries received in such fights. Whatever the truth of the matter, their accounts are endlessly replicated in contemporary travellers' tales, and perhaps unsurprisingly British reviewers home in on the episodes wherever they appear: the *British Critic* calls attention to Janson's account in *A Stranger in America*, the *British Review* finds the custom described in John Lambert's *Travels* (1814), the *Quarterly Review* notes Henry Bradshaw Fearon's horrified treatment in his *Sketches of America* (1819), and so on. It is left to the *Monthly Magazine*, in 1826, to attempt to call time on this urban legend:

> I have lived in the United States of America for nearly thirty years, during which time I have had as fair opportunity of knowing the truth as – to say the least of it –any traveller could have; and yet, I never saw a case of gouging there, nor ever a man who had seen a case; no, nor a man who would say that he had ever seen a creature who *had been* gouged. (ns 2: 609–10)

Even if such incidents do occasionally occur, the reviewer continues, they are 'not at all characteristic of the American habits, nor a fortieth part so frequent *any where*, as they are represented to be *every where*' (610). For good measure, he points out that the worst fighting he has ever seen was among Devonshire men, who kick each other's shins and reinforce the toes of their shoes for the express purpose of inflicting maximum damage. This forthright attempt to repeal one of the 'strange errors ... touching America' that had taken on a life of their own is a good example of the sceptical intelligence that accompanied the thirst for knowledge shared by all readers of travel literature and serviced by the reviews.

The *Monthly*'s article, which points to a gulf in understanding between the people of America and the British reading public caused precisely by the poor standard of British travel writing on the new republic, appeared at a time when there was something of a vogue for sweeping judgements of Americans as a 'race,' which reached a high-water mark of controversy with the publication of Fanny Trollope's *Domestic Manners of the Americans* in 1832.[11] Christopher Flynn, as mentioned above, has highlighted an emerging project of 'comparative ethnology' focused on white Americans, but the pejorative cast of this project as described by Flynn looks much less definitive when one takes on board the evidence of reviews and other periodical material. The *Weekly Entertainer* began an essay on 'The Anglo-Americans' in 1818 with the startling claim that the 'manners, habits, and customs of the Americans, bear so great a resemblance to our own, that to detail the one is almost to give a description of the other' (1st ser. 57: 148). The somewhat ironic justification of this statement involves highlighting the existence of a class structure in America every bit as unequal as the one that emigrants left behind them in Britain; but the tone of the article is not completely negative – the author notes that the Americans are distinguished for 'their enterprize, courage, and perseverance, in almost everything they undertake,' and are no more or less vain than the English (153). In a more tendentious piece on 'The American Character' in 1823, the *Literary Chronicle* claimed that the Americans were still so new a mixture of different nations that they had not yet acquired a distinct character. Despite this, the article goes on to proclaim that the American 'lives only in himself, and for himself, and regards all disinterested acts as so many follies,' and that the mainspring of the American republic is, indeed, an 'unbounded love of money.' In another characteristic formula, Americans are accused of illogical vanity based on unfeasible ambitions for the future: 'Unable ... to boast of what they have been ... they boast of what they are one day destined to become' (3: 681–2). In 1824, an article entitled 'The English and the Americans Compared' in the populist *Mirror of Literature, Amusement, and Instruction* emphasized the youthfulness of the American people compared with the longevity of the English and the former's focus on posterity as opposed to the latter's obsession with ancestry. The author draws contrasting portraits of each national type, the Englishman showing 'his high opinion of his country by silence; the American his, by talking'; Englishmen possessing 'more mind, more wisdom, more judgment, and more perseverance,' Americans 'more genius, more quickness of perception, more adventurousness'

---

[11]   It is worth saying that Trollope's book had a deep and lasting cultural impact, unlike some of the other travel books featured in this chapter. I do not mean to give a false impression that all these books were of equal historical significance; but all received extensive coverage in the periodical press, and therefore are of equal value for my purposes in tracing the contours of historical reception.

(4: 186–7). While at times favouring the English, overall the article sees a broad moral equivalence between the two types.

The ongoing, sometimes acrimonious debate about American manners is encapsulated in the reception of two books that appeared in 1828 and 1829, respectively, Fenimore Cooper's *Notions of the Americans* and Basil Hall's *Travels in North America*. These works were the subject of measured criticism in the *Edinburgh Review*, whose reviewer, William Empson, affirmed that 'the whole Bodleian cannot contain two books whose principles, sentiments, and conclusions, have so little in common' (49: 477). Cooper's book, slated elsewhere in the periodical press for blindly patriotic praise of the author's countrymen, is treated sympathetically by Empson, although he satirizes Cooper's attempt to portray a 'transcendentalism about common sense' (516) as the essence of the American people. Conversely, Empson takes Hall's observations of American society and institutions seriously, but finds his account of American manners and of Anglo-American relations unbalanced and impolitic, and cannot avoid treating sarcastically the circumstance whereby travels that were undertaken to dispel 'anti-American heresies' imbibed in the author's youth have resulted in a book with entirely the opposite agenda. Attempting to steer a middle course, but lapsing inevitably into condescension at times, Empson acknowledges certain 'social defects' among the Americans but insists that these be considered in the context of the environment that has shaped them, and that they are in any case more than outweighed by the 'zeal, hospitality, and kindness of their deeds' (513–4). His hope is that improved knowledge of America and Americans will mitigate the growth of international animosity and jealousy, and he plainly holds dear the belief – it was a keynote of the *Edinburgh*'s treatment of the United States – in a nascent 'special relationship' between the two countries.

To sum up, there was undoubtedly a lot of British travel writing on America that did little to promote intercultural communication and understanding, but there were elements in the periodical press that countered the more extreme utterances and give witness to more liberal attitudes among the wider reading public. Irving was probably right about the prejudices and misinformation peddled by 'English Writers on America,' but British reviewers sifted and interpreted what they read with care, and assumed similar tolerance and open-mindedness among the wider reading public.

Emigration: The 'American mania'

Throughout the Romantic period, the theme of emigration runs through transatlantic travel literature like the place name in a stick of Brighton rock,[12] so

---

[12]   Stephen Fender, in his major study of the literature of emigration, claims that 'Hardly a British book of travels in America published in the first half of the nineteenth century ... failed to include the question of emigration among its observations on the new country' (38).

it is hardly surprising that it is also a prominent theme in the reception of those books in the periodical press. What is more surprising is that so little notice has been taken of this phenomenon in criticism of British Romantic writers. Michael Wiley has rightly pointed out, in a notable recent effort to correct this deficiency, how many of the major names from the period either emigrated to the United States, planned to emigrate, or 'speculated imaginatively upon emigration' (56);[13] for many students of Romantic literature, however, emigration features, if at all, only as an intriguing byway in the early career of Coleridge, in the shape of his and Southey's ostensibly hare-brained Pantisocracy scheme.

Bernard Bailyn has written that 'The westward transatlantic movement of people is one of the greatest events in recorded history' and that from 1500 to the present its 'magnitude and consequences are beyond measure' (5). Included in any global estimate of this movement of people are more than three million enslaved Africans carried to the Americas in British Empire ships in the century and a half prior to abolition in 1807 (Richardson 440). Included too, during the eighteenth and early nineteenth centuries, were large numbers of Europeans, a significant proportion of them British and Irish, variously composed of the indigent and desperate, economic migrants, men from professional or commercial backgrounds, political and religious exiles, and so on, who crossed the Atlantic, more or less voluntarily, in search of a better life. During the eighteenth century the pattern of emigration changed, with a huge rise in the numbers of Scottish and Irish emigrants compared to the English, and a steady increase in the proportion of skilled and semi-skilled workers and of men from professional or commercial backgrounds, although up to half of all migrants in the period went as indentured labourers (Horn 50) – a contractual arrangement repeatedly excoriated by hostile traveller-observers as a form of white slave trade. Although reliable statistics are hard to come by, it seems that emigration rose sharply after Independence in 1783, and continued in the face of government-imposed obstacles and economic boom and bust through the generation-long turbulence in Europe, albeit declining during the Napoleonic wars and virtually coming to a halt with the outbreak of the War of 1812.

Up to 1815, British government policy, based on mercantilist principles, had been to discourage emigration: in the words of one historian, 'Men still equated population with power and wealth and saw each industrious emigrant as a further loss of national strength' (Johnston 2). In time of war, the argument for retaining human resources resounded even louder; hence various devices such as the Passenger Act of 1803, which limited the number of emigrants that ships could carry and made such cargoes unprofitable for many operators. In the years after Waterloo, however, the climate of opinion shifted: economic depression, worsening unemployment and poverty, and the threat of large-scale disorder prompted the government and opinion-formers to reassess the merits of regulated emigration, although they attempted to regulate it in the direction of British colonies (Canada

---

[13]   See also Chandler 454–63.

and the Cape Colony) rather than the United States.[14] Once the spectre of serious unrest had receded, so did governmental support for emigration: 'they acted only when social order was threatened, and they lost interest as soon as the danger was diminished' (Johnston 56). However, the post-war exodus continued whatever the government said or did, ebbing and flowing in response to political and economic circumstance but going in one unambiguous direction, and by the late 1820s had assumed the character of a mass movement. As such, it had, according to Maldwyn Allen Jones, 'a distinct air of irrationality, even of frenzy, and many of those who took part in it were simply carried along by a force they did not understand' (80). Jones's words resonate with those of an article published in the *Literary Magazine* in 1805, at a time when the war effort was suppressing emigration. Too many people, the journal complained, had been taken in by misrepresentations of the advantages of America and deserted their homeland – a country where, it was bizarrely claimed, man was 'subordinate, happy with himself, and at peace with his neighbours' (4th ser. 1: 348); finding a cure for what it called 'the American mania' was said to be all-important.

The *Literary Magazine*'s attack on the 'general delusion' regarding the United States came in the shape of a review of Richard Parkinson's *Tour in America*, the reception of which provides a fair measure of the emigration debate in the first half of the period. Parkinson, a Lincolnshire farmer and agriculturist, emigrated to America in 1798 with a letter of introduction to George Washington, in the hope of making 'a rapid fortune' (1: 2) from rented land on Washington's Mount Vernon estate. This farm not being to his liking, he was offered, and declined, numerous other offers of land, before settling on 300 acres near Baltimore. Despite the fact that his farm was successful, at least by his own account, he seems rapidly to have agreed with a fellow Englishman that America was the 'devil's own country' (1: 167), and after two years acquiesced in his wife's desire to return to England. He published his *Tour* ostensibly to prevent others 'running headlong into misery, as myself and many others have done' (1: v). It is, without a doubt, one of the worst travel books published in the Romantic period, its value determined solely by the 'instruction' it provided in the science of agricultural improvement. Its content being otherwise restricted to a montage of familiar anti-American themes, such as the pernicious effects of the doctrine of liberty and equality on social relations, its high point was a sixty-page section of plagiarized captivity narratives designed to illustrate the dangers of farming in the western territories: if the barren soil does not finish you off, Parkinson implied, the Indians will. Given the execrable quality of Parkinson's mongrelized text, it is an indication of how seriously opinion-formers took the emigration issue that the periodicals gave it so much attention.

The aggregate response to Parkinson's *Tour* was one that called into question official policy on emigration and challenged negative representations of the

---

[14]   There were several modest schemes of assisted emigration. These made little dent in the problem, but the government took the view that the announcement of a decision to promote emigration 'was more important than its subsequent execution (Johnston 37).

United States. The *Literary Magazine* was in fact fairly isolated in its admiration of the book. Parkinson was more typically read 'against the grain,' although many reviewers strove to be fair-minded. The *Annual Review* conceded that the work benefited from limiting its observations to subject-matter on which the author was qualified to speak, but argued that overall it presented a caricature of an 'unbetterable' country, and was manifestly trying to 'curry favour with the tories of England, by ascribing the evils of North America to its republicanism' (4: 82). Parkinson was accused of disingenuousness in seeking new legislative barriers to emigration: if America is as unattractive as he makes out, the journal reasoned, why would so many 'necessitous' people continue to pack their bags? The *Monthly Review* did not object to Parkinson's position on emigration as such, but believed him guilty of 'illiberal prejudice and misrepresentation,' effectively breaking the compact between travel writer and reader: instead of the 'narrative of an impartial observer' he had subjected his audience to 'the effervescence of angry disappointment' (51: 42). The *Literary Journal*, as one would expect from an organ founded by the Utilitarian philosopher James Mill, took a coolly analytical approach to Parkinson's argument, dissecting the situations and motives of different kinds of emigrant: in the *Journal*'s view, the small tenant farmer threatened with relegation to wage-labour who went to America expecting the hard life to which he was already accustomed would not be disappointed, whereas farmers with more capital who expected to make a quick killing would soon be disillusioned. Parkinson, the author claimed, was very definitely in the latter camp, and although many of his observations were 'deserving of attention' (5: 1075) his expectations of a young and underpopulated country were plainly unrealistic. In a similar vein, the *Edinburgh Review* condemned Parkinson's bias and calmly rationalized his grievances:[15] 'In the whole of his numerous details and anecdotes, we can discover nothing asserted of that country, which might not have been predicted from a little consideration of its peculiar circumstances; and no inconvenience imputed, which is not susceptible of an effectual remedy, either at the present moment, or in the rapid progress of its improvement' (7: 33). Parkinson was unlikely to deter either the poorer classes or 'capitalists' from emigrating, the journal concluded.

The most hostile – and the most entertaining – response to Parkinson came from the *Critical Review*, which compared the author to Sterne's Smelfungus (his caricature of the ill-tempered traveller in *A Sentimental Journey*), exuding ignorance and spleen in equal measure. However, the *Critical*'s masterstroke is to point to some of the many contradictions in the *Tour*, such as Parkinson's contempt for the barren soil of America contrasted with his evident success in cultivating it, and to conclude that it is intended as 'a burlesque upon arguments against emigration': 'the author continually seems to be in a violent passion, but

---

[15]   The fact that the *Edinburgh*, with its highly selective reviewing policy, decided to cover a dreadful book like Parkinson's is indicative to me not of the journal's delight in a good hatchet job but of the urgency with which it viewed the topic of transatlantic emigration.

we have no doubt that he is all the while laughing in his sleeve at the credulity of his readers' (2nd ser. 7: 25). The review becomes an exuberant demolition job, as it elaborates a cruelly ironic case for Parkinson's own 'rich vein of irony,' along the way making preposterous comparisons with Cervantes, Rabelais, and Swift, and praising the author as 'in his heart ... a true American' (27). It was perhaps Parkinson's misfortune that none of the journals that might have been expected to warm to his dissuasive appeal to potential emigrants seems to have noticed his publication. The *British Critic*, for example, had zealously towed the anti-emigration line in its reviews of a series of works published in the 1790s and early 1800s, including Thomas Cooper's *Some Information Respecting America* (1794), Jardine's *Letter from Pennsylvania* (1796), Wansey's *Journal of an Excursion to the United States of America* (1797), and Volney's *View of the Climate and Soil of the United States of America* (1804). It read with, or against, the grain of the text as the situation demanded. Cooper's book, for instance, an important source for Coleridge and Southey in devising their Pantisocratic scheme, was turned completely on its head: whereas Cooper had promoted America (and specifically Pennsylvania, where he happened to have 300,000 acres of land to dispose of himself)[16] as a country offering freedom from material want and anxiety, and from religious discrimination and political oppression, the *British Critic*'s reviewer condemned him as a mere 'auctioneer' and found 'little encouragement for emigration' in his picture of a land where there were 'no manufactures,' 'no room for the exertion of arts,' and 'little prospect of the poor man attaining independence' (1st ser. 5: 27, 29). The *British Critic*, however, passed over Parkinson's *Tour*, as did the *Gentleman's Magazine*, which might have been sympathetically inclined. It is worth underlining, though, that Parkinson's reviewers, the *Critical*'s hatchet-man excepted, all gave credit to his observations in the field of husbandry or found other points in his favour: for a book which, to the modern eye, is singularly devoid of aesthetic merit, this is testimony both to the impartiality of the liberal press and to the premium placed on empirical knowledge-gathering in an expanding world.

In the years of political and economic crisis after Waterloo, as noted above, official attitudes to emigration started to shift, just as emigration itself resumed, and soon reached unprecedented levels, after its artificial suppression during the War of 1812 and the endgame of the Napoleonic wars. There was no overnight change in opinion: William Cobbett referred to widespread 'alarm' on the subject of emigration in a series of articles on emigration to America, apparently written in response to constant enquiries from readers, in his *Weekly Political Register*; the *Caledonian Mercury* also used the word 'alarm' to describe the national mood and tried to allay this by pointing out the advantages both to the emigrants themselves and to the mother country of transporting labour 'from the overstocked market of Europe to the understocked market of America' (28 Dec. 1818: 3). While the government would eventually recognize the force of this argument by providing

---

[16] For discussion of Cooper as a 'radical travel writer' who was 'interested in more than the sale of [his] books' (190), see Verhoeven.

limited assistance to emigrants, the real source of the anxiety seems to have been that the 'American mania' was no longer confined to the most destitute members of society. Cobbett referred to 'most valuable and most respectable men' packing up to go to America (22 Jun. 1816: 769), while the *Bristol Mercury* said that it had been 'the subject of much complaint ... since the termination of the war' that 'multitudes of persons of moderate fortune have gone to live abroad' (8 Mar. 1819: 3)[17] Emigration was a national talking point, and just as newspapers rapidly took the temperature of the debate, so the literary journals constantly returned to the subject as they reacted to the latest travel narratives, tourist accounts, and, indeed, the emerging sub-genre of emigrant guides.

A substantial review article which appeared in the *British Review* in 1819, on the 'State of Literature, Religion, Slavery, etc. in the United States of America,' covering seventeen books in a variety of genres, acknowledges the growing independence of American cultural production and provides a fair-minded assessment of achievements in scientific fields as well as poetry and the indigenous periodical press. The *Review* is predictably less sympathetic to what travellers reveal of the proliferation of different religions in a country where religion 'is considered a mere personal affair' (82), the iniquities of slavery, and the grudging efforts to civilize those 'Indians' not yet 'exterminated by the sword of American aggression' (100). This leads the reviewer to conclude his lengthy reflections with the hope that, whatever defects the British constitution might have, 'he, who cherishes any regard to pure and undefiled religion, for solid liberty, for moral virtue, will not readily abandon it for ideal happiness, and an uncertain abode in the great western wilderness' (100). That last phrase reads rather oddly as the coda to an extended treatment of 'native American' literary culture, but it registers a quiet anxiety over emigration and a desire to fight back in defence of conservative and patriotic interests.

Among the seventeen books surveyed in this review is Henry Bradshaw Fearon's *Sketches of America* (1818), the outcome of a journey undertaken by the author, on behalf of thirty-nine English families, to investigate the rights and wrongs of emigration. Fearon was equivocal in his conclusions, and this vacillation did not go unnoticed by his reviewers, including Sydney Smith in the *Edinburgh Review* – a journal which found itself in the unusual position of attempting to quell the enthusiasm for emigration by emphasizing that England, though highly taxed, was by the same token a very 'habitable and comfortable' country. 'Severe and painful poverty will drive us all anywhere,' Smith concedes, but 'a wise man should be quite sure he has so irresistible a plea, before he ventures on the Great or the Little Wabash' (31: 150). The subtext of Smith's remarks seems to be to allow the truly indigent to try their luck in America, but to persuade those respectable 'men of moderate fortune' to stay.

An oddly similar note is struck in John Barrow's critique of Fearon in the *Quarterly Review*, but the tone is, as one would expect, much harsher. Barrow

---

17   See Chandler 459–63 for further discussion of this topic.

blames the emigration trend on well-off people who are too impatient to wait for their country to recover from the ravages of a long war. The thirty-nine families for whom Fearon has acted as a scout or outrider are 'cold-blooded, calculating men' unwilling to hazard everything as many poorer 'agriculturists' have done but perfectly willing, once the reconnaissance has been completed, to sacrifice '*love of country*' and the 'ties of blood' in order to shield their wealth from 'the claims of their native land' (21: 125). America's much-vaunted 'liberty and equality' is derided in light of the 'abominable' facts of slavery that Fearon is forced to confront, and Barrow also focuses on Fearon's description of the arrival of a shipload of indentured labourers: these are the individuals, he says, whom Fearon would hypocritically seduce into emigrating – people who would 'rise, from labourers in their own country, to "redemptioners" on board a pestilential hulk, and, if they survived the passage, soar to a state of slavery in the free soil of Kentucky or Virginia' (146). As Barrow acknowledges, Fearon confesses that his prejudices in favour of America have been sorely tested during his trip, and Barrow turns this to his advantage in highlighting the contrast between the author's constant praise of the American government and his routine disparagement of American people: 'We hear over and over again, that it is an *easy*, *cheap*, and *reasonable* government; and yet all the materials of it, all the members of the several departments of it, are accused of ignorance, vulgarity, brutality, and corruption' (163). The American character thus again becomes a stick with which to beat the new republic – here as a clinching argument against emigration – in a dystopic reversal of the Godwinian vision of moral regeneration in a pristine land that had inspired radicals in the 1790s.

At one point, Barrow takes delight in noting Fearon's astonishment at hearing that significant numbers of Americans are relocating across the border into Canada. He does not pursue the theme of Canada as an emigrant destination, and the main thrust of the article is to present a patriotic case against the 'patriophobia' of the apostles of emigration. However, this was precisely the period when, as noted above, it became official policy to divert the tide of emigrants towards British colonies, Canada in particular. Now whereas sometimes, in dealing with cultural traits, the United States and Canada are merged in a generalized discussion of 'transatlantic manners,' when reviewers engage with a politically sensitive issue like emigration, the distinction is invariably kept firmly in view. It is far from coincidental that, the year after Barrow's broadside against Fearon, the *Quarterly* published a review (by Richard Whately) of three books under the heading 'Emigration to Canada' that goes out of its way to present this option in a favourable light. Whereas Barrow had mocked the notion that the 'extreme poor' would benefit from uprooting themselves and trying their luck in the 'new Eden,' Whately quotes with approval the view of James Strachan (in his *Visit to the Province of Upper Canada*) that Britain is in a situation at present where emigration would be a useful expedient to relieve a distressed population – even more so if economic misery has bred political dissatisfaction. For not only does Canada offer families the possibility of rising 'to comparative wealth' on the same amount of work that would just keep their heads above water in Britain, it is also a land where 'the chief reform called for is to convert forests into cornfields,' and where 'the whole structure of society is to be built up, without being previously pulled down' (23: 400). Whately assiduously draws practical information from the three books under review to assist a haemorrhage of British subjects which would, he argues, eventually help the mother country by increasing demand for British goods.

There had been support for emigration to Canada in the periodical press before the post-war crisis – the *Annual Review*, for example, had used its reviews of George Heriot's *Travels through the Canadas* and Charles Janson's *A Stranger in America* to press the case for regulated emigration in that direction – but the desperate situation after Waterloo and the surge in transatlantic human traffic concentrated commentators' minds. Consequently, books like John Howison's *Sketches of Upper Canada* (1821) united reviewers across the ideological spectrum. It would have been no surprise that the liberal *Edinburgh Review* supported efforts 'to direct the current of our surplus population towards the unsettled districts of Upper Canada' (37: 250) and was therefore keen to extract from Howison's text information likely to be of use to potential working-class emigrants; but the conservative *Blackwood's* also responded warmly to Howison, approving his positive account of the emigrant's chances of success and quoting at length from his practical advice to settlers. Both reviewers attend also to other aspects of Howison's *Sketches*, such as his landscape descriptions, but it is noticeable that both begin with the material – the advice to emigrants – that is supplementary to Howison's text: they read with a purpose, and, given the importance of periodicals in disseminating awareness of these expensive travel books, the seriousness of that purpose should not be underestimated.

The quarterlies at war

The hot topic of emigration was therefore capable, in the troubled post-war years, of producing a measure of convergence between the *Edinburgh Review* and its London-based rival, the *Quarterly Review*, two journals often pictured as implacable enemies, launching verbal missiles at each other across a veritable Hadrian's Wall of print journalism. This caricature is not entirely inaccurate, of course. *The Edinburgh*, launched in 1802, stood out from the crowd with its rigorous selection policy, its uncompromisingly evaluative approach, and its readiness to subordinate the reviewing function to opinionated discussion of issues raised by the publication in question. Establishing itself in the public mind as a Whig journal, it rapidly achieved cultural pre-eminence. But if the *Edinburgh*, in Marilyn Butler's words, 'set out to break the mould of existing journal culture' (131), the *Quarterly* set out to break the *Edinburgh*. Founded in 1809 by a group of British nationalists (including Walter Scott) under the patronage of George Canning, its aim was to counter the influence of the *Edinburgh* with a liberal-conservative organ of equal weight and quality, imitating key features of the *Edinburgh*'s revolutionary approach and using books on a variety of subjects to

– in the words of publisher John Murray – delicately insinuate 'honnied drops of party sentiment ... into the unsuspecting ear' (Cutmore, *Conservatism* 203). In correspondence, Murray and Scott repeatedly used military metaphors to describe the journalistic confrontation that lay ahead – Scott, for instance, looking forward to taking their 'foe' by surprise when the 'first bomb bursts upon the public.'[18] In the post-war period both periodicals reached the height of their success, achieving circulations of 12–14,000, considerably higher than any of the longer-established reviews.

These two publishing behemoths were at odds on most of the big social and political questions of the 1810s and 1820s, including most obviously the war against France, and the subject of America also highlighted political differences. These became particularly acute during the War of 1812. The *Edinburgh* saw the war as entirely the product of Britain's calamitous foreign policy, which, in seeking to cripple the French economy, damaged its own trading interests as well as those of the United States and jeopardized the entire symbiotic relationship between the two countries. At a late stage in the war, the journal accused the government of exploiting peace in Europe (and the military resources thus released) to turn a dispute over international trade into a legally indefensible war of conquest. In complete contrast, the *Quarterly* defended the controversial Orders in Council of 1807, towed the government line on impressment, condemned America's alleged partiality for Bonaparte and French principles, and (with an eye on Canada) described any territorial ambitions as being entirely on the American side. Extreme as the opposition between the two journals thus appears to be, it is worth noting that on the other side of the Atlantic they appeared indistinguishable to some observers: Robert Walsh's *Appeal from the Judgments of Great Britain Respecting the United States of America* (1819), an outpouring of resentment at the 'calumnies' of periodical writers stretching back at least five years,[19] lumped the *Edinburgh* and *Quarterly* together as publications that had 'taken the lead in the war of defamation and derision, against the American people and institutions' (214). On rather different grounds, Marilyn Butler has argued (developing an observation made by James Mill in 1824) that both journals, by virtue of their cultural elitism and their commitment to 'aristocratic' rule, could be seen as Establishment in the broadest sense – especially when placed alongside the 'crop of radical weeklies' that emerged in the post-war period (Butler 136–7).

One aspect that united the quarterlies was their shared enthusiasm for travel literature. Both journals valued it as a source of new knowledge and a discursive adjunct to Britain's foreign relations and colonial interests. Both would seem to have compromised their principle of strict selectivity in order to give the most

---

[18] See Wheatley, 'Plotting' 27–8, for further examples.

[19] John Barrow's merciless review of Charles Ingersoll's *Favourable View* of the United States in the *Quarterly Review* in 1814 can be regarded as the initial provocation, while Sydney Smith's review of a bundle of American travels in the *Edinburgh Review* in 1818 brought matters to a head.

generous treatment possible to the genre. Both quarterlies, too, took a keen interest
in North America: under Jeffrey's editorship, the *Edinburgh* devoted more than
thirty substantial articles to American travels, as well as numerous pieces on other
genres of Americana; at the *Quarterly*, John Barrow presided over the reviewing
of travel books, and among his prolific output of more than two hundred articles
over a period of thirty years were thirty-two on North and Central America –
excluding his important pieces on Arctic exploration (Cameron 142–3).[20] It was
a fundamental part of the *Quarterly*'s strategy to combat the *Edinburgh* without
ever mentioning it by name. It seems curiously consistent with this plan that, in
the realm of travel literature at least, they rarely contested the same terrain. Over a
fifteen-year period from the launch of the *Quarterly* there are very few examples
of the two journals reviewing the same travel book. I glanced at one of these,
Fearon's *Sketches*, in the previous section; in the remainder of this section, I shall
focus on two more notable examples.

The first case I want to consider is the publication of the first official narrative
of the Lewis and Clark transcontinental expedition of 1804–06 – the so-called
Biddle edition, published first in Philadelphia in 1814, then in England the same
year by Longman, and the nearest either national audience would get to the exact
words of Lewis and Clark before the twentieth century. The *Edinburgh*'s review
was by the mathematician and geologist John Playfair, a frequent contributor
otherwise best known as a defender and popularizer of James Hutton's *Theory of
the Earth*; the *Quarterly*'s review, twice the length, came from the indefatigable
pen of Robert Southey, who contributed ninety articles during this most durable of
his associations with a literary journal.

There are certain striking similarities between the two reviews. Although
Playfair begins by announcing that he will not follow the account of the expedition
in a methodical way, both reviews in fact employ what might be termed a 'rich
guided tour' method, involving generous chronological summary with occasional
lengthy quotations and passages of commentary or evaluation. Given that the
published narrative was well over 600 pages long (in the London edition), there is
an astonishing degree of overlap between the two reviews. It is hardly surprising
that both should highlight major milestones of the expedition, such as the arrival
at the Great Falls of the Missouri, or include dramatic incidents, such as the
encounters with grizzly bears or Shoshoni guide Sacagawea's unexpected reunion
with her brother. However, the convergence goes beyond such predictable areas of
agreement, encompassing a large proportion of what the reviewers select from the
mass of ethnographical information about Native American peoples collected by
Lewis and Clark on Jefferson's instructions. Some of this material is of a plainly
titillating nature; some of it consists of sober descriptions of domestic life and

---

[20]   For the *Edinburgh*'s general interest in travel literature, see Demata; for a fuller
analysis of its reviews of American travels, see my own essay in *Symbiosis*. Cameron
provides an excellent survey of Barrow's coverage of travel books, stating that 'No
significant explorer in Africa, Asia, Australia, or the Americas escaped his scrutiny' (143).

forms of subsistence. That two such different intellectuals as Playfair and Southey arrived independently at such close and comparable redactions of a voluminous text shows a remarkable shared understanding of readerly expectations and of the reviewer's craft.

There are, nevertheless, subtle differences between the two reviews, and these have a lot to do with the personal and professional traits of their authors. Playfair's training as a geologist is evident from the beginning of his article, where he launches immediately into an analysis of the 'peculiar character of the Missouri' (24: 413) and its role in the 'degradation of the land' (414) and criticizes the explorers for not taking more regular and exact measurements to allow for a calculation of the gradient. This geological perspective surfaces repeatedly in the course of his review, most notably in the passage dealing with the Gates of the Missouri, where he disputes the narrative's assumption that some momentous convulsion must have occurred to produce such a deep and perpendicular chasm: it is much easier for untrained minds, Playfair muses, 'to call in the agency of some unknown power which may produce its effect at once, than to sum up the slow workings of a river that must be extended to many ages' (426).

Southey is not uninterested in rock formations, but his article is more preoccupied with their visual and imaginative appeal than with scientific causes. As with Playfair's, the opening of Southey's review establishes the distinctive tone of his response to the Lewis and Clark story, recalling as it does some of the many myths and legends surrounding the region they set out to explore, including the claim of the upper Missouri to conceal the descendants of the legendary Welsh prince Madoc. The mass of hard information he extracts and synthesizes in the course of his review has the aim of discrediting such preconceptions, of substituting fact for fable, or perhaps of renewing the imaginative appeal of the American West by grounding it in well-attested natural wonders and the curiosities of a diverse indigenous population. Certainly Southey shows no desire to prolong falsely romanticized notions of American Indians: his comment on the description of one dance, rendered in Latin by Biddle owing to its sexual content, is that 'we shall no longer be pestered with rhapsodies in praise of savage life' (12: 328); but this generalized rejection of noble savagery co-exists with an exact interest in different native languages and customs in a more complex effort of understanding.

Throughout, Southey's review is more bookish, comparative, and digressive in approach than Playfair's; he also shows more interest than the latter in the human drama of the expedition – in episodes of danger and misadventure – and a much more absorbed attention to matters of natural history (including the possible threat to the survival of certain species as a result of European intervention). Perhaps the other really characteristic note that he strikes is a gently mocking tone applied in particular to the explorers' colonial arrogance in the naming of places – a practice seemingly taken for granted by Playfair. Having noted the naming of the Three Forks of the Missouri after prominent American Congressmen, Southey cannot resist exclaiming when a similar procedure is applied to three tributaries flowing into the Jefferson: 'Philosophy, Wisdom, and Philanthropy, uniting to form the –

Jefferson! – how beautiful an allegory, how delicate a compliment! – I guess our President will approve of that!' (346) However, these side-swipes do not amount to a significant anti-American impetus in the article; Southey seems well-disposed to the United States[21] and strains no sinews to score political points at its expense. In this he is on common ground with Playfair, but the two reviews do diverge ultimately in terms of their geopolitical vision: whereas Playfair acknowledges that the United States, having already acquired more territory 'than they are able to occupy ... are constantly in search of new acquisitions,' and foresees that 'a few years will place an American colony somewhere about the mouth of the Columbia' (437), Southey makes greater allowance for the rival interests of Britain, Russia, and Spain and deems it unlikely that American territorial ambitions will be realized in these western extremities. Both reviewers grasp the significance of Lewis's and Clark's accomplishment, but, partly mirroring the corporate worldview of their employers, they annotate it in different ways.

The theme of westward migration makes an easy transition to my second pair of reviews, this time of Morris Birkbeck's *Notes on a Journey in America*, which appeared in London in 1818 following its publication in Philadelphia the previous year. Birkbeck, a Surrey farmer who crossed the Atlantic in 1817 to found the Albion settlement in Illinois, has been rightly described by James Chandler as 'massively famous in his own time, and almost unknown in ours' (469), and his book as having fuelled 'general alarm and 'national paranoia' (459) over emigration to America. Responses in the *Edinburgh* and *Quarterly* again pitted against each other two formidable reviewers: in the *Edinburgh*, Henry Brougham, one of the 'Gang of Four' friends who founded the journal, and a prominent Whig politician; in the *Quarterly*, almost inevitably, John Barrow, whose position as Second Secretary to the Admiralty gave him unique insider knowledge for reviewing travel literature and a special interest in Britain's 'imperial geography' (Cameron 141). These were big guns to bring to bear on what Brougham called a 'modest little tract' (30: 120) and Barrow accurately yet contemptuously described as a 'little volume, printed with an ordinary type on coarse paper' (19: 54).

It was, nevertheless, a book that Brougham also described as equal to anything produced in the past twenty years for the 'importance, the novelty, or the interest of its contents' (120). The reason for this had little to do with the intrinsic qualities of Birkbeck's writing; rather, it was because of the surge in transatlantic emigration discussed in the previous section, and Birkbeck's book – which narrates his quest of 'a new settlement in the western wilderness' (Birkbeck 5) as a retreat from 'the approaching crisis – either of anarchy or despotism' in England to 'a society whose institutions are favourable to virtue' (8–9) – was one indicator among others that people of a more respectable background, as well as the destitute and desperate,

---

[21] W. A. Speck argues that Southey disliked the *Quarterly Review*'s tendency to disparage the U.S., citing a review in which he claims that the two countries are 'natural friends,' despite the Americans having by now evolved a 'distinct national character' (Speck 167).

were answering the call of America. As such, reviews of Birkbeck's *Notes* in the periodical press are a signal example of how the reception of travel literature could be mediated by extrinsic political or cultural factors. Both Brougham and Barrow read Birkbeck shrewdly and purposefully, to very different ends; it is interesting that, in doing so, they quote many of the same extracts, articulating their differences as much through tone and implicature as through explicit annotation.

Brougham does, as he himself claims, give 'a tolerably fair outline of Birkbeck's work' (139), but he also puts it to work in deliberate ways. He uses Birkbeck as ammunition in the cause of domestic reform, conceding some validity in the latter's account of Britain's political and economic injustices as motives for leaving the country; he quotes at length from Birkbeck's description of the condition of slaves in Virginia to reinforce the *Edinburgh*'s long-running campaign for abolition; and he interprets Birkbeck's picture of the young republic's population growth and internal emigration, apparently violating all known laws of the 'growth of nations' (122), as an augury of future American supremacy. Most obviously, he uses Birkbeck as a text on which to address the emigration issue, on which his stance is even-handed or equivocal: he acknowledges the legitimacy of the alleged motives for departure, and concludes that Birkbeck has offered a 'tempting' view of emigration to 'men of moderate fortunes and industrious habits' (134–5); yet his neutral-seeming presentation of extracts dealing with some of Birkbeck's less appealing impressions of America has covert designs on the reader, and his patriotic discourse on the irrational strength of local attachment – the 'friendly treachery' of our memory that overpowers every 'unpleasing reality' (135) – appears designed to talk down the threat of emigration at the same time that he registers its potency.

Barrow's review in the *Quarterly* makes no pretence at impartiality. He concedes that the *Notes* give 'an interesting and in some measure a faithful picture of the country through which [Birkbeck] travelled' (78), but counterbalances what would normally count as significant praise of a travel book with overt detestation of the author's moral and political principles. He satirizes Birkbeck's hostility to organized religion and all but the most rudimentary systems of government, ridicules his rhetorical presumption in talking of desires and aspirations as though they were present-day realities,[22] and attacks the self-interestedly flattering portrait of his own Albion settlement (the book concludes with details of the lands that Birkbeck and his colleague, George Flower, propose to offer for sale to 'a number of our countrymen' [Birkbeck 153]) as a 'puffing advertisement' (71). He takes delight in highlighting apparent contradictions in Birkbeck's argument. Whereas Brougham marvelled at the westward flow of migrants, Barrow derides the notion of a 'New America' distanced from 'Old America' by just a few short years; and while Brougham saw the prevalence of emigrants like Birkbeck as a guarantee of its stability, Barrow finds in his book contrary signs of the imminent disintegration of the Union. Most tellingly of all, Barrow reads Birkbeck against the grain, lacing

---

22   Birkbeck himself identifies 'anticipation' as a figure of rhetoric uniquely American: 'By its aid, what *may be* is contemplated, as though it were in actual existence' (39).

his extracts with heavy sarcasm or undercutting them with literary allusions. Twice he punctures Birkbeck's portrait of life in the back-settlements with references to Book 4 of *Paradise Lost,* casting Birkbeck as the 'lost Archangel,' looking back with 'jealous leer malign' from the 'pestilential swamps of the Wabash' to the 'broad sunshine of peace and prosperity' bestowed on the England he foolishly deserted (70, 76–7). This rather improbable celebration of England in 1818 is underscored by the patriotic lines from Book 2 of Cowper's *The Task* that end the review, and encapsulate its attitude to the British diaspora: 'England, with all thy faults, we love thee still,' Barrow quotes, but with the proviso that England will gladly spare any number of Morris Birkbecks to 'wage war with the bears and red Indians of the "back-woods" of America' (78).

These four utterly distinctive reviews – the scientific curiosity of Playfair, the omnivorous intelligence of Southey, Brougham's liberal politics, the imperial hauteur of Barrow[23] – ably represent the vitality and diversity of reviewing in the periodical press. They demonstrate that beneath the fiction of a journal's corporate identity (shored up by authorial anonymity), which literary historians have tended to accept unquestioningly, were and are individual, historical readers. The reviews, moreover, are rich and rewarding acts of reading: they may be public, self-conscious acts, caught up in wider currents of debate and controversy, but they are readings nonetheless, and they tell us something of the way voyages and travels were read in the Romantic period, why it was such a culturally significant genre, and how North American travels in particular were filtered, interpreted, and disseminated among a reading public consumed by curiosity about the transatlantic continent.

A child in time: The future of the United States

In the thousands of pages devoted to North American travels in the periodical press in the Romantic period, there was one other important theme that reviewers could not help but address: in addition to new geographical or anthropological knowledge, fresh sources of 'amusement,' perspectives on American manners and the American character, and the running controversy of emigration, they returned time and again to questions of national destiny and the future of Anglo-American relations. It is right, therefore, to conclude this chapter by glancing at key aspects of this matrix of concerns.

At the simplest level, what comes over most vividly in reader responses to American travels is sheer astonishment at the preternatural development of the infant republic and the rapid growth of its population. This demographic sublime appears quite early in the period, but the shock and awe intensify in the 1810s and 1820s. Part of Brougham's anxiety (if that is what it is) in his review of

---

[23] Attributions of authorship for articles in the *Edinburgh Review* are made on the authority of Houghton; for the *Quarterly Review*, I rely on Jonathan Cutmore's excellent *Contributors.*

Birkbeck stems from a feeling, shared by other *Edinburgh* contributors, that the United States is rewriting the laws governing the progress of human societies laid down in their Enlightenment textbooks. Two trips to America, separated by a few years, will, he suggests, impress upon the visitor 'the whole mystery of the generation as well as the growth of nations,' and he ransacks his thesaurus for terms to connote the scale and speed of this process. Westward expansion adds to the spectacle of what has already been achieved the vista of almost limitless future potential: 'New America' becomes 'Old America' in the blink of an eye as a 'broad, deep, and rapid stream of population' descends on the Pacific Ocean, casting into humiliating shade 'the scarcely perceptible progress of our European societies' (30: 122). The transformation of the landscape entailed in this relentless colonization – what an article in *Blackwood's* in 1826 refers to as an insatiable desire to extend the 'dominion of intellect' over 'vast and boundless forests' (20: 307) – is another recurrent theme. And in an extraordinary essay, nominally a review of five travel books, in the *Eclectic Review* in 1829, a potent combination of statistics and rhetoric amplifies the historical uniqueness of the transatlantic experiment. The United States, the reviewer declares, already possesses territory exceeding that with which the great empires of the past came to an end, and its population has risen from less than two million to nearly twelve million since the middle of the previous century: 'Nothing in the history of the world presents any parallel to this expansion of the human race' (3rd ser. 2: 370).

The 'four stages' theory of human progress espoused by eighteenth-century philosophical historians prescribed that 'societies undergo *development* through successive *stages* based on different *modes of subsistence*' (Meek 6), these modes being hunting, pastoralism, agriculture, and commerce. America, considered as the home of Native Americans, presented no obstacle to this theory; indeed, it was early encounters with 'Indians' ('first stage' hunters) that helped germinate the theory in the first place: as John Locke had said, in the beginning all the world was America. As Christopher Flynn has argued, however, as the home of newly independent Anglo-Americans apparently hurtling through the four stages to a position where they would rival the great European powers in the not-too-distant future, the United States posed more of a problem. In the post-war period, especially, readers digesting travellers' reports of the country struggled to come to terms with developments. The *British Review*, for instance, comments in 1815, after summarizing accurate data on agriculture, manufacturing industry, commerce, and transport infrastructure, that 'the Americans are by no means in that retrograde state ... in which the British nation have sometimes been taught to suppose them, but, on the contrary ... they are in many respects entirely independent of their mother-country' (6: 403). Its publishing industry, however, is said to be less impressive, dominated by reprints of works first published in England, and this mark of difference is underscored in a series of reviews published four years later, in which the United States is described as having no 'learned men' of note and no prospect of evolving a native literature or music (13: 510); in these fields, it seems, it will always be a net importer.

It seems almost a last-ditch consolation for British readers at this time that, however remarkable America's strides in other areas, in cultural, and especially literary, terms she is still raw: the periodical press may be flourishing, with twenty-nine literary journals at the last count, but the 'muse of poetry ... seems with difficulty to have made her way across the Atlantic' (*British Review* 14: 65). Sydney Smith's notoriously offensive list of rhetorical questions from an 1820 essay in the *Edinburgh Review* – 'In the four quarters of the globe, who reads an American book? or goes to an American play? or looks at an American picture or statue?' (33: 79) – resonates in much contemporary writing. Reviewers are generally willing to explain these deficiencies according to the principles of Enlightenment social science – that is, as corroborating stadial history: the *British Review* concedes that scholarly and artistic activity are out of place in a country 'where wealth has not yet been separated from the soil' (13: 510), and the *Edinburgh Review* similarly (and repeatedly) takes the line that cultural prowess requires 'hereditary opulence' and the emergence of a cultivated, leisured class (2: 447) – an aristocracy, in effect. Even the *Quarterly Review* is concerned to point out that a country with so mobile a population, so engrossed in trade, could not be expected to compete with 'the arts, the elegances, the refinements, and general intelligence' (27: 98) of the nation that emigrants have left behind. America may have rocketed to the fourth stage, but it takes a far more mature fourth-stage society to acquire such graces. During the Romantic period, the idea that Britain could take pride in the accomplishments of America, as its estranged yet talented and energetic offspring, lost ground as the picture of a people culturally and linguistically independent of their biological roots came into ever sharper focus. Romantic reviewers were obliged to confront not only the reality of America's rising material prosperity and its practical achievements, but also the growing vitality of its intellectual life. Despite Smith's undiplomatic verbal excesses, there were plainly eminent American authors in natural history, botany, law, medicine, and many other fields; literature, however, seemed to most readers an exception and was therefore asked to shoulder the burden of keeping the infant republic, that 'crude and impatient minor' (*Edinburgh Review* 49: 524), in its place.

British complacency regarding its own overflowing cultural capital helped to mitigate the dawning realization that the United States was destined to become, in the words of the *British Review*, a 'most powerful empire' (6: 418). The author of this prophecy envisioned its fulfilment 'some centuries hence,' but other reviewers took a more abridged view of futurity: in 1814, for example, the *Edinburgh Review* predicted that America would become 'one of the most powerful and important nations of the earth' within the space of a single lifetime (24: 262). This arresting prospect led the *Edinburgh* to insist, time and again, on the importance of cultivating friendly relations with the United States. This was partly for reasons of enlightened commercial self-interest: surely it must be to Britain's advantage to have another great trading nation as its own best customer (and the damage done to both countries' economies by the War of 1812 only sharpened this perception). But a deeper motivation lay in the grim geopolitical outlook of the journal's editor, Francis Jeffrey. In Jeffrey's view, the French Revolution had laid the foundations for a contest between democracy and tyranny – a contest both ideological and military – that could last fifty to one hundred years; America, he believed, would have 'prodigious power and influence,' either as a 'mediator or umpire' or an 'auxiliary and ally,' in how this looming crisis would be resolved (33: 404). John Clive claims that the *Edinburgh*'s advocacy of close ties with the United States thrived in the context of French domination of Europe, but that in the post-war era it saw no place for the country in the new international order (104). Quite the opposite is true: Jeffrey's vision, first outlined in private correspondence with his father-in-law in 1818,[24] was consistent through the next decade, and when he edited a selection of his contributions to the *Edinburgh* in the 1840s he added a note restating his position on the importance of America not only to Britain's security and prosperity but also to 'that of the better part of the world' (*Contributions* 2: 167).

Clive's comment might more justly be applied to the *Quarterly Review*, in which John Barrow asserted that 'the true interests of Great Britain and the United States are intimately blended with each other' (7: 213), when the two countries were at war, but lapsed into his characteristically belligerent posture when they were once again at peace. The *Edinburgh*, by contrast, never ceased to remind its readers, as it did again in 1828, of the 'hundred reasons' why Britain and America 'should hold the other in the light of the most favoured nation,' and it was not alone among the weightier and more serious periodicals in holding this line. The *Eclectic*, very different in ideological complexion as it was, echoed many of the *Edinburgh*'s arguments in a magisterial review published the next year, putting on them the kind of spin one would expect from the leading journal of Dissent. The anonymous author insists that America, more than a generation after Independence, remains bound by 'language, laws, literature, and religion' to the mother country, whose 'moral empire will thus be co-extensively advancing beyond the limits of her political sway' (3rd ser. 2: 368). Whatever animosities may flare up from time to time, these fundamental sympathies must eventually prevail:

> Policy, religion, the voice of nature and of God, enjoin the strictest amity between the two grand portions of that favoured race to whom Divine Providence appears to have committed the moral empire of both hemispheres, and, with it, the responsibility, as the depository of the true faith, of spreading the Gospel, and extending the reign of the Prince of Peace, throughout the world. (398)

The religious zeal energizing this statement may not have held much appeal beyond the *Eclectic*'s self-selecting community of the devout, but the basic political convictions it articulates seem to have been widely shared by the end of the Romantic period. Historian Paul Johnson has suggested that this period witnessed the beginning of the much-debated and ever-controversial 'special relationship' between Britain and the United States (41–3), and in the responses of educated and semi-professional readers to reports of transatlantic travel there is, as I have tried to show in this chapter, plenty to support his case.

---

[24]   See Cockburn 2: 183–4.

Chapter 3
Northern Exposure:
Romantic Readers and
British North America

In Chapter 1 I briefly took note of key developments in British North America from the end of the Seven Years' War through to the 1840 Act of Union. By 1800, there were seven formal colonies under British rule, together with a huge wilderness penetrated and exploited by fur trading companies. A population of approximately half a million (including Native peoples) was overwhelmingly rural in character, with Quebec itself holding no more than eight thousand inhabitants. The colonial economy, such as it was, remained centred on fish and furs, but most settlers practised what was essentially subsistence agriculture. The circumstances of First Nations communities varied enormously, from the surviving remnants of peoples in the eastern colonies whose ways of life were adapted to, or dependent upon, their white neighbours, to the Inuit in the far north who still existed beyond direct contact with Europeans. Although the European population was concentrated in small areas of a vast landmass, most British North Americans, it has been said, 'had relatively little contact with each other or with the outside world,' a situation that 'perhaps suited many of them who were British neither by origin nor by choice' (Conrad 310).

This rather anomalous situation of an unimaginably large territorial possession of very modest population and pretensions, whose contributions to the British economy 'did not justify the costs of colonial defence' (Marshall 386), began to alter over the next few decades. Emigration, chiefly from Scotland and Ireland but with sizeable numbers from England and Wales too during the post-war economic slump, boosted the population of Upper Canada and the Atlantic colonies. 'By 1820,' Helen Cowan observes, 'small tradesmen, mechanics, men of every occupation were joining the throngs of emigrating small farmers, and every port in the north and west was sending hundreds annually to Nova Scotia and Quebec' (52). The economic importance of Canada rose during the Napoleonic wars as its inexhaustible supplies of timber – essential for shipbuilding and other purposes – replaced resources cut off by the French blockade of Baltic ports. Nevertheless, throughout the Romantic period, British North America, and the territory to the west to which it would eventually lay claim, was a country the interior of which remained largely unknown to Europeans; the very outlines of the subcontinent were only slowly filled in on the map. It was a country that was brought under control, and brought to the attention of British readers, first by exploration, then by emigration and colonial settlement, and only in marginal ways by touristic, recreational, or aesthetic travel.

Land-based exploration throughout the period was financed and conducted almost exclusively by the fur trading companies, whose primary motives were, unsurprisingly, economic rather than scientific. I shall examine the reception of narratives of two of the most remarkable such expeditions later in this chapter. Dissemination of knowledge of important travels in this part of the world was not, it is worth saying, always reliable or timely. A book of much interest to modern scholars like Alexander Henry's *Travels and Adventures in Canada and the Indian Territories* (1809), with its dramatic rendering of the siege of Fort Michilimackinac during Pontiac's War and its sympathetic account of Native customs following the author's adoption into a Chippewa (Ojibwe) family, was published several decades after the events it recounts and seems not to have attracted much attention, at least in the literary press. Equally, seminal explorers such as Simon Fraser (1776–1862), who first journeyed the length of the great river that now bears his name, and David Thompson (1770–1857), who explored and mapped five million square kilometres of North America and discovered the true course of the Columbia River, did not publish accounts of their travels in their own lifetimes and therefore did not affect public awareness and imagining of Canada in the way that others did.[1]

Valuable explorations of the Northwest also took place by sea in this period, led by the third voyage of James Cook between 1776 and 1779, which mapped the west coast of Canada and cleared the Bering Strait to reach the northwestern extremity of mainland North America at Icy Cape, and, as Glyndwr Williams points out, set new standards not only in 'empirical observation' but also in 'prompt publication' (564). Certainly, the proliferation of editions of Cook's narrative, and of rival accounts by other members of the expedition, meant that awareness of his achievements permeated all levels of the reading public in the Romantic era. George Vancouver's expedition of 1791–95 systematically filled in the details in Cook's survey, but his *Voyage of Discovery* (1798) reached a smaller and mostly underwhelmed audience, not least because of its length and tedious detail.[2] Cook's voyages stimulated the coastal fur trade in the Pacific Northwest, and more than three hundred ships visited the region over the next fifty years as Britain, France, Spain, and the United States vied for access to sea otter pelts to trade in China for luxury goods. Some of these voyages, such as those by Nathaniel Portlock, George Dixon, and John Meares, produced publications in due course, but never with the same impact as Cook.

---

[1]   Simon Fraser's journals first saw the light of day, in abridged form, in L. F. R. Masson's *Les Bourgeois de la Compagnie du Nord-Ouest* (1889), while full publication awaited W. Kaye Lamb's edition of the *Letters and Journals* in 1960. David Thompson's *Narrative of his Explorations in Western America 1784–1812*, which he worked at constantly in the second half of his life, did not appear until J. B. Tyrrell produced a limited edition in 1916.

[2]   Anna Larpent was even-handed in her opinion: she was 'much entertained' with the book and thought its descriptions 'made with such plainness such simplicity & such an air of truth that they are highly interesting' but considered its 'nautical and geographical parts ... so minute that they tire a common reader' (*Diary*, 7 November 1799).

Among travel books that made more impression were *The Life and Adventures of John Nicol, Mariner* (1822), the redacted story of an ordinary seaman whose twenty-five years' service included a visit to the northwest coast, and several versions of the *Adventures and Sufferings* of John Jewitt, an English blacksmith held captive for three years by the Nuu'chah'nulth people on Vancouver Island after a trading dispute ended in the massacre of all but two of his ship's company. Nicol's and Jewitt's pacey, 'unvarnished' narratives attracted interest and admiration in the periodical press.[3] Meanwhile, in the frozen Arctic seas at the top of the continent, the renewal in 1818 of the quest for a Northwest Passage pioneered by Frobisher, Davis and others in Elizabethan times generated a series of perilous and sometimes calamitous voyages that gripped the imagination of the public to an unprecedented degree. I shall focus on the reception of key texts in this major episode of North American exploration later in this chapter.

There was therefore a significant quantity of exploration literature produced about British North America in this period, representing a still broader span of activity that saw Britain assume a transcontinental presence and begin to knit its disparate colonies and territories together. Much of the exploration was carried out, and much of the literature written, by men born in Britain, and most travel narratives were aimed at a British audience (though some were piratically republished in the United States, usually in New York or Philadelphia).[4] The works that impacted most deeply on British readers were of a kind to assist the formation of enduring myths of Canadian life and identity – that association of national experience with 'Romantic' locales of 'wilderness, North, water,' and with ideas of survival or 'doomed exploration' linked to 'intolerable anxiety,' of which Margaret Atwood has written (137–8, 42), or that powerful construct of a 'deadly, inhuman North characterized by mystery, danger, and adventure,' leading at worst to 'isolation, madness, violent death,' that Sherrill Grace, writing from a modern Foucauldian perspective, appears to resent but recognizes nonetheless as 'naturalized' and 'essential to Canada' (33, 15).

In addition to the steady stream of exploration writing emanating from British North America, there was a body of tamer literature focusing chiefly on Lower and Upper Canada, and oriented at least in part to the interests and needs of prospective emigrants. Some of these travel books were shaped around a tour of existing settlements and embraced topographical or aesthetic descriptions of the major towns and surrounding natural scenery – including, most obviously, Niagara

---

[3]   For an overview of Canadian explorations by land and sea up to the mid-nineteenth century, see the two excellent survey essays by Victor Hopwood in the *Literary History of Canada*.

[4]   Publication in Canada itself was not a serious option, of course; there was no chance of Alexander Mackenzie's *Voyages from Montreal* being published in Montreal. Although Canadian publishers on the British model began to emerge in the early nineteenth century, progress was slow and output was dominated by works of a practical nature. For the primitive state of the Canadian publishing industry in the period, see Gundy.

Falls, which became established as a tourist destination during the period and was attracting thousands of visitors a year by the 1830s. In this chapter I shall begin by looking at responses to Canada as a picturesque site or emigrant destination, before moving on to consider works of exploration or 'extreme travel.' Having surveyed miscellaneous evidence of private reading experiences in Chapter 1, and concentrated on the periodical press in Chapter 2, here I shall attempt, in a limited way, to bring the two into conversation: periodical reviews will dominate, but occasionally it will be possible to counterpoint public and private reactions.

The emigrant's welcome

In the early decades of the nineteenth century a number of works appeared that took the form of a tour of Upper and Lower Canada, usually incorporating a great deal of factual information about the progress of these colonies and sometimes taking care to assess the prospects for emigrants. In some cases, the authors were following the extended itinerary of what Philip Stansbury, in his more exacting pedestrian version of the circuit, called the '*Grand Northern Tour*,' which began in New York and embraced 'the Springs, the Lakes, the Canadas, and the New England States' (v).[5] Isaac Weld, discussed in Chapter 2, took a route very like this after his initial excursion to Virginia. Other travellers' accounts of the St Lawrence and Great Lakes region included George Heriot's *Travels through the Canadas* (1808), Hugh Gray's *Letters from Canada* (1809), John Lambert's *Travels through Lower Canada and the United States of America* (1810), Francis Hall's *Travels in Canada and the United States* (1818), John Howison's *Sketches of Upper Canada* (1821), and John Duncan's *Travels through Part of the United States and Canada* (1823). These books found variable favour with the periodical reviewers. Here I shall highlight characteristics of the British response to these views of Britain's colonial outpost in North America, focusing on the books by Heriot and Howison, which attracted more notice than the others.

Heriot's *Travels through the Canadas*, the work of a Scottish-born colonial administrator who served as deputy postmaster general of Canada between 1799 and 1816, is an oddly constituted book: it begins with a chapter on the Azores, proceeds with a tour of Lower and Upper Canada that extends as far as Lake Superior,[6] includes a lengthy disquisition on Canada's economic and political history, and devotes the entire second half to a compilation of material on 'The Manners and Customs of Several of the Indian Nations of North and South America.' In the periodical press, readers had little time or sympathy for this latter part of the work, which was recognized as derivative and not unfairly condemned

---

[5]   Stansbury was American and took a very different position on the relative merits of Canada and the United States to the writers I focus on in this section; he considered Canada a 'subjected nation' and sadly denied 'the excellences of our republican form of government' (vi).

[6]   In fact, upstream of Niagara it seems uncertain whether Heriot's account is based on personal observation.

as 'a strange and heterogeneous jumble of manners and customs, soils and countries, rivers and trees, beasts and birds,' all thrown together 'in the true spirit of modern book-making,' by the *Universal Magazine* (9: 221). The denunciation of travel narratives as mere exercises in book-making was a common feature of reviews: indeed, Ina Ferris has argued that the critique of 'crass commercialism' and the 'unseemly rush into print' (460) reflected general unease over the credibility and authenticity of the genre and was symptomatic of a wider anxiety over the proliferation of print at the end of the eighteenth century. Seen in this light, Heriot's mauling by the press was not only predictable and well deserved but also redolent of deeper concerns and insecurities.

One aspect of Heriot's *Travels* towards which reviewers were generally more favourable was the quantity and quality of its factual information about the growing colonies: in a manner wholly consistent with the formal responses to American travels examined in Chapter 2, they highlighted those central chapters in which Heriot surveys Canada's commercial progress, describes the mechanics of the fur trade, and summarizes improvements in agriculture and transport. *La Belle Assemblée* considered these 'full of the most interesting and important information' (3 supp.: 41), while the *Annual Review* quoted generously from this part of the book. However, the 'thirst after information' to which *La Belle Assemblée* referred was far from disinterested: Heriot's researches were valued above all because they underpinned a cover story of Canada's rapid advancement under British rule since 1763, with the *Annual Review* and *Universal Magazine* both culling the same data to demonstrate the contrast between French enervation and British innovation. The *Annual Review* was keen to reinforce this nationalistic reading in the context of emigration trends: although Heriot himself does not explicitly address this theme (he does, however, point out that 'Every person in Canada may have within his power the means of acquiring a subsistence,' and that the climate is 'favourable to human health, and to the increase in population' [Heriot 252–3]), the *Annual*'s reviewer commented that he 'draws such a portrait' as is likely to 'allure settlers to the British colonies' in preference to the United States (6: 30).

In contrast with Heriot, John Howison's *Sketches of Upper Canada* advertises in its full title its inclusion of *Practical Details for the Information of Emigrants of Every Class*. Howison (1797–1859), another well-travelled Scot, practised medicine from 1818 to 1820 in St Catharines in Upper Canada; he was therefore on hand to witness the steady stream of his compatriots arriving in the colony, propelled by the post-war economic slump back home, and to lament 'the helpless condition of most of the emigrants ... and the indifference which the supreme government have ever manifested about the welfare and prosperity of the colony' (Howison 61).[7] Reviewers differed in their general view of emigration, but all

---

[7]   In the immediate post-war years the British government offered assisted emigration to groups of Scottish, Irish, and English workers, mainly in an attempt to channel what was seen as an inevitable exodus away from the United States, but the numbers involved were always dwarfed by unassisted emigration.

responded positively to Howison's 'practical details' and foregrounded this part
of his book. Magazines as ideologically diverse as *Blackwood's*, the *Eclectic*, and
the *Edinburgh Review* acknowledged that in the current climate emigration was
a logical recourse for the labourer seeking security and independence, or, as the
Edinburgh put it, 'the man of small income and increasing family' (37: 251).

The unanimity on this point did not prevent some reviewers from disparaging
Canada in more general terms. The *Eclectic* accepted that the country might be
fit for the 'overflowing population' of the nineteenth century, but was repelled by
its 'anonymous tracts of savage country, its forests, swamps, and mountains,' not
to mention the absence of historical or cultural associations that made it a 'moral
vacuum in which the mind finds itself unable to breathe' (18: 353). The recently
established middlebrow weekly, the *Literary Gazette*, worked the same theme
with heavier sarcasm, while underlining those social benefits that any emigrant
not driven overseas by penury would be needlessly forsaking:

> There is something, doubtless, in being the lord even of desolation; in cutting
> one's own wood for fuel, and labouring one's own soil for subsistence, and
> carrying an axe, and shooting deer, and herding with wild Indians; but for these
> delights what are the sacrifices? Our native home and country, the society of
> human beings like ourselves, the protection of equal laws, and all the blessings
> of civilized communion. (253: 739)

The *Gazette* reviewer's stance, in particular the mock-heroic reference to becoming
a 'lord ... of desolation,' has much in common with Robert Cruikshank's satiric
print, *The Emigrant's Welcome to Canada* (Figure 3.1), which appeared at the
same time as Howison's *Sketches*. Cruikshank depicts an inappropriately dressed
emigrant, laden with silk stockings and dancing pumps, being greeted in an icy
landscape by a well-insulated Jack Frost, who gives him a friendly tweak on the
nose (almost certainly an allusion to an Inuit custom reported by John Ross in
the narrative of his polar voyage). The other elements of the scene, such as a sign
indicating 'Fine Land to grow wheat if you can plough it,' heavy-handedly make
the point that hopes of an easy livelihood in Canada are likely to be disappointed.
Such hopes, it has to be said, were not fuelled by Howison or other guides to
emigration, who promised 'abundant means of subsistence' (Howison 172), but
only in return for 'a few years' hard labour' (257); nor were they encouraged by
reviewers, who preferred to reproduce practical and realistic advice in the form of
substantial excerpts. It might be argued that Howison's ironic allusion to Milton's
Satan ('Better to reign in hell than serve in heaven') in defending Upper Canada as
an 'agreeable place of residence' (268) outdoes the hostile *Gazette* in ambivalent
affirmation.

Despite finding Howison's discussion of the pros and cons of emigration
reasonable and helpful, reviewers were critical of other aspect of the *Sketches*.
Glaring contradictions in the author's account of settler communities – the
occupants of the Talbot settlement are said to be a 'lawless and unprincipled
rabble' (169), yet Howison also comments on the prevailing 'harmony' (174), the

Fig. 3.1   Robert Cruikshank, *The Emigrant's Welcome to Canada* (c.1820). Library and Archives Canada, Acc. No. 1970–188–2056 W.H. Coverdale Collection of Canadiana.

politeness of social intercourse, and the hospitality shown to new arrivals – did not go unnoticed. The *Edinburgh* argued the impossibility of men falling into worse habits in 'one of these forest hamlets' than they would have acquired as poor labourers in an overcrowded city, and disdainfully left the author to 'reconcile these inconsistencies' (37: 265, 267), while the *Monthly Review* conceded that Howison was 'too honest to suppress facts because they happen to contradict his opinions,' while pointing out that his own description of the settlers belied his 'piteous moanings over the degraded state of man' (99: 181). As these liberal reviewers perceived only too clearly, Howison had tied himself in knots because his realistic appraisal of the material benefits of emigration and his first-hand experience of an easy-going, cooperative settler way of life could not entirely overcome his ingrained dislike of the lack of social subordination and 'civilized' distinctions in manners. The *Monthly* found it incredible that his remarks on the 'revolting' consequences of transatlantic democracy were 'penned on the frontiers of the largest, the freest, the most enterprizing and most prosperous Republic that the world ever saw,' where there was no 'insolent domination on one side and crouching sycophancy on the other,' and where 'the principles of political and civil liberty' were 'better practised than in any one of the old governments of Europe' (177). A Tory periodical such as *Blackwood's*, as might be expected, took a different view, agreeing with Howison that equality was the 'greatest curse' of transatlantic society, and that the absence of 'superior models' of behaviour had a brutalizing effect that was especially noticeable in Canada (10: 545).

Ideological differences notwithstanding, the formal reception of Heriot's and Howison's tours confirms the bias towards empirical observation, adjusted to transient historical circumstances (as in the case of emigration), already noted with respect to the United States in Chapter 2. Readers are assumed to possess a thirst for information, and their professional counterparts see it as their responsibility to satisfy that thirst, providing generous excerpts or summaries on such matters as climate, agriculture, and trade while taking care to evaluate the accuracy and reliability of different travellers' reports.

Conversely, one feature of the tours of Lower and Upper Canada that reviewers showed little interest in, or patience with, was descriptions of natural scenery. This may appear surprising, given the centrality of Niagara Falls to the 'Grand Northern Tour' and their rapid development as a tourist spectacle. John Towner has shown that in North America generally there was 'a rapid transition from eras of discovery and exploration to larger scale tourism developments' (166), and Niagara epitomized this trend. Isaac Weld, visiting the Falls in the 1790s, was already able to view them from several defined 'stations' and was led to the foot of the Falls (on the Canadian side) via 'Mrs Simcoe's ladder' to peer into the caverns behind. He devoted a chapter to the Falls and favoured them with four of his illustrations: two of these depict white men clearly rapt in contemplation of the sublime spectacle; another, interestingly, shows three 'Indians' in the foreground with their attentions elsewhere, picturesque accoutrements to the scene but not themselves aesthetic observers (Figure 3.2). Heriot, whose description of the site extends over two chapters, has three colour plates of the Falls and the nearby whirlpool, including one view taken from the base of the American Falls. Howison, a later visitor, enjoyed improved tourist facilities, including easier access to the foot of the Horseshoe Falls via 'a spiral staircase enclosed in a wooden building' (96), and was able to enjoy the whole spectacle from the water using a ferry provided 'for the convenience of travellers' (98). Despite being a comparative latecomer, he was not deterred from offering his own verbal representation of the scenery, nor from recycling some now familiar anecdotes (an Indian carried over the edge in his canoe was doomed to reprise his fatal descent in many retellings) and reflections (such as the rate of erosion and gradual retreat of the Falls upriver).

Although travel writers therefore felt compelled to practise their literary art on this natural spectacle, professional readers had little time for any of it. The *Annual Review*, seeing the Falls 'toss and tumble over fifteen pages' in Heriot's *Travels*, decided that they had led him to 'overstep the boundary which separates sublimity from bombast' (6: 24). The *Edinburgh Review* stated the 'inflated' raptures and 'unintelligible sensations' that Heriot had bestowed on the 'watery parts of his subject' reached fever-pitch at Niagara (12: 213), while the *Universal Magazine* suggested that his 'incomprehensible' effusions would have provided Pope and Swift with a perfect specimen of 'true bathos' (8:423). As for Howison, *Blackwood's* was unusual in admiring his 'chastely and tastefully powerful' description of the Falls, written 'as if his spirit were ... penetrated with the mighty and mysterious influences of elemental nature' (10: 540). In contrast, the *Edinburgh* was scornful of his 'big words and sounding epithets' and offered an alternative sketch of a rapidly modernizing touristic space: the visitor no longer had to brave the 'pathless forest' to visit the 'great cataract' but was 'carried to its very brink in a mail-coach,' and 'he views it with very different emotions, when he sees perched on the Table rock, instead of the wild Indian in his savage habiliments, a bevy of giggling damsels from Albany or New-York, with pink pelisses and green parasols' (37: 260). Howison, the writer implied, had given a highly selective and artificially 'primitivized' view of Niagara – very much of a piece with the Weld illustration (Figure 3.2). In fact, Weld's drawing, already an anachronistic misrepresentation of a burgeoning tourist site, seems with hindsight to have fathered a canon of imitators enamoured of the same inauthentic formula. Unbeguiled, the *Monthly Review* did not deign to mention Niagara until the very end of its article, and cited the passage merely as an example of stylistic bad taste: Howison's description was 'all splash, dash, roar, and foam' – he had 'out-Heroded Herod, and beaten *Bombastes Furioso* out of the field' (99: 185).

Given the close association of the Romantic era with emotional responses to nature and the enthusiastic pursuit of the sublime, it is worth noting just how intolerant Romantic readers could be of what they considered 'bad' – sloppy, formulaic, or inflated – writing about nature. In the arena of travel books, nature writing was low on their scale of priorities, probably because it offered too little by way of a contribution to knowledge and too much by way of rhetorical self-indulgence. On the evidence available, there was little difference between public

Fig. 3.2   Isaac Weld, *View of the Horse-Shoe Fall of Niagara*; illustration for *Travels through the States of North America* (1799). Library and Archives Canada, Acc. No. R9266–2179.

and private responses to travel literature in this respect. In terms of the mantra discussed in the last chapter, nature description was not instructive, and was entertaining, more often than not, for the wrong reasons.

As a useful counterpoint to generalizations about how people read this sub-genre of Canadian travels, it is interesting to consider William Beckford's notes in his copy of Edward Talbot's *Five Years' Residence in the Canadas* (1824), preserved in the Bodleian Library. Talbot presents another version of the northern tour, journeying up the St Lawrence via Quebec and Montreal, then around the northern shores of Lake Ontario to his eventual place of residence at what was then the new settlement of London in southwestern Upper Canada. Also included in the book is a great deal of miscellaneous information on Canada's natural history, its development as a colony, and its social organization. Following his standard practice, Beckford kept tidy and concise notes on his reading on the flyleaves (three pages in each volume), writing down page numbers followed by a quotation or near-verbatim excerpt, sometimes adding an observation or humorous gloss of his own. This method confirms, firstly, that Beckford read these books straight through, rather than 'dipping into' them; it is also a fascinating guide to what he found of particular interest in the books, or wanted to make a note of for future reference.

Beckford completely ignores Talbot's mandatory description of Niagara Falls and seems to take no interest in the chapters on emigration or all the documentary material on Canada's political and legal institutions. In fact, most of the narrative of the tour itself appears to pass him by. Many of his notes focus on what the eighteenth century called 'curiosities of nature' – unusual or remarkable aspects of Canadian flora and fauna: he copies out, for example, brief excerpts regarding the behaviour of the skunk, butterflies said to be as large as bats, and the magnificent appearance of red and white pines. In some instances he laces the extract with his own comments. In his note concerning 'a very tiresome sort of Pheasant,' the word 'tiresome' is not Talbot's, while he shows his mischievous sense of humour by taking a sentence of Talbot's that disputes another writer's observations on wolves ('This sentence contains no less than five positive assertions every one of which is diametrically opposite to the truth') and turning it against Talbot's own statements. Beckford copies out Talbot's conventional description of the beaver as 'a perfect architect & a wonderfully practical advocate for maintaining the bonds of society,' and adds his own satirical gloss: 'He is your animal for the execution of [Robert] Owen's plan.' In terms of the natural landscape, only two passages catch Beckford's eye. He likes Talbot's description of the 'sombre gloom' that 'hangs like the shadow of darkness over the greater part of this extensive continent,' and he notes the picture – said by Talbot to be one of the few things in Canada capable of evoking a 'sadly-pleasing recollection' of a glorious yet vanished past – of 'a poor old oak tired to death of conveying annual nutriment to its decaying boughs.'[8] It is

---

[8]   In fact, Talbot's phrasing is the more impersonal 'an aged oak whose trunk has become weary ...'. Beckford's 'poor old oak tired to death' further sentimentalizes the image and leads one to suspect that he is actually making fun of the author.

interesting that these two short passages combine to give an impression of Canada as a vast, forbidding wilderness, essentially void of human history – a national stereotype that is crystallized in Beckford's miserly selections from the tour.

The second volume of the *Five Years' Residence* deals at length with the 'manners and customs' of the Canadian people, and here Beckford's excerpts bring his personality still more to the fore. He picks out passages that argue the impossibility of true female gentility in Canada and make fun of the Canadians' (supposedly) relaxed sexual morality. He relishes the observation that unmarried mothers are treated with as much respect as vestal virgins, and to Talbot's description of the willingness of Canadian men to put up with their wives' infidelities he adds the laconic comment, 'comfortable arrangements.' Talbot's hostile account of a Methodist camp-meeting is evidently much to his taste ('Ravings, rantings, & roarings' is his concise summary), and he clearly agrees with Talbot that religious enthusiasm is as open to abuse as the American doctrine of 'Liberty and Independence.' His notes overall express a mix of national snobbery, political conservatism, and sexual chauvinism – unaggressive and lightly worn, but pronounced all the same.

Beckford's note-taking, in what seems to have been a careful and thorough reading of this Canadian tour, shows a different mentality to any discoverable through formal reviews. There is no 'scientific' imperative of information-gathering here: he is interested in novelty and strangeness, but in what seems a fairly random, casually selective way. It is a kind of browsing mentality – sometimes idle and uninvolved, but intermittently fully engaged. This travel book, like many others, allowed Beckford to exercise his laconic wit and gently caress his aristocratic prejudices, and he enjoyed this sufficiently to read through to the end. Just as one has to assume that the kinds of criteria deployed by reviewers in their professional encounters with travel texts had something in common with the interests and preferences of private readers, so there is no reason to suppose that Beckford's mental grazing was not replicated in hundreds of individual reading experiences – or at least that it was not *one way* Romantic readers consumed such texts.

For the sake of 'a few furs': Hearne and Mackenzie

In a very different geographical, conceptual, and generic world to the northern tours and emigrant literature perused in the previous section were the writings of those undertaking primary exploration and helping to extend the boundaries of British North America. It was the fur trading companies that largely drove and financed exploration: the Hudson's Bay Company, established in 1670, which 'owned' the vast territory draining into the Bay and was thereby the largest private landholder in the world, came under pressure in the 1780s from the North West Company, a conglomerate of Montreal-based traders which had taken over the French trading and transportation network following the Treaty of Paris in 1763. Initially reluctant to sponsor exploration for exploration's sake, and secure in the supply of furs brought by First Nations people to its trading posts on the Bay, the Hudson's Bay Company was forced to become more enterprising and move inland to fight the competition from the rival company, whose members had always pursued a policy of aggressive westward expansion and preferred to deal directly with Native hunters. A period of fierce and sometimes violent economic warfare ensued until the companies amalgamated in 1821. In the eyes of a leading historian of the fur trade, Harold Innis, the latter development was inevitable because the large capital investment on which this industry depended created an irresistible movement 'toward cut-throat competition and monopoly' (251). Innis also observes that the area over which the North West Company extended its operations, at the height of its power, was roughly coterminous with the eventual boundaries of the Dominion of Canada, and that it was therefore the 'forerunner of confederation'; indeed, the belief that Canada is unique in owing its emergence as a nation to a single industry is still a popular foundation myth.[9]

The necessary counterpoint to this affirmative story of the confluence of economic and political goals is well articulated by Eric Wolf, who focuses on the consequences of the fur trade and relentless westward expansion for indigenous populations:

> Wherever it went, the fur trade brought with it contagious illness and increased warfare. Many native groups were destroyed, and disappeared entirely; others were decimated, broken up, or driven from their original habitats. Remnant populations sought refuge with allies or grouped together with other populations, often under new names and ethnic identities. (193)

As the British steadily built a transcontinental trading empire, more and more First Nations began the journey from – to borrow Urs Bitterli's terminology for intercultural encounters – 'contact' to 'collision' (in which the property or cultural identity of the weaker party is under threat) to 'conflict' (which takes various forms, including violence, competition for resources, and disease). Although some Native groups managed, at least for a time, to use trade goods to supplement their existing subsistence activities and traditional way of life, ultimately the internal and external social relations of indigenous peoples were profoundly altered: they reconfigured their ways around the trading post and European goods, and they became essentially 'specialized labourers in a putting-out system' (Wolf 194) operating on an international basis.

As one would expect, the objectives and working practices of the fur trading companies, and their necessary interactions with First Nations groups and individuals, feature prominently in the writings of explorers in British North America in this period. While most explorers maintained field notes and journals, only a minority wrote up their travels for publication within their own lifetime. Those that did had to straddle the expectations of their sponsors and institutional authorities, on the one hand, and the interests and expectations of a wider reading public, on the other, and very often they reveal themselves (for example,

---

[9] See Grace 65–6 for a summary of alternative theories of Canadian origins.

through awkward disclaimers) to be acutely aware of this tension. Owing to the pressure to conform with company policy or wider cultural frameworks, there could also be conflict, as Bruce Greenfield argues, 'between loyalty to the places from they departed and to which they returned and an honest reporting of the actual experiences of the places and peoples they "discovered"' ('Rhetoric' 58). Greenfield has also written persuasively of the manner in which travellers give final shape and significance to their journeys, coordinating and structuring a multitude of contingencies into a purposeful narrative geared to the economic and political motives of the expedition:

> In the field, the journal is the tool the explorer uses to extend to the 'trackless' forests and prairies the order that he, the 'civilized' traveler, has sustained within himself. The narrative's published form is an assertion of the power the explorer exerts over new lands and peoples, portraying them as part of his own story. (*Narrating* 18–19)

While this characterization of exploration writing makes compelling sense, Greenfield runs the risk of overstating the degree of 'power' achieved both by the explorer *in situ*, in challenging and sometimes life-threatening situations where survival was dependent on the cooperation or tolerance of local people, and by the explorer, usually a reluctant and inexperienced writer, as a fabricator of text.

Where I part company with Greenfield is where he presents the project of Euro-imperialism as explaining everything not just about the activities of explorers but also about the reception of their published writings. It was, he claims, 'only the widely shared understanding that Europeans and Euro-Americans were fundamentally concerned with, even defined by, their global expansion that enabled the traveller to undertake his mission and to gain a public hearing when he returned' (*Narrating* 11). Was it really *only* that? Were there no other reasons why the contemporary reading public gave explorers a 'hearing' than reconfirmation of their status as citizen-subjects of a global superpower? Does a shared sense of cultural power and complicity with the goal of furthering the rule of European knowledge *completely* account for whatever curiosity they felt about those explorers' stories? Such claims should at least be empirically tested against evidence of actual reception.

In this section I examine the reception of two notable explorers of the late eighteenth century, Samuel Hearne and Alexander Mackenzie. Both achieved celebrity for their accomplishments, and their publications were influential in more ways than one, but their names, though doubtless appearing somewhere in the curriculum of Canadian schoolchildren, are otherwise familiar now only to a coterie of scholars with interests in Canadian history and literature. Ray Mears, the bushcraft expert who in 2009 broadcast a BBC television programme on Hearne in an attempt to resurrect his reputation, describes him not unfairly as 'little known here in the UK' (95), and the same could be said of Mackenzie.

Hearne, a Naval veteran of the Seven Years' War by the age of twenty-two before joining the Hudson's Bay Company in 1766, was sent on an overland expedition to discover the truth concerning substantial copper deposits said to lie near the mouth of the Coppermine River; at a time when the Company was being accused of insularity and obstructionism, his aims were to 'promote an extension of [its] trade' (Hearne lxiv), investigate the possibility of a 'passage through' the continent (lxix), and take possession of any exploitable land in the name of the king. In completing his mission in 1772 (without finding the legendary copper), Hearne became the first European to reach the northern coast of North America; he also disproved the existence of a navigable route from Hudson's Bay to the Pacific Ocean and pioneered the method of wilderness exploration by living off the land and using the skills and knowledge of indigenous people. Hearne continued working for the Hudson's Bay Company until 1787; returning to London, he spent his remaining years preparing his story for publication, but *A Journey from Prince of Wales's Fort in Hudson's Bay to the Northern Ocean* (1795) only saw the light of day after his death.[10]

Modern critical debate on Hearne (most of it published in highly specialized academic journals) has been preoccupied with his account of the massacre of sleeping Inuit by the Chipewyans attached to Hearne's expedition, who, in a manner revelatory of its leader's passive and dependent position, transform it from a journey of discovery into a war party. In a seminal essay, I. S. MacLaren explores the differences between the published version of the Bloody Fall massacre and Hearne's field notes, and argues that the sadistic and sentimental excesses of this episode are of dubious provenance and were manufactured to suit the 'Gothic taste of the age' ('Samuel Hearne's Accounts' 41). In later articles, he has furthered his discussion of the massacre, said to have 'transfixed' English-Canadian literary studies, and of the material history of Hearne's text, seen as a construct of 'imperial publishing history' ('Exploration/Travel' 57–8); with the benefit of new manuscript evidence, he has strengthened his challenge to the authority of the 'published Hearne' ('Notes' 25) and posed additional questions that require bibliographic research. On a different track, beginning from the premise that there is no fully substantiated account of the massacre in European, Inuit, or Indian sources, Robin McGrath invokes the Inuit oral tradition to demonstrate not only that such a massacre probably occurred (as 'one of a series of such encounters' [98], but that Hearne probably 'was present' at the event (105).

Needless to say, from the point of view of a study of contemporary reception, this whole area of enquiry is somewhat beside the point: Romantic readers knew only the published version of the *Journey*, and it is their responses to that work that need assessing. Another area that critics have been particularly interested in is Hearne's exposure to the Chipewyan people and their way of life (he devotes a full chapter to 'A Short Description of the Northern Indians'), and the question of whether he was able to transcend the biases of his own culture. Did Hearne escape the prison-house of ideology and adjust his mindset to that of the Native people who partnered him on his expedition, or did he filter everything he experienced

---

[10]   Editorial involvement in the text of the *Journey* was discounted by Hearne's modern editor, Richard Glover, but is still disputed by scholars.

through the lens of an ethnocentric superiority complex? Kevin Hutchings has provided a balanced summary of these contrasting positions and put forward a more nuanced argument that sees Hearne's text as the product of intercultural dialogue, its colonialist mentality subject to 'contextual uncertainties' (52); with a particular focus on how Hearne's treatment of the 'Indians' both confirms and contradicts the 'four stages' theory, he contends that Hearne's 'narrative perplexity' might be considered an 'early manifestation of critical *self-reflexivity*' (73).

This line of research is vital and fascinating, but the vocabularies of postcolonial and poststructuralist criticism in which it finds a natural home can seem as remote from the reading experience of Hearne's contemporary audience as the scholarly pursuit of textual variants. Nevertheless, a strong interest in the representation of 'Indians' or 'savages' is something that Romantic-period readers have in common with modern scholars. Although most reviewers duly noted Hearne's geographical discoveries and his conclusions respecting a Northwest Passage, in terms of pure column inches they were far more interested in what he said about the customs and beliefs of the Chipewyans and in several striking anecdotes he presented concerning members of his party. There was a marked pattern to this readerly interest: the same incidents or aspects of Chipewyan culture were constantly extracted, summarized, or discussed. Hearne's description of Native women – the relative standard of beauty by which they are judged, the qualities looked for in an Indian wife, the life of physical toil and domestic drudgery to which they are inured, the sexual morality that governs their behaviour – provided much of the raw material for many reviews, including those in the *Edinburgh Magazine*, *English Review*, and *Gentlemen's Magazine*. The story of an assault by Matonnabee (the Chipewyan leader whose assistance was crucial to the safety and success of Hearne's expedition) on the former husband of one of his wives, and an account of 'the custom among those people for the men to wrestle for any woman to whom they are attached' (Hearne 67), proved irresistible to reviewers. An episode of related interest was the party's encounter with a solitary Dogrib woman, an escaped slave, who had been living alone for at least seven months, trapping animals to feed herself and making clothes that showed 'no little variety of ornament' (Hearne 169). For the *English Review*, this confirmed Shaftesbury's observation that 'a love of cleanliness and decorum in dress' was 'implanted in the mind by the hand of nature' (28: 123); the *Critical Review* admired the woman's 'fortitude and ingenuity' but thought its readers should find the story a useful reminder of how 'happily removed from the barbarity of savage manners' (20: 135) they were. Tim Fulford argues that Hearne finds in this woman's ability to survive in 'the harshest of environments' an instance of sublimity, and that this 'aesthetic sensibility' is used to demonstrate his 'moral superiority' (172) to the Indian men who treat their womenfolk in a brutal and possessive way. Whether this passage really has the covert agenda of assuring white readers 'that British government was better for Indian women than rule by Indian men' is questionable, but Fulford is right to highlight Hearne's fondness for portraying Native women as 'pitiable victims' and thereby adapting them to 'a popular sentimental category' (167). The evidence of contemporary reception is that, in doing so, Hearne (or whatever composite author was responsible for seeing the *Journey* into print) shrewdly judged the 'taste of the age.'

Among other passages that caught the eye of reviewers, there were several more that reinforced the theme of the sad oppression of Indian women: a woman compelled to begin a long march immediately after childbirth; the general indifference shown to women in labour; an encounter with a consumptive woman, incapable of travelling, who had simply been left behind by her people, to either recover or die (Wordsworth's use of this incident will be examined in Chapter 4). The popularity of this entire constellation of extracts plainly speaks to the enduring strength of the eighteenth-century cult of sensibility, as well as channelling an ostentatious display of compassion and empathy among a predominantly male corps of reviewers at a time when traditional gender constructions had loosened. And then there was the massacre, the epitome of 'Indian barbarity' for many readers. The tensions and contradictions that modern critics find arising from Hearne's collusion in this event (Fulford, for instance, considers he is in danger of becoming a Romantic Kurtz, sinking into savagery in a Canadian heart of darkness [69]) were not, on the face of it, evident to contemporary readers. The *English Review*, *London Chronicle*, and *Monthly Review* all quoted extensively from this narrative climax, including the memorable scene of the torture of a young Inuit girl who died agonizingly at Hearne's feet, while the *Gentlemen's Magazine* and the *Analytical Review* alluded to the massacre as an important component of the book but affected to spare their readers' feelings by not reproducing the gory details. All appear to assume that fellow readers will simply be appalled by the spectacle of Native savagery. If the *Heart of Darkness* analogy has anything to say about historical reception, however, it may be that Romantic readers played Marlow to Hearne's Kurtz, mesmerized by a sense of 'remote kinship' with the violent passions on display. Perhaps, for male reviewers and readers at least, this offset the tender feelings evoked by countless scenes of suffering women with powerful expressions of an atavistic masculinity.

Overall, professional readers offered a range of positive responses to Hearne's treatment of the 'Northern Indians,' thought to be based on 'much careful observation' by the *London Chronicle* (1 Sep. 1796: 217), and providing for the *Monthly Review* such a 'striking picture of the miseries of savage life' that readers would be led to appreciate more fully 'the inestimable blessings of civilized society' (20: 247). The reviewers would all have concurred with the *Monthly*'s opinion that the 'gratification of a liberal curiosity' concerning a 'savage' nation hitherto little known to Europeans was the main benefit of Hearne's *Journey*; by comparison, Hearne's services to geographical discovery, economic growth, or geopolitical development scarcely warranted a mention.

Perhaps the most interesting responses are those in the *English Review* and *Critical Review*. The former's reviewer is repelled by what the Bloody Fall massacre reveals of the Indians' 'animal ferocity,' but by aligning this with 'the smooth barbarity of courts' (28: 119) the reviewer interprets events along Christian lines as evidence of a propensity for evil inherent in all human beings, rather than the mark of a primitive stage of human evolution that Europeans have consigned to a distant past. For him or her, the *Journey*'s interest is ultimately of a philosophical nature: ceremonies described by Hearne as having taken place after the massacre are the product of guilt, and confirm the presence of an innate moral conscience in the unlikeliest of quarters. Although Hearne is not himself a philosopher, the *English* says, he provides valuable resources for philosophical speculation, and allows us to draw conclusions regarding universal moral laws that underlie the varieties of human character and behaviour.

The *Critical Review* is unimpressed with Hearne's philosophical credentials, but considers that he has made a valuable contribution to what would now be called social science. Through a plain and factual presentation of the 'barbarity of savage manners' Hearne has provided, for this reader, valuable ammunition for combatting the Rousseauesque noble savagery that was so current in literary culture – what he refers to as 'fanciful descriptions of the state of nature' (20: 135). As a contribution to that ongoing Enlightenment project of compiling 'the history of mankind in different parts of the world,' Hearne has offered 'a true insight' into 'the life of a North American' (127).

Despite ideological differences and alternative emphases, there was considerable uniformity among professional readers in their response to the *Journey*. It is interesting to compare these public reactions with the more private thoughts of a reader encountering the same text, and for this purpose it is fascinating to have available an annotated copy of Hearne in the National Library of Scotland. Unlike the Rhodes House copy discussed in Chapter 1, which contains just a single marginal comment illustrative of an amused but rather condescending form of attention, this copy is extensively annotated. Most of the notes are in the same hand and are neatly written in pencil; on internal evidence they are not contemporary with publication of the book but were probably written around 1817 or soon thereafter.[11] Some of the annotations take the form of subject headings or brief summary comments, allowing the unidentified reader to locate key passages easily at a later date, and there is much cross-referencing of other parts of the text, almost as though an index is being compiled as the reading proceeds. This suggests a much more careful and attentive reading of a work of travel literature than other sources might indicate was the norm in this period. There are also many more substantial 'supplementing' notes (to recall Heather Jackson's classification of marginalia), which take issue with Hearne or develop points made in the text, sometimes with reference to other sources. In line with another common form of note-taking discussed by Jackson, the annotator enjoys making links with other literary works – there are quotations from Edgeworth's *Castle Rackrent*, Pope's 'Essay on Criticism,' Burns's 'Unco Guid,' and Shakespeare's *Hamlet* – but these constitute only a small proportion of the complete series.

An overview of this reader's annotations reveals a close correspondence between his or her interests and those of the reviewers. Of fifty-seven marginal notes distributed throughout the book fewer than ten are not directly related to

---

[11]	The notes include a reference to the fifth edition of Malthus's *Essay on the Principle of Population* (1817). There is also an allusion to Walter Scott's *Waverley* (1814), but nothing to suggest the reading took place later than the 1810s.

the 'Indians,' and the same passages that dominate the reviews are marked or commented on by this individual reader: Indian ideas of female beauty, the treatment of women during and after childbirth, Matonnabee's assault on his wife's former husband, the custom of wrestling for possession of women, Indian jugglers, the forsaken consumptive woman, the solitary Dogrib, and Matonnabee's reported suicide all attract comment. Sometimes the reader merely notes characteristics of the Indians as they are expressed in the text: they are 'voracious & thoughtless' (25),[12] possessed of 'Selfishness and inhumanity' (51) and 'hostile propensities' (147), show 'Little natural affection' (107), yet are capable of 'generosity' (99) and feelings of 'honour' (109). It is as though he or she is assembling an ethnic character profile from the piecemeal evidence furnished by Hearne's account. More often, however, the notes assume a discursive form, showing that this reader is not merely 'entertained' but engaged and stimulated by the narrative. References to Malthus, clearly a respected yet far from sacrosanct figure for the reader, are a case in point. On page 66 Hearne, narrating the discovery that a store of provisions along the route has been stolen, comments that 'the Indians, not expecting to meet with so great a disappointment,' had not practised economy with the food in their possession; this elicits a note that such 'want of economy in the consumption of food will account for many of the evils which Malthus ascribes to excessive population,' along with a list of page references to the *Journey* that offer further illustration of this improvidence. On page 83 (Figure 3.3), a passage that has proved of considerable interest to Hearne's postcolonial critics, in which he claims that although it is the duty of every 'Company' man to encourage 'a spirit of industry among the natives' (by which he means devoting all their energies to the fur trade), this is not in fact 'for the real benefit of the poor Indians,' seems to have got this contemporary reader thinking. Hearne's observation that by following their traditional subsistence lifestyle the Indians 'are seldom exposed to the griping hand of famine' causes a disagreement:

> The improvidence of these traders would produce frequent famine, however weak the principle of population, or however abundant the supply of food. To weaken the principle of population would increase the relative plenty of food, & occasion a still more wasteful & improvident consumption.

A few pages later, Hearne's description of how an Indian woman is kept in seclusion for a month after childbirth, during which time the father never sees the child, draws the comment that this is an 'Opportunity to murder the child, if the father is a tyrant,' followed by chapter and verse from Malthus. Evidently this reader had a strong interest in political economy and was keen to test Malthus's controversial population theory against what travellers like Hearne reported of societies at a much earlier stage of development. A travel book here serves not only as the stimulus for reflection, debate, and self-definition through reasoned disagreement, but as the very physical medium in which those processes are carried out.

---

[12]   The NLS Hearne is a copy of the (first) London edition of 1795; page references in the discussion that follows are to this edition.

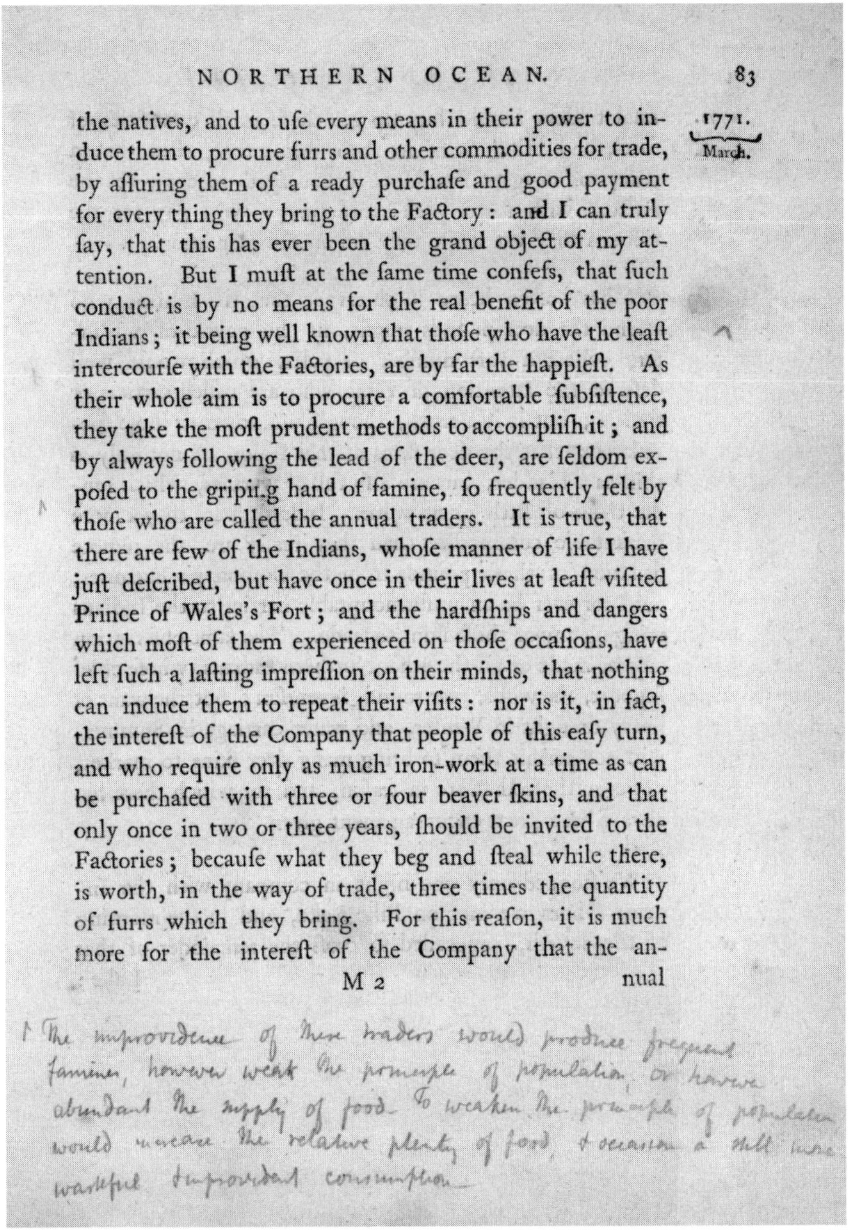

NORTHERN OCEAN.　　83

the natives, and to ufe every means in their power to induce them to procure furrs and other commodities for trade,
by affuring them of a ready purchafe and good payment
for every thing they bring to the Factory : and I can truly
fay, that this has ever been the grand object of my attention.　But I muft at the fame time confefs, that fuch
conduct is by no means for the real benefit of the poor
Indians ; it being well known that thofe who have the leaft
intercourfe with the Factories, are by far the happieft.　As
their whole aim is to procure a comfortable fubfiftence,
they take the moft prudent methods to accomplifh it ; and
by always following the lead of the deer, are feldom ex-
pofed to the griping hand of famine, fo frequently felt by
thofe who are called the annual traders.　It is true, that
there are few of the Indians, whofe manner of life I have
juft defcribed, but have once in their lives at leaft vifited
Prince of Wales's Fort ; and the hardfhips and dangers
which moft of them experienced on thofe occafions, have
left fuch a lafting impreffion on their minds, that nothing
can induce them to repeat their vifits : nor is it, in fact,
the intereft of the Company that people of this eafy turn,
and who require only as much iron-work at a time as can
be purchafed with three or four beaver fkins, and that
only once in two or three years, fhould be invited to the
Factories ; becaufe what they beg and fteal while there,
is worth, in the way of trade, three times the quantity
of furrs which they bring.　For this reafon, it is much
more for the intereft of the Company that the an-
　　　　　M 2　　　　　　　　　　nual

*The improvidence of thefe traders would produce frequent
famines, however weak the principle of population, or however
abundant the fupply of food to weaken the principle of population
would increafe the relative plenty of food, & occafion a ftill more
wafteful improvident confumption —*

Fig. 3.3　　Manuscript note to Samuel Hearne, *A Journey from Prince of Wales's
Fort in Hudson's Bay, to the Northern Ocean* (1795). Courtesy of
The Trustees of National Library of Scotland.

Many other annotations show this reader's fondness for 'thinking out loud' in the margins of a book. Against Hearne's account of the application of war paint and other preparations for the massacre appears the sardonic comment: 'Contrast with the gaiety of civilized war – many ways of dressing the same thing – We have the same passion for mischief, but our taste is more elegant' (152). It is interesting that when Hearne describes a near-naked Indian conjuror apparently swallowing a bayonet, which he assumes is a trick although he is unable to see how it is performed, our reader is much more open-minded: 'There seem to be talents peculiar to barbarous nations, as there is a delicacy of touch peculiar to the blind – We cannot either explain or conceive them, in our happier condition' (194). In a similar vein, Hearne's remark, during a discussion of the Northern Indians' longstanding hostility towards the 'Esquimaux,' that 'Their hearts ... are in general so unsusceptible of tenderness, that they can view the deepest distress in those who are not immediately related to them, without the least emotion' (340), inspires a corrective observation at the bottom of the page:

> Habit will reconcile the heart, as it will reconcile the senses, to what is naturally most offensive – There is no evidence of natural hardness of heart – We might as well say that the hardness of hand in a day-labourer was natural –

In such annotations, it cannot be determined whether this private reader is talking to himself/herself, or to the book, or to other potential readers. But the picture that emerges is of a serious, thoughtful, unprejudiced individual who engages with travel works chiefly on an intellectual level: although a lighter side is occasionally evident in notes deploying literary quotations, he or she seems principally interested in the ethnological content of the text and in pondering its philosophical and moral implications. It is one piece of evidence that the type of reader projected by periodical reviews of travel literature – a reader keen to learn about the 'manners and customs' of unfamiliar or newly 'discovered' peoples – was not an editorial fantasy.

Anna Larpent read Hearne's *Journey* in January 1797, and her diaristic reflections on Hearne, a unique window on an individual Romantic reader's reception of a major exploration narrative, can be usefully juxtaposed with those of the anonymous annotator considered above. In some respects her stance is comparable, displaying a keen interest in the lives of the 'Indians,' albeit accommodating these ethnological observations to her characteristic religious worldview: Hearne, she notes in her journal for 11 January, gives 'a plain narrative of what passed – & an unprejudiced account of these nations,' and it is 'curious to read of such varieties; to view a country so different from ours; to observe how an almighty wisdom operates over all its works – fitting each part to the whole providing for its strange incomprehensible diversities!' Also part of that strange diversity are the flora and fauna of the Canadian tundra, and Larpent states that she has 'marked passages for extracts' from Hearne's lengthy chapter on the natural history of the region. This is confirmation of David Allan's observation that women readers of the period were not only 'greatly interested in scientific material' but also interested enough to commit such material to their commonplace books as part of their general drive for self-education and self-improvement (94). However, Larpent's overall response to the representation of the Chipewyans – perhaps provoked by the Bloody Fall massacre, though she is not explicit on this point – is much less dispassionate than our previous reader's: 'the mind revolts,' she confesses, 'from contemplating such a disgusting picture of uncivilized human nature. Treachery – cruelty – Nastiness – Not <u>one</u> quality which casts a pleasing hue over their beastly characters & manners.' This appears a very partial and disproportionate judgement on Hearne's Native companions, especially given the portrait of his guide, Matonnabee, as a man of 'benevolence and universal humanity' (Hearne 224). Nevertheless, it shows that the tensions critics have located in Hearne's text, a product of his struggle to establish a coherent identity at a time when there was no settled colonial discourse for handling the varied relationships between colonizers and indigenous people (allies, enemies, trading partners, lovers, anthropological objects), translated directly into reader response: some readers identified more with the strain of scientific rationality in Hearne's narrative, some with the strain of crude opposition of 'civilized white man' and 'savage Indian.'

There is also a neat subversive turn in Larpent's entry on Hearne. In effect, she acknowledges that the passions of her compatriots are as extreme in their own way as the 'beastly' behaviour of the 'savages' – just as incomprehensible and just as irrational:

> it is also interesting to see the passions of men Ambition, Avarice, Curiosity, conquering difficulties that appear almost insurmountable, & bringing knowledge to the student whether of zoology, of Botany Geography or of the history of Mankind & above all to the Philosopher – how much does luxury risk! – how much money is spent, how many pass years in this inhospitable clime among Savages – for what? <u>A few furs.</u> denied to our more southern regions – probably because the want of them <u>for us</u> is fictitious.

Given her rank in society, Larpent was undoubtedly more than familiar with the end-products of the fur trade; that she could dismiss the objectives of this huge, complex, labour-intensive industry, its operations encompassing a whole continent and ultimately defining the boundaries of Britain's largest colony, as 'a few furs' is a revealing index of this woman's quietly robust personality. John Brewer's claim that Larpent was a 'passive recipient' of information when reading works on traditionally masculine subjects ('Reconstructing' 236) seems wide of the mark in this context: here she shows the same 'critical assertiveness' that Brewer says that she reserves for imaginative literature, ridiculing the entire institutional and economic framework of Hearne's expedition. In fact, Larpent's readiness to absorb new information while keeping a sceptical distance from the colonial adventurism that was responsible for generating so much new knowledge not only shows her independent spirit but also is a chastening reproof to modish generalizations about the social construction of Romantic readers. Travel writing may have been approved for female consumption partly because, as Jacqueline Pearson argues, it bolstered patriarchal and nationalistic values, but women readers were plainly capable of resisting such rhetorical coercion.

Anna Larpent, as one would expect of someone who seems to have read every significant work of travel literature published between 1790 and 1830, also worked her way through Alexander Mackenzie's *Voyages from Montreal* (1801), in October 1802.[13] Mackenzie achieves his place in the history of exploration as the first documented person to cross the continent of North America – a feat accomplished fully twelve years before the much better-known Lewis and Clark expedition. Born in 1762 on the Outer Hebridean island of Lewis, he and his family joined a mass emigration from the Highlands and Islands to North America, arriving in New York just months before the American Revolution broke out. Moving to Montreal to escape a conflict in which his father was to die (on the loyalist side), Mackenzie began his career in the headquarters of the Canadian fur trade, eventually becoming a partner in the powerful North West Company. It was as a key player in the Northwest frontier trade, based at Lake Athabasca, that he set out on two voyages, in 1789 and 1793, in search of a navigable route to the Pacific via inland waterways. His first voyage took him not to the Pacific but to the Arctic Ocean, along the length of the river to which his name would become attached. His second voyage brought him, by birchbark canoe, arduous portages, and a final 180-mile trek across the Coast Range using a First Nations' trade route or 'grease trail,' to Pacific tidewater at modern-day Dean Channel, where he inscribed a memorial to his achievement on 22 July 1793.

Early the next year Mackenzie left the Northwest, never to return. He devoted the next few years, indeed the rest of his life, to developing the commercial benefits of his exploration – most immediately by extending the territory of the North West Company but, in the longer term, promoting his larger vision of a British trading empire capable of penetrating the markets of Russia, China, and Japan. Mackenzie lobbied persistently for state support for this project, but the British government was too preoccupied with the Napoleonic wars to give much time to his grand schemes, and the merger with the Hudson's Bay Company that he strenuously advocated did not happen until after his death in March 1820. In the meantime, Mackenzie succeeded in preparing the journals of his two voyages for publication, with the unlikely assistance of William Combe (author of the picturesque satire, *The Tour of Doctor Syntax*) as ghostwriter. There was a measure of public anticipation about this publication – Isaac Weld regrets the delay, for instance, in his *Travels* (1799) – and the production in short order of two British and two American editions, along with French and German translations, indicates commercial success on a scale unmatched by many travel books. (Such assertions should nevertheless be placed in the context of the material evidence

---

[13] For a full examination of the reception of Mackenzie's *Voyages*, see Jarvis, 'Curious Fame.' Here I shall summarize my findings as reported in that article and incorporate sources I was not aware of at the time of writing.

concerning the pricing, sales, and accessibility of travel literature discussed in Chapter 1. To suggest, as Mackenzie's more enthusiastic biographers do, that *Voyages* was a 'bestseller' [Smith 148] or 'sold briskly at every bookstall' [Gough 179] is comically inappropriate. The very term 'bestseller' is an anachronism when applied to a period in which new book publishing continued to operate on the model of small sales and high prices.) The accolade of a knighthood less than two months after publication (presumably in the pipeline for some time) reinforces the impression of official esteem and a significant impact on public consciousness.

The impact may have been ephemeral, however. W. Kaye Lamb states that after an initial flurry of interest Mackenzie's book 'was largely forgotten for the better part of a century' (50), and it is difficult to disagree with him. One source of hard evidence is the borrowing registers of the Bristol Library Society, a private subscription library whose members are known to have had a particular relish for travel writing.[14] These registers show that *Voyages from Montreal* was purchased on publication, borrowed 12 times in 1802 and 11 times in 1803; there was then a steep falling-off, with the result that in 1806, and again in 1807, the registers record only a solitary borrower. The interest generated by the book, perhaps buoyed by the knighthood and Mackenzie's sudden celebrity, seems to have been intense but short-lived.

Perhaps part of the reason for this decline in reputation is the fact that Mackenzie's book, as even his most fervent admirers would admit, is not at all times the most riveting of travel narratives: it has its occasional thrills and spills, but there is nothing resembling the Bloody Fall massacre in Hearne's *Journey* to shock or titillate the reader. Such was his determination to write the kind of plain and factual account that explorers had to write to win credence that Mackenzie even declined obvious opportunities to stir readers' emotions: on completing his quest and becoming the first European to cross North America by land, he merely notes without elaboration, still less celebration, that 'At about eight we got out of the river, which discharges itself by various channels into an arm of the sea' (373). The monotonous recording of compass directions and distances covered was also likely to bore the general reader as much as it irritated periodical reviewers.

This was certainly Anna Larpent's experience. Her diary entry for 16 October 1802, when she was still working her way through the *Voyages*, hesitates between unenthusiastic praise and mild criticism:

> Mackenzie's route through a most comfortless country – Now & then meeting with wretched Indians & given as a Journal is very dry – it seems true & simple – & offers a view of that part of the world & occasionally of human nature without civilization

Perhaps Larpent, who was both intrigued and revolted by Hearne's dramatic and characterful account of his interactions with Native peoples, would have preferred fewer details of Mackenzie's route and more attention to 'uncivilized' human

---

[14]   See Chapter 1, and Kaufmann, 'Some Reading Trends.'

nature. On 20 October, having completed the book, she writes a rather breathless summary, punctuated almost entirely by dashes, of the final stages of the second voyage, suggesting that she became more absorbed by the narrative at this stage; this is plausible, since it is during the crossing of the Coast Range that Mackenzie and his companions came closest to death on the treacherous Fraser River, had a major falling-out amongst themselves ('it is wonderful how he kept them in order,' says Larpent), became the first Europeans to make contact with some First Nations groups, and encountered real hostility from the Heiltsuk people in particular. Larpent concludes her entry with another ambivalent assessment of the book:

> Mackenzie's voyage & journey seems to open much information to the geographer & to open views to trade he certainly proves that there is a passage over land across America N. West to the Pacific Ocean he also points out how the country may be settled & the trade extended his own steadiness & perseverance were great, & he tells his story simply with a great air of truth ... certainly to a common reader the detail of his route is dry. but when it is associated with the spirit of the Enterprize one reads on with some enthusiasm & are [*sic*] entertained.

Ventriloquizing the fair-minded criticism of a professional reviewer, Larpent here gives ample credit to the practical and scientific benefits of Mackenzie's work; it is in passages like this, perhaps, that she moves beyond what she called her 'self-conversation' and tries, as Claire Colombo puts it, to 'write into existence an alternate public realm' (298) in which she could participate on an equal footing. However, her personal response is clear enough in the repeated reference to a preponderance of 'dry' detail and her statement that she reads with enthusiasm only when the plain narration of the journey is infused with the 'spirit of the Enterprize.' In the preface to *Voyages*, Mackenzie warns his readers that there is little to 'gratify the curiosity of such as are enamoured of romantic adventures,' and claims only the 'approbation due to simplicity and to truth' (59). Larpent acknowledges that claim in every particular – 'he tells his story simply with a great air of truth' – but gives the impression that she favours those parts of the text harbouring elements of romantic idealism.[15]

Larpent provides valuable evidence of a 'common reader' responding to this major work of exploration both while she was reading it, and in the form of summary reflections. The record of historical reception lacks anything of comparable substance outside the periodical press. Later explorers of the Canadian North and Northwest were familiar with Mackenzie's work, and such men as Simon Fraser, David Thompson, and John Franklin paid tribute to it in their own writings. In the broadest perspective the most significant reader of *Voyages from*

---

[15] Scholars who resurrected Mackenzie's reputation in the twentieth century had no problem reading grand literary designs into his life and work, with Roy Daniells, for instance, comparing his two voyages to the mythological voyage of Jason and the Argonauts in search of the Golden Fleece (198–9).

Montreal was Thomas Jefferson, whom it propelled into organizing the Lewis and Clark expedition – thus furthering the United States' westward expansion and ultimately guaranteeing its transcontinental destiny. Whereas Mackenzie struggled to interest the British Colonial Office in his warnings about American ambitions, his book was frequently invoked as Jefferson made arrangements for his own journey of discovery, and in June 1803 he ordered a more portable '8vo edition of McKenzie's travels with the same maps which are in the 4to edition' (Jackson 56), presumably for Lewis to take with him. Few travel books of the period could have been implicated in events of such huge economic and geopolitical consequence.

These men and the institutions they represented had very specific and limited reasons for reading Mackenzie. For further evidence of how individuals responded to his travels, aimed as they were at the general reading public, it is necessary to look at the reviews. One striking facet of the latter is their common vocabulary for assessing the author's personal qualities: Larpent's reference to his 'steadiness & perseverance' is echoed in praise of his 'bold and persevering spirit' (*Monthly Review* 38: 225), his 'fortitude, patience, and perseverance' (*European Magazine* 41: 116), his 'intelligence, his spirit, and perseverance' (*Critical Review* 37: 379), and his 'diligence and intrepidity ... temper and perseverance' (*Edinburgh Review* 1: 157). The one word linking all these judgements, 'perseverance,' encapsulates the single-minded determination that, in Mackenzie's narrative, overcomes all threats to his survival and the recalcitrance of his companions, and elevates the completion of his journey into a moral imperative: as Bruce Greenfield observes, 'Absolute defeat is a possibility in Mackenzie's narrative, but the possibility of a story different from the one he sets out to tell is never recognized' (*Narrating* 54). Mackenzie's perseverance is as much a textual construct as it was (presumably) a character trait, projecting him as solely responsible for the success or failure of the expedition. The apparent modesty of his denial of pretensions to 'literary fame' and his representation of his work as a contribution to scientific geography are less than fully convincing, because the narrative he presents shows the accomplishment of vital commercial and political goals to be entirely dependent on his personal energies. The evidence of contemporary reviews is that most readers, to some degree at least, bought into this 'highly selective picture of the explorer as hero' (MacLulich 66).

Reviewers were also of one mind in their preoccupation with Mackenzie's observations on Native customs and beliefs, both in the course of the narrative and in his occasional ethnographic interludes.[16] On the face of it this is surprising, given that Mackenzie himself seems to set little store by these parts of his book: his reference in the preface to the constant need to 'watch the savage who was our guide, or to guard against those of his tribe who might meditate our destruction' (59) is not the sign of a man who took a close interest in other cultures, except

---

[16]   I leave aside the question of whether some of these passages (those contained in the first section, 'A General History of the Fur Trade') were in fact written by Mackenzie's cousin Roderic. See Lamb 33.

insofar as their members assisted or impeded his main objectives. However, in terms of the thirst for new knowledge that was one of the principal reasons for the popularity of travel literature in the period, there was promising material in Mackenzie's descriptions of his interactions with indigenous groups, especially the Northwest Coast Nations encountered in the second voyage (his is the first substantial written record of the Nuxalk people) – and these were the parts of the book that reviews tended to favour and to highlight via extracts. The *Monthly Review* picked out the account of a murder committed among the Beaver for reasons of sexual jealousy, and also focused on the fishing methods and domestic practices of the Nuxalk. The *Annual Review* and *European Magazine* fastened, suspiciously, on the same violent incident, despite its occupying a mere two paragraphs, the former including it among a number of 'curious facts respecting the Indians and their country' (1: 28), the latter generalizing about the similarities between these 'Indians' and the 'the savages of the islands and coasts of the South Seas' (41: 199). The *Critical Review*, which in general was dismissive of 'travels through a country distinguished only for variety of wretchedness' (35: 122), inhabited by 'Scattered tribes of savages' (37: 367), nevertheless took an interest in the 'more numerous and more civilised' coastal communities: the apparently feudal structure of a Nuxalk village, the wooden houses decorated with painted figures and carvings, and the funereal customs, are all 'too curious to be overlooked' (37: 377). The *Edinburgh Review* also dwelt on Mackenzie's description of the Nuxalk, and was intrigued by the contrast between these people, with their 'traces of improving art and civilization' (1: 157), and the Chipewyans and Cree who seemed to have made 'no sensible progress' (1: 146) in the two hundred years since first contact with Europeans.

The general tenor of professional readers' interest in these aspects of Mackenzie's travels appears to be one of moderate curiosity, in a mix of the intellectual and vulgar connotations of that term discussed in Chapter 2. If Parker Duchemin is correct in his hostile assessment of Mackenzie's interactions with First Nations – emphasizing his assumptions regarding 'generic' behaviour ('when an individual Indian performs an action which either obstructs or advances his ends, he takes it to be characteristic of his "tribe"' [60]) and his overall perception that they are 'too witless or ignorant to improve their condition' (67) without European intervention – there is little to suggest that contemporary readers did anything other than read with the grain of his writing.

Viewed as a whole, the reviewers' public response to Mackenzie had a lot in common with Anna Larpent's private reflections. Having acknowledged the author's strength of character, and indulged their curiosity concerning the 'savages' who occasionally impinge on his journey, they were left to contemplate the significance of his completed mission, and on this the consensus was unflattering: although the *Monthly Magazine* placed Mackenzie 'among our first nautical adventurers' and declared (rashly) that he had 'settled, perhaps for ever' the question of a Northwest Passage (13: 652), the *Edinburgh* thought 'the importance of his geographical discoveries' (1: 157) negligible, while the *Critical's* acerbic commentator believed that Mackenzie's extraordinary exertions were exceeded only by the futility of their end-product, in that 'the whole of this northern continent may be resigned without a sigh, or even the slightest regret' (37: 381).

The most unusual note in the reviews was struck by Francis Jeffrey in the *Edinburgh*:

> There is something in the idea of traversing a vast and unknown continent, that gives an agreeable expansion to our conceptions; and the imagination is insensibly engaged and inflamed by the spirit of adventure, and the perils and the novelties that are implied in a voyage of discovery.

Mackenzie's 'small band of adventurers,' he went on to say, 'carry back the imagination to those days of enterprize and discovery, when the Genius of Europe broke into all the continents of the world, and performed and discovered wonders' (1: 141). Here is an appeal to the imaginative allure of travel – a 'Romantic' conception of travel expanding the mind and re-fuelling the spirit – that is extremely rare in periodical reviews of travel literature at this time, although there are expressions of it, as we have seen, in the testimony of private readers. Unfortunately, most readers, Jeffrey included, seem to have felt that Mackenzie's plain, sober, and faithful report on his voyages failed to live up to its imaginative potential.

Interlude: Romancing the beaver

Although travel literature (and periodical reviews of travel books) played a major role in mediating a world rapidly opening up through scientific exploration and colonial expansion, it was not the only means by which that world, and North America in particular, was brought closer to a curious public in Britain. Museums, public exhibitions, and material culture were also important vehicles for familiarizing people with exotic landscapes and their natural and human inhabitants. Troy Bickham, in his study of British representations of American Indians in the eighteenth century, has written interestingly of the role of museums and other public collections in allowing middle- and upper-class people to engage with Native Americans and their way of life, at a time (in the second half of the century) when displays were moving away from their earlier cabinet-of-curiosities format and acquiring a greater emphasis on informed pedagogy, authenticity, and scientific organization. Zoology, botany, and geology were just as central to such displays as the representation of human cultures. As Bickham says, 'Exhibitions of ethnography and natural history generally were designed with two purposes in mind: to transport the viewer virtually to the represented people, and to reinforce notions of British cultural and technological superiority' (42); visitors, he adds, 'regularly remarked on the "reality" of the displays' (43).

The British Museum, founded in 1753 and opening to the public (initially on a discretionary, ticket-only basis) four years later, was attracting 'clientele from all classes of society' by 1810, when the number of visitors 'had reached what was considered a staggering 120 a day' (Caygill 26). The original collection, based on the private cabinet of Sir Hans Sloane, contained 210 items of North American origin, including some forty from Hudson Bay and the Arctic archipelago (King 234); along with many Native American weapons, utensils, and ornaments, *The General Contents of the British Museum*, an early visitor's guide, lists a birchbark canoe (202), the head of a buffalo from Newfoundland (7),[17] some narwhal tusks ('Horns of the Unicorn Fish'), and the 'Head and Paws' of a walrus (196) to help 'transport' the viewer to this geographically remote location. These exhibits were considerably augmented in the late eighteenth and early nineteenth centuries by the spoils of exploration. The Museum's minutes record the acquisition of 'An ample collection of natural and artificial curiosities brought home by [Archibald] Menzies from North West America and the South Sea Islands' in 1796, and Joseph Banks 'presented numerous animals, most of them in spirits' gathered on Cook's three voyages (Miller 75). John Ross's Arctic expedition of 1818 brought the Museum a polar bear (said to have considerably boosted attendance) among other items, while William Parry donated 'dresses and implements of Esquimaux, various dried Arctic plants, six skins of quadrupeds, and thirty Birds, with some eggs' (Caygill 23) in 1824 following his second Polar voyage. Exhibits like these gave tangible form and visual corroboration to the novelties set before the reading public in the world of travel texts.

The rage for accumulation and display of natural and human objects from the frontier of exploration was brilliantly satirized in two prints inspired by the return of John Ross's otherwise unsuccessful Arctic expedition of 1818. Both present versions of the transportation of specimens collected on the voyage to the British Museum, as reported in *The Times* on 8 December of that year:

> Yesterday morning the curiosities, &c., brought from Baffin's-bay, by Captain Ross, were landed at Whitehall-stairs, from the boats of the *Isabella* and *Alexander* discovery ships. There are four dogs and two bitches, the former larger than the latter; three are almost black, one black and white, and two brownish, and appear nearly of the same species as those of Kamschatka, with heads and tails resembling a fox ... Among the curiosities was an amazingly large skin of a white bear, about 7 feet in length: a sledge of bone,[18] about 5 feet long and 2 high, with the whip, &c. used by the newly-discovered inhabitants; specimens of mineralogy and botany, and some very remarkable star-fish. The whole of the productions were conveyed to the British Museum, for the inspection of the public. (2)

George Cruikshank's *Landing the Treasures* (1819; Figure 3.4) shows a procession, led by Ross, approaching the gates of the British Museum, where curators are jumping up and down in eager anticipation. This print makes the polar

---

[17]   From the description, this is more likely to be a musk-ox than a buffalo or bison.

[18]   This sledge is still on display in the North American gallery at the British Museum.

bear, carried by seven seamen and Ross's diminutive nephew, James Ross, its centrepiece, although the 'treasures' also include a barrel of the infamous 'red snow,'[19] a dead gull carried by (and to be named after) Captain Sabine (astronomer to the expedition), molluscs, 'Worms found in the Intestines of a Seal,' a tree stump, a block of granite, a narwhal tusk, and a number of 'Esquimaux dogs.' Particularly striking is a bizarre caricature of the Greenlandic Inuit interpreter, Hans Zakaeus, who accompanied the expedition. Two sailors in a boat on the right-hand edge of the print ask, on the understanding that the dogs are destined for the taxidermist, what will happen to 'Jack Frost' (the Inuit), and one replies: 'Cut his throat & stuff him also, I supposes.' Whether this is intended as a sly comment on the implicit violence of the objectifying practices of ethnography is debateable, but the aside is a disturbing one and unsettles the exuberance of the burlesque. Meanwhile, an overweight, curmudgeonly citizen on the far left of the picture provides a normative response to the grotesque march: 'I think as how we have Bears, Gulls, Savages, Chump wood. Stones & Puppies enough without going to the North Pole for them.' With all these terms carrying a secondary reference to a stereotype of Georgian satire, the effect is to use the foreign and extraordinary to provide an ironic reflection on the spectator's 'normal' reality, in the tradition of *Gulliver's Travels*.

Charles Williams's *Curious Dogs* (1819; Figure 3.5) puts Ross, sitting proudly on his sledge, at the centre of the picture, with several of the accompanying sailors riding bears. The fact that Ross is sitting on his log book, which in turn is resting on a crate of rum, may be intended as a sly innuendo concerning the central failure of the Arctic expedition, namely Ross's discontinuation of the journey through Lancaster Sound on the grounds that he had seen a chain of mountains completely blocking further progress. Among the souvenirs en route to the British Museum in Williams's drawing are a basket of red snowballs, another basket of snowballs of a gratuitously blue colouration, and samples of 'Polar Iron' and 'Polar Ice.' Embroidering the procession of curiosities, Williams depicts one sailor carrying a huge mammoth tusk (which was not among the spoils of the expedition), while in the background Ross's ship, mounted on wheels, has a colossal whale strapped to its mast (Ross's crew did kill a 46-foot whale and bring it on board for examination, but they had to jettison the carcase). Once again the fate of the 'Esquimaux dogs' is a major point of interest, with one seaman holding a flag bearing the legend, 'Dogs to be killed to save the Nation the expence of feeding, and stuff'd with straw for the British Museum.' Less complex than Cruikshank's, this print is seemingly designed to ridicule the accomplishments of the (government-sponsored) expedition, the self-importance of Ross, the dubious value of imperial acquisitions

---

[19] See Chapter 1. There was plenty of media interest in the red snow. The *Morning Chronicle* reported on the latest speculation regarding its origins on 5 December and 8 December 1818, and the provincial press took up the story too: the *Lancaster Gazette*, for instance, looked forward on 12 December to hearing the results of chemical analysis, even though 'Our credulity is put to an extreme test' by the phenomenon.

Fig. 3.4   George Cruikshank, *Landing the Treasures, or Results of the Polar Expedition* (1819). © Trustees of the British Museum.

(Ross proudly bears a flag naming the Prince Regent 'Sovereign of the Pole'), and possibly the superficial character of what it takes to be the public appetite for 'curious' relics of foreign travel. Both prints provide a vivid illustration of the sort of reception (amused, sceptical) to which explorers (and their written accounts) were vulnerable, as well as the nature of popular interest in British North America, including its northernmost extremities.

One animal that Ross did not have the opportunity to bring back for stuffing and public exhibition is the animal that nonetheless became synonymous with Canada, namely, the beaver. Not that the public were denied the chance to familiarize themselves with beavers and their unique behaviour – at least dead beavers, or their dismembered body parts. Among the early donations to the British Museum was 'the trunk of a tree gnawed asunder by the Beaver' (Caygill 17), while the Leverian Museum in Leicester Square, a private museum second only to the British Museum for its ethnographic collections, displayed the jaws and feet of a beaver in its natural history section (*Companion* 37). The impresario Stephan Polito had a pair of live beavers in his travelling menagerie, which acquired a permanent base at the Royal Menagerie at Exeter 'Change from 1810 to 1814. Perhaps most impressive was the London Museum in Piccadilly, which boasted a large apartment called the 'Pantherion' in which stuffed quadrupeds were exhibited (in Linnaean groupings) 'as ranging in their native wilds and forests,' surrounded by model trees and plants, and 'the whole being assisted with a panoramic effect of distance and appropriate scenery, affording a beautiful illustration of the luxuriance of a torrid clime' (*Companion to the London Museum* iv). Although hardly associated with torrid climes, there was a beaver in the Pantherion, along with many other Canadian mammals, such as a porcupine and a wolf from Hudson Bay, all accessible to anyone who could afford the shilling entrance fee. London Zoo, which opened in 1828 (initially only to members of the Zoological Society), had a pair of beavers donated by Lord Dalhousie, Governor-General of British North America, and it was claimed at the time that these seemed 'happy and contented' despite one being totally blind and the other partially-sighted (Bennett 170). As with the natural history of Canada generally, therefore, there were plenty of opportunities for people to engage with the country's iconic animal outside the printed page.

However, at risk of stating the obvious, the most immediate and tangible form in which the beaver was encountered was not the museum exhibit but clothing – specifically hats, since this was the use to which the vast majority of the large numbers of beaver skins imported annually to England (80,000 by the mid-eighteenth century) was put. In his study of the growth of the North American fur trade and the violence this entailed (both between rival traders and by stimulating destructive competition between indigenous groups), Eric Wolf wryly reminds us that 'The target of all these conflicts and accommodations was the profit to be made from trapping a small fur-bearing animal weighing about 1½ pounds' (163). That small fur-bearing animal sustained a hat industry that was unique in

Fig. 3.5   Charles Williams, *Curious Dogs, from the North Pole; or the Return of the Arctic Expedition!!* (1819). © Trustees of the British Museum.

facing no serious competition for its raw materials,[20] and was the main source of demand for a fur trade that was itself unique in playing such a pivotal role in the evolution of Canada as a nation: 'from the very beginning,' as A. Radclyffe Dugmore summarizes, Canada's development 'was inextricably interwoven with the life or, I should say, the death of the beaver' (178).

The English hat industry, with a strong base in Southwark and Bermondsey but spreading to provincial centres of production in the eighteenth century, contributed significantly to what Neil McKendrick has called the 'commercialization of fashion' in the last quarter of the eighteenth century: by this period, he says, a powerful combination of 'social imitation, social emulation, class competition and emulative spending' (52) was at work, and clothes were the first mass consumer product to be noticed by social commentators, with numerous observers remarking on the rage for fashion spreading downwards with the ensuing obliteration of social distinctions. David Corner's study of business correspondence relating to the London hat trade shows 'the existence at this time of a fashion-conscious consumer market' (169), with producers eager to gain intelligence regarding the styles in demand in different parts of the country. At a time when headwear was much more common than it is now (in the eighteenth century, women wore a hat, bonnet, or cap at all times during the day, including indoors), beaver-felt hats were luxury products, advertised extensively via newspapers and trade cards to upper-class and aspirational middle-class consumers. The young Dorothy Wordsworth, when writing to her close friend, Jane Pollard, on 8 May 1792, that her brother Richard had brought her 'a very handsome Gown, and has since sent me a Beaver Hat' (*Letters* 1: 73) in preparation for a stay in Windsor, was clearly delighted at becoming well equipped for the radical change of scene and society she was about to experience ('I fancied myself treading upon Fairy-Ground' [82], she later reported). It only reflects the standards of the time that a woman who, in her journals and poetry, would later come to epitomize a loving, non-appropriative relation to nature clearly gave no thought to the fact that several small fur-bearing animals had died to produce the hat she so proudly wore in aristocratic company in Windsor. In her account of a Scottish tour with her brother in 1803, Dorothy Wordsworth describes Loch Lomond as 'an outlandish scene' and says that 'we might have believed ourselves in North America' (*Journals* 1: 252). Her knowledge of North America was, of course, derived entirely from books; but as a consumer of fashion North America had long been close to her skin, as it was to every well-dressed man and woman of the period.

Owing to the fact that, as Dugmore argues, in no country 'has an animal played such a conspicuous part' as the beaver has in Canada, it is worth dwelling a little longer on this creature, which features in nearly all travellers' accounts of the country and its inhabitants and attracts corresponding interest in the reviews. The beaver had a key place in many First Nations' creation myths, but it also accrued a rich mythology in French and British colonial travel writing which proved

---

[20]   See Crean 385.

remarkably resilient to the accumulating evidence of close encounters with the animal acquired through the fur trade. These latter myths centred on the alleged social instincts and architectural abilities of the beaver, and a few examples from later eighteenth-century texts will suffice as illustration. The much-reprinted *Wonders of Nature and Art* (1750) is a reliable benchmark of beliefs concerning the beaver's dam-building skills:

> These creatures ... observe a wonderful Polity, and their Manner of living and building their Habitations shews an extraordinary Instinct implanted in them by the great Author of Nature ... [Dams are formed by] thrusting down Stakes five or six feet long, and as thick as a Man's Arm, deep into the Earth; and these they wattle across with tender pliable Boughs, and fill up the Spaces with Clay ... When the Beavers have completed their Causey or Dike, they begin to form their Cells, which are round or oval Apartments, divided into three Partitions or Stories, raised one above another ... The Materials are the same as they are for the Dike; and as their Teeth supply the Place of Saws, they cut off all Projections that shoot from the Stakes beyond the Perpendicular of the Wall; after which they work up a Mixture of Clay and dry Grass into a Kind of Mortar, and by means of their Tails they lay it over the Building both within and without. (4: 169–71)

More than four hundred beavers, the author says, have been found 'in different Apartments communicating with each other' (171), creating the impression of a substantial condominium. The respected and much-cited traveller and naturalist, Thomas Pennant, in his *History of Quadrupeds* (1781), maintained the beaver's reputation as the 'most industrious of animals' (2: 384) and revelled in the use of architectural metaphors: beavers' houses are built on 'piles,' the tops are 'vaulted' so that the inside is a 'dome,' the walls are 'neatly plaistered as if with a trowel,' and there are 'two or three stories in each dwelling' (385). The measurements of beaver property development are prone to a kind of inflation: here, the dams are a hundred feet long, each house contains up to thirty beavers, and, most strikingly of all, 'a community of two or three hundred' (385) is said to assemble for the purpose of dam- and house-building.

It is in this vision of organized, cooperative labour, with each group of beavers carrying out their appointed task under the supervision of an 'overseer' who issues instructions via 'smart strokes' of his tail, that Pennant articulates another key aspect of colonial beaver mythology. Buffon's *Natural History*, a monument of Enlightenment natural history which went through countless editions and was translated into many languages, reflects the same popular conception that beavers possess a kind of intelligence that 'supposes common projects and relative views; projects which, having society for their basis, and, for their object, a dike to construct, a town to build, or a republic to found, imply some mode of making themselves understood, and the capacity of acting in concert' (22). Beavers, it seems, have an almost human-like ability to make choices, whether this be the choice of a mate during the 'season of love' (35), or the choice to build a dam in association with 'the whole community' (29). Talk of founding a republic does not appear to be loosely figurative, as Buffon compares their social arrangements favourably with those of their human persecutors:

> Their union is cemented by common labours; and it is rendered perpetual by mutual convenience, and the abundance of provisions which they amass and consume together. Moderate appetites, a simple taste, an aversion to blood and carnage, deprive them of the idea of rapine and war. They enjoy every possible good, while man knows only how to pant after happiness. Friends to each other, if they have some foreign enemies, they know how to avoid them. (33)

In light of this, it is perhaps surprising that Buffon rejects the idea, advanced by other naturalists, that beavers group in odd numbers so that there will be a casting vote when they debate matters of importance. Nevertheless, the main strands of European myth-making about beavers – their prodigious building feats, their capacity for organization, their communitarian ethos – proved remarkably resilient through the Romantic period.

In an essay focusing on colonial travellers in New France before 1763, Gordon Sayre articulates the dual emphasis of their accounts of the beaver, as 'a natural and social marvel when alive, and ... a valuable commodity when dead' (659). In a deeper layering of meaning, he argues that at one level the beaver was treated as an ethnographic object in a manner similar to the ubiquitous chapters on the 'manners and customs of the Indians' beloved of travel writers, and, as with the latter descriptions, served 'to rhetorically reconstitute the undisturbed indigenous life which was being disturbed by the invading Europeans.' On another level, though, the social life of beavers was made to resemble not the 'anarchic equality' (670) of Indians but 'civilized and particularly colonial society' (660). Hardworking, peaceful, self-disciplined, independent yet ready to cooperate for the common good, beavers were the colonial settler's ideal alter ego. Sayre suggests that when the fur trade shifted into British hands 'the significance of the beaver for the ideology of settlement lessened' (679). I would suggest, on the contrary, that British travellers and writers in the late eighteenth and early nineteenth centuries seem just as prone to fantasy and exaggeration regarding *castor canadensis*.

There are, however, exceptions. Samuel Hearne's treatment of the beaver is especially interesting in this connection. Hearne, who had plenty of first-hand experience of hunting beavers with his Chipewyan companions, systematically debunks all the fanciful or erroneous stories told about the animal by 'romancing travellers.' Beaver houses generally contain no more than 'four old, and six or eight young' animals, says Hearne, and the legions of authors who have written of houses divided into different apartments dedicated to different uses were either ignorant or 'guilty of attempting to impose on the credulous' (Hearne 148). The physical characteristics of the beaver make it inconceivable for the animal to carry out the elaborate building works frequently ascribed to it: it would be 'as impossible,' for instance, 'for a beaver to use its tail as a trowel ... as it would have been for Sir James Thornhill to have painted the dome of St Paul's cathedral without the assistance of scaffolding' (150). Despite all the reports of beavers 'assembling in great bodies, and jointly erecting large towns, cities, and commonwealths,' Hearne insists drily that 'even where the greatest numbers of beaver are situated in the neighbourhood of each other, their labours are not carried on jointly in the erection of their different habitations, nor have they any reciprocal interest, except it be such as live immediately under the same roof' (152).

Over more than ten pages of occasionally mocking but otherwise quietly reasonable prose, based on his own observations both of wild beavers and several kept in captivity 'till they became so domesticated as to answer to their name' (156–67), Hearne demolishes seemingly imperishable 'fictions' about this animal, while giving due credit to its considerable 'sagacity' (150) and remarkable 'workmanship' (146). As he states, these fictions mostly stem from French colonial travel writers of the seventeenth and early eighteenth centuries, although they were taken up and recycled enthusiastically by the British, especially in works of natural history. If it is true that a wildly fictitious natural history of the beaver was hard to dislodge because it offered a sanitized and sentimental view of a natural world even as that natural world was being invaded and despoiled by the industrial hunting required for the fur trade, or because it modelled the kind of virtuous and productive existence to which early settlers aspired, then it is perhaps significant that Hearne, now seen by many critics as uneasy about aspects of the colonial project and as having questioned the inherent rightness of the cultural assumptions he brought to the Canadian wilderness, is one of the few writers capable of deromanticizing the beaver. If, as Kevin Hutchings argues, he shows a 'troubled ambivalence concerning the morality of an abstract "industriousness" [urged upon First Nations by fur traders] that in reality transforms happy people into what he himself calls "slaves"' (Hutchings 71), then it seems appropriate that he should also look more rationally and sceptically at the animal that symbolized that very industriousness and became the metonym of a new country built upon that creature's commodity value.

To summarize, natural history played a significant part in British public awareness of Canada in the Romantic period, aided by the rapidly growing museums and exhibitions sector; it was also a much more prominent element in travel writing about Canada than in the equivalent body of literature about the United States, and drew correspondingly more attention from reviewers. One particular animal, the beaver, owing to its central role in the industry around which Canada grew, acquired a special status in the literature and became a popular topic among professional readers. Apparently symbolizing (however improbably) many of the virtues that colonial ideology ascribed to early settlers, anthropomorphic images of happy, hard-working, community-focused beavers circulated freely and seemed inseparable from the textual construction of Canada – perhaps because they put an acceptable face on the ecocidal practices of a trade that sustained the burgeoning culture of fashion in London and the provinces. The occasional injection of realism from an ambivalent insider like Hearne, which did not go unnoticed by reviewers, took a long time to alter perceptions: a pseudo-scientific guide to London Zoo published in 1830, while dismissing some popular notions as 'too absurd to require refutation' (Bennett 164), nonetheless still indulged fantasies of beavers forming 'populous villages' (158).

Arctic dreams: The search for the Northwest Passage

In the introduction to his *Journey ... to the Northern Ocean*, Hearne defended his employers, the Hudson's Bay Company, against the accusation that they had no interest in, or gave no support to, exploration; his own expedition, he believed, was a refutation of this charge. However, the Company's reputation in this area remained low, and in the years immediately following Waterloo Sir John Barrow, from his powerful position in the Admiralty and using the cultural influence afforded him as a leading reviewer for the *Quarterly*, renewed the criticism: in his review of Lord Selkirk's *Sketch of the British Fur Trade in North America* in the October 1816 issue, he pointed out that the Company's case for an exclusive charter had been predicated on the search for a Northwest Passage, but that this had not only been 'totally neglected' but 'thwarted by every means in their power' (16: 144). Although government-sponsored exploration, most famously in the form of Cook's three voyages, was vigorously pursued in the late eighteenth century, the Company, Barrow complained, had done nothing to assist 'the spirit of discovery in the north' (163).

It was in this review that Barrow first espoused, on both scientific and economic grounds, a renewed search for a Northwest Passage – a quest largely abandoned since the great voyages of Frobisher, Davis, Hudson, Baffin, and others in the late sixteenth and seventeenth centuries. In the summer of 1817 he was encouraged in this project by reports (brought back by whaling ships) of retreating ice in Baffin Bay, which seemed to Barrow to concur with other evidence of significant climatic change – in effect, the end of what is now referred to as the 'Little Ice Age' – that had major implications for polar navigation. In his review of Lieutenant Chappell's *Narrative of a Voyage to Hudson's Bay* in the October 1817 *Quarterly*, Barrow summarized the arguments for a general audience and considered the prospects for two new official expeditions to try to penetrate the putative 'open polar sea' en route to the Bering Strait. In one of the most spectacular examples of the reviewing strategy for which the *Quarterly* (along with its rival, the *Edinburgh*) achieved notoriety, Barrow's essay dismissed Chappell's book in its opening paragraph in order to focus exclusively on its own agenda, but this high-handed approach did nothing to lessen the impact of the piece, which stirred public interest in this new phase of Arctic exploration. In terms of the contemporary reception of travel literature, for the next few years the attempt to find a way *around* North America gripped the public imagination more than anyone's travels in any part of the continent itself, known or unknown.

One of the reasons for this was that there was much more than geographical discovery at stake. In the *Edinburgh Review*, John Leslie, professor of mathematics and (later) natural philosopher at Edinburgh University, likened Barrow's reasoning to the 'dreams of romance' (30: 5) and attempted to prove in dense scientific prose that despite natural fluctuations in temperature, the extent of sea-ice, and other factors, 'no material change has taken place for the last thousand years in the climate of Europe' (30). In setting up its stall in this way (which seems eerily to anticipate the discourse of so-called 'climate change deniers' today), and in talking down both the prospects and the practical and commercial value of the recently-departed expeditions, the *Edinburgh* seems to have misjudged the mood of the nation – or at least of a large segment of the reading public. After the runaway success of Scott's *Lay of the Last Minstrel* and *Lady of the Lake*, the fortunes of romance (as a genre) were on the rise, and the public appeared to have a taste for romantic schemes combined with the expectation of scientific progress. Moreover, the *Edinburgh*'s liberal politics was a factor in its lukewarm response to the Arctic venture, in the eyes of more conservative commentators: in Janice Cavell's words, 'patriotism was associated with support of the explorers, while radical opinions, unrest, and selfishness were described as the characteristics of those who opposed their enterprise' (67). Over time, Barrow would become expert at cultivating such attitudes, helping to construct a discourse in which maritime adventure was central to British history and destiny, and Arctic exploration was the theatre in which the national character found its purest expression.

In the short term, though, Barrow's ambitions were dealt a blow by the premature return of the ships that had departed in April 1818. Barrow, whose *Chronological History of Voyages in the Arctic Regions* (1818) – which drew on the mystique of the great Elizabethan navigators to legitimize a renewed quest for the Passage – was designed to whet the public appetite for news of the ships' completed mission, was particularly dismayed at the failure of the expedition led by John Ross. In what follows, I shall examine the reception of Ross's published account of his voyage, rushed out in a bid to defend his actions and salvage his reputation, and compare the responses to two remarkable expeditions from the next phase of the Arctic enterprise.

Ross's instructions were to ascertain the existence or non-existence of a passage between the Atlantic and Pacific by way of Davis Strait, which meant establishing whether Baffin Bay was really a 'bay' at all. He quickly came to the (false) conclusion that it was indeed closed at the northern end, which put extra importance on the possible outlet via Lancaster Sound, long thought (rightly, as it would turn out) to be the likeliest way through. In a move that would do lasting damage to his career, Ross turned back soon after entering the Sound, claiming that he 'distinctly saw the land round the bottom of the bay, forming a chain of mountains connected with those which extended along the north and south sides' (Ross 1: 245). Unfortunately, 'Croker's Mountains,' as Ross named them in honour of the Secretary to the Admiralty, turned out to have been an optical illusion. Although Ross claimed that 'the general opinion' was that Lancaster Sound 'was only an inlet' (241), after his return it soon emerged that very few members of the expedition were prepared to corroborate his sighting of land. A letter by an unidentified officer on the *Alexander* published in *Blackwood's* reported that on entering the Sound 'every creature on board anticipated the pleasure of writing an overland despatch to his friend, either from the eastern or the western shore of the Pacific' (4: 342), and he spoke of their huge disappointment when they saw the *Isabella* turn round when not 'the least appearance of land was visible' (343) from their own crow's nest. This testimony was backed up by other published accounts, while Ross's second-in-command, William Parry, said nothing in public but let his superiors know of his unhappiness at the way the expedition had been conducted.

Barrow evidently decided quickly that Ross had failed in his duty, and took it personally; the outcome was an exceptionally savage review in the *Quarterly* of the book that Ross was 'virtually instructed to write' in lieu of a naval inquiry (Ross, *Polar Pioneers* 68). In this review, Barrow (anonymously, of course) denies any 'personal hostility' in his criticism, but in stating that the leadership of a voyage of discovery requires a 'peculiar tact, an inquisitive and persevering pursuit after details of fact not always interesting, a contempt of danger, and an enthusiasm not to be damped by ordinary difficulties' (21: 214) he blatantly accuses Ross of lacking these qualities. He devotes considerable space to falsifying Ross's claims on logical and scientific grounds: he argues, for instance, that Ross could not have seen an impenetrable wall of ice barring their way through Lancaster Sound from the exact position he admits to having been at. But it is the attack on Ross's character that gives the review its bite: he is said to have been 'Impenetrably dull or intentionally perverse' (248) in interpreting his official instructions, to have shown a 'want of perseverance' (251) in having forgotten all the preparations for overwintering in the Arctic in his rush to come home, and even to have fallen short in the essential attributes of manliness: Barrow scoffs at his talk of 'danger,' and suggests that, compared to the great voyages of discovery undertaken by men like Magellan and Cook, Ross's summer cruise around Baffin Bay was a mere 'voyage of pleasure' (252).[21]

Elsewhere, Ross's book came in for similar treatment, but in milder terms and without the same level of *ad hominem* criticism. The *Monthly Review* noted the disagreements between Ross and his fellow officers regarding the conduct of the voyage, and its reader agreed with Barrow in thinking it not 'physically possible' (89: 352) that Ross could have established beyond doubt the continuity of land around Baffin Bay from the position in which the ship was placed; but although Ross was accused of a 'dereliction of the search' (352) the journal did not collude in the character assassination. The *British Review* mocked Ross's 'singularly modest declaration' that he had 'set at rest forever' the question of a Northwest Passage (13: 416) and ridiculed his firm assertions regarding the termination of bays said to be 140 miles distant, but it also found serious fault with the vague, 'crude and unphilosophical' instructions (418) he had been given. *Blackwood's* acknowledged

---

[21]   Ross's biographer finds Barrow's remarks 'most ungenerous' (Ross, *Polar Pioneers* 59) and 'grossly unfair' (69). For a fuller account of his 'relentless persecution' of Ross and contrasting glorification of Parry's and Franklin's 'heroic quest,' over eighteen substantial articles in the *Quarterly*, see Wheatley, 'The Arctic.'

that the events in Lancaster Sound had left a 'disagreeable impression' with the public (5: 150), and rather charitably attributed the implausibilities in Ross's account to hasty publication, or merely asserted that they were 'drawn without sufficient evidence' (151). Unsurprisingly, the *Edinburgh Review* defended Ross, insisting that he had 'done his duty with great diligence' (31: 337) and accepting his conclusions.

These reviews all give witness to the serious interest contemporary readers took in the results of Ross's expedition as scientific travel. However, most reviewers had one eye on the general reader (the *Edinburgh*'s review, probably written by the eminent geographer Hugh Murray, was a notable exception), and therefore made plenty of room for the more 'entertaining' or 'amusing' aspects of his account. Since these were few and far between, what this amounted to was a predictable convergence on the phenomenon of red snow (as featured in the prints examined in the previous section [Figures 3.4 and 3.5], and in Hester Piozzi's correspondence, discussed in Chapter 1), and an equally predictable concentration on the expedition's dealings with a particular Inuit community, christened the 'Arctic Highlanders,' encountered at a northerly point on the west coast of Greenland. Middlebrow periodicals like *La Belle Assemblée* and the *Literary Gazette* focused most of their discussion on these two areas of interest, which were also amply covered in the more serious reviews. The *Quarterly* condemned Ross for manufacturing a whole chapter on this artificially designated 'tribe' on the basis of two or three short (translated) interviews but nonetheless spent several pages picking apart his description of their appearance and behaviour. A similar approach was taken by the *Monthly Review* and *British Review*: the familiar double-sided strategy here was to provide lengthy quotation or paraphrase of this part of the book in order to maximize supposed entertainment value for the journal's readers, but to maintain a critical distance with a filter of irony or by finding occasional fault with the author's explanations and conjectures. In this way the demands of respectable intellectual curiosity and vulgar amusement were reconciled.

One interesting feature of the reception of Ross's *Voyage of Discovery* is the way in which the book's material properties and production values became the target of an intense form of displaced hostility. John Barrow was sufficiently overt in his hostility not to need such rhetorical sleight-of-hand, but still took time to criticize the coloured prints accompanying the narrative: 'strangely exaggerated as to their grouping, figure, and dimensions,' they reflected a pervasive 'looseness of description' (21: 216). The *Eclectic Review* was equally scathing about the 'bad taste' and 'tawdry style' of Ross's illustrations, picking out the 'childish' polar bear leaping off an iceberg and the too fiercely tinted crimson cliffs as particularly offensive (16: 58). The *British Review* commented on the 'enormous price' of the book, rendered inevitable by the numerous engravings rather than the quantity of new and valuable information: 'people of the present day look for something besides show,' this reader explained, whereas Ross's *Voyage* offered 'little else than details of the equipment of the expedition, the general orders and their fulfilment, and the correspondence and communications among the officers'

(13: 421). In noting the fundamental disagreements between Ross and two of his officers who had also published accounts of the voyage, the *Monthly Review* observed that Ross took precedence in at least one department, having produced 'a gay and handsome quarto' rather than a 'plain and homely octavo' (89: 338). The unmistakable implication was that Ross had put more care into bookmaking than into effective decision-making. For all these readers, it seems to have been much easier to tear into bad style or over-luxurious book production than into the character of a well-decorated naval officer; but the subtext of these remarks is that a man responsible for fabricating such a book, all style and no substance, might also be capable of fabricating other things – like 'Croker's Mountains.'

In the winter of 1818–19, even as Ross's reputation was going into freefall, his second-in-command, Edward Parry, was selected to lead the next Arctic expedition. Parry's instructions were to proceed to Lancaster Sound, and 'in the event of its proving a strait opening to the westward ... to use all possible means ... to pass through it ... and if it should be found to connect itself with the northern sea ... to make the best of your way to Behring's Strait' (Parry xx). Parry followed his instructions, and, passing through the imaginary barrier of Croker's Mountains, entered waters 'never before traversed by Europeans' (Delgado 61). The expedition reached 112° west before their progress was halted by ice, by which point they were nearly out of the Arctic archipelago. Forced to retreat to safe anchorage on Melville Island, the *Hecla* and *Griper* became the first British ships to pass an entire winter within the Arctic circle, for nearly three months of which they were in total darkness. Parry took great care in preparing the ships for the winter and was equally assiduous in monitoring the health of his crew and maintaining their morale – for example, by organizing regular theatrical productions and running a weekly newspaper called the *North Georgia Gazette*. After fully ten months in captivity, with further westward progress still impossible, Parry decided to turn for home, although he formed the view that a Northwest Passage existed and was likely to be found at a lower latitude, closer to the northern coast of mainland America. On his return to England, Parry was given a hero's welcome.

Parry published his *Journal* of the voyage the following year, and the perceived success of his expedition was reflected in periodical reviews from across the ideological spectrum. Comparisons with Ross were odious yet inevitable, and John Barrow did not shy away from making them: he begins his review in the *Quarterly* by recapitulating the inadequacies of Ross's voyage and reminding readers of the journal's undiminished faith in the existence of a Northwest Passage. He makes abundantly clear the patriotic significance of the fact that it is the British Navy, following its military triumph in the Napoleonic wars, that has begun to open up the fabled route to the East. Unsurprisingly, Barrow takes particular delight in noting the substitution of 'Barrow's Strait' for 'Croker's Mountains' – the transformation of 'the magnificent and insuperable range of mountains, which a former expedition had assigned to one Secretary of the Admiralty, into a broad and uninterrupted passage, bearing the name of the other Secretary' (25: 180). He also gives extravagant praise to Parry in suggesting that, while the latter's personal and professional qualities put him on a par with Cook, in some respects his achievements outshine those of his illustrious precursor.

Barrow was not alone in pointing up the comparison with Ross: the *British Critic* began its review by recalling the situation of that 'unfortunate navigator' and praised Barrow himself (in his official capacity) for persevering in the quest, 'of high importance to science' (15: 608), after Ross's initial failure. Although Parry did not succeed in penetrating as far as Bering Strait, he had valuably extended the boundaries of geographical knowledge, and reviewers broadly accepted his conclusions regarding the existence of a Northwest Passage, even if they differed on its potential utility. The conservative *Gentleman's Magazine* declared that he had shown the way 'to unravel the mazes of this hitherto inexplicable labyrinth' (90: 616), while the independent *Eclectic* considered the existence of the Passage established 'beyond all rational scepticism' – reflecting well on both Parry and Barrow, his most 'strenuous advocate,' in face of 'all the discouragements which Captain Ross's representations were evidently designed to perpetuate' (16: 65). Even the radical *Examiner*, which was unlikely to look kindly upon pet government projects, reacted positively: it deemed the 'field of exertion ... a barren one,' and predicted any Northwest Passage would be 'practically useless,' but was unstinting in its praise of Parry and took pleasure in a broader vindication of the national character: the voyage was said to demonstrate 'the intrepidity, perseverance, and honourable spirit of enterprise which it is possible to infuse into every class of our countrymen' (669: 332–3).

Just as Parry's status as an explorer and leader of men was enhanced in contradistinction to the ignominy of Ross's premature return and the public disunity of his expedition's members, so the reception of Parry's narrative seemed to prosper in inverse proportion to that of Ross's.[22] In every respect, from the content of its scientific findings to the quality of its maps, charts, and engravings, it was deemed a superior production. In terms of desiderata, Janice Cavell has argued that by 1824, following publication of a whole raft of narratives and journals spawned by the search for the Northwest Passage,

> a consensus on the evaluation of Arctic writing had emerged among reviewers. The desired qualities were empiricism and modesty; the narratives might be overly detailed and at times repetitive and dull, but this was no real cause for censure. Instead, an abundance of factual material, listed in a sober scientific fashion, was a guarantee of authenticity. (114–5)

---

[22] *Blackwood's*, having been the first journal to air doubts concerning Ross's judgement, was unusually even-handed in its later treatment of the two men. In its review of Parry's *Voyage of Discovery*, it points out that whereas Ross was the first to go in search of the Northwest Passage, Parry benefited from his experience of the previous voyage as Ross's second-in-command. As for their books, *Blackwood's* makes the fair point that Ross's apologetic tone is accounted for by the fact that he knew his reputation was low with his employer and the public, whereas Parry had enjoyed public acclaim and knew that his credit as an author was considerable.

In addition, she suggests, reviewers valued those narratives that revealed the author's character: perseverance and faith were the two leading attributes, and these were taken as representative 'of all that made Britain great' (115). The reception of Parry's *Voyage of Discovery* indicates that it had a significant role in shaping and reinforcing this consensus, since, in the eyes of professional readers, it ticked all the relevant boxes. The *Literary Chronicle* praised him for giving 'a plain and faithful account of the facts' which was 'circumstantial without being tedious, explicit without being commonplace, and interesting without the least art or attempt at effect' (3: 305); its reviewer prized equally the evidence of Parry's 'enterprizing and undaunted character' and 'the modesty with which he narrates his success' (344). The *Monthly Review* allowed that the constant reiteration of daily struggles with ice and the detailing of scientific observations could become monotonous, but said that the 'discerning reader' would accept their value to the 'professional navigator' and 'natural philosopher' (96: 142); Parry was commended for his 'plain, unvarnished, and modest' narrative, 'devoid of the tricks and pretensions of authorship' (282). These judgements are representative, and their conformity to Cavell's abstract criteria is striking. While the general stylistic criteria are perfectly consistent with those we are already familiar with, the emergence of a criterion concerning the explorer's character as an embodiment of perceived national virtues is a notable development.

Of course, professional navigators and natural philosophers (to pick up the *Monthly*'s phrases) were presumably a relatively small subset of the any periodical's audience, so 'discerning readers' must have found additional sources of pleasure in narratives like Parry's. The uniformity among reviewers in terms of passages quoted and episodes summarized leaves little doubt that in Parry's case it was the novelty of his account of an Arctic winter, and all the circumstantial detail of his crew's northern exposure, that readers found compelling. The beauties of the polar landscape, the pyrotechnics of the aurora, the exploration of Melville Island, the daily routine of exercise and essential housekeeping in an extraordinary setting, the trials of sensory deprivation amid 'the death-like stillness of the most dreary desolation' (Parry 125), the perils of snow-blindness and frostbite, the glorious incongruity of the amateur theatricals: these elements of the narrative were presented and discussed in one periodical after another. It is safe to assume that reviewers were of one mind with ordinary readers in their fascination with such things, which provided imaginative transport to a strange and unsettling environment where human beings experienced extreme sensations and faced unprecedented physical and mental challenges. It is worth repeating the point that owing to the high price of Parry's luxurious quarto volume many readers on low or middling incomes would have been dependent on periodical coverage for access to his narrative; reviewers and editors were well aware of this and were unembarrassed about supplying what readers wanted. The *New Annual Register* states that Parry's voyage has aroused such deep interest that his book must already have found its way into 'every body's hands capable of affording the cost, or having access to public libraries' (41: 47) – but provides 'some interesting extracts' nonetheless, presumably in the knowledge that those categories do not include all potential readers.

The *British Review* made a particularly eloquent and sustained appeal to the interests of the general reader in its treatment of Parry's narrative. The reviewer begins by contrasting the 'voluptuous regions of the south,' as described by Continental tourists, with their safely consumable scenes of the sublime and the picturesque, with the wilderness described by Parry, where there is 'nothing to redeem the unmingled terrors of scenes impressing on us an appalling certainty of almost total privation, – scenes of utter desolation, apparently the sepulchre of nature' (18: 65). 'Forbidding' as these materials are, she or (almost certainly) he is sure that the general reader, however bored by 'learned details' (66), will be drawn to the beauties of the polar landscape and 'participate in' (65) the abnormal and sometimes terrifying experiences that Parry's crew undergo. A familiar montage of quotations and summary then follows, along with a scattering of citations from the early books of *Paradise Lost*, which has the effect of casting Parry's 'daring adventurers' as figures in a romance epic, situating their ordeal within a larger and still unfinished metanarrative of Arctic exploration that is part of Britain's national story. In responses like this, one senses that the appeal of the best travel literature to Romantic readers lay in combining scenes of novelistic singularity and intensity with the guarantee of proximity to real-life experience.

It is interesting that the *British Review*, with its declared bias towards the general reader, makes no mention at all of the illustrations in Parry's *Voyage of Discovery* – perhaps because it prefers to assume that it is addressing readers who cannot refer to the extravagantly priced original. Nevertheless, for those readers who could afford or otherwise access the published volume, the fine prints, which attracted much favourable comment in other periodicals, must have enhanced the imaginative experience. *The Examiner* was particularly impressed with a print depicting the *Hecla* and *Griper* housed over for the winter, surrounded by a curtain of ice for purposes of insulation: 'The very soul is frozen by the inspection, except that portion of latent heat which is supplied by an involuntary feeling of self-complacency, at a contemplation of the difficulties which may be surmounted by the ardour, the courage, and the sagacity of man' (699: 333). Another remarkable illustration, remarked upon by several reviewers, depicted the ingenious but incredibly laborious process of 'Cutting into Winter Harbour' (Figure 3.6) – literally, sawing a channel more than 4000 yards long through the sea-ice just wide enough to allow the ships to pass through to safe anchorage, attaching 'sails' to large chunks of ice to float them out of the way. The *British Review*, *Monthly Review*, *Gentleman's Magazine*, and *Blackwood's* were among those periodicals that featured this passage, and the latter two journals specifically mentioned the plate. Evidently there was curiosity value attached to this episode, but equally clearly it was taken to represent a level of perseverance, diligence, and ingenuity that redounded to the credit of the national character.

At almost the same time in 1819 that the *Hecla* and *Griper* set sail for Lancaster Sound, another expedition under John Franklin left England bound for

The Crews of H.M.S. Hecla & Gripes cutting into Winter Harbour
Sept. 26. 1819

Fig. 3.6   William Westall, *The Crews of H.M.S. Hecla & Griper Cutting into Winter Harbour*; illustration for W. E. Parry, *Journal of a Voyage for the Discovery of a North-West Passage* (1821). Library and Archives Canada / C-028782.

a trading post on Hudson's Bay. Franklin's mission was to proceed overland to the northern shore of mainland America and further the search for a Northwest Passage by charting the Arctic coast; it was thought that he might meet up with Parry's ships, but if not, he would leave his co-explorer information in specially constructed cairns. Having followed the fur traders' route into frontier territory, during a period in which intense rivalry between the Hudson's Bay Company and North West Company had a negative impact on the expedition's preparations and provisioning, it was not until June 1821 that Franklin and his companions (three fellow British officers and a seaman, a crew of French-Canadian *voyageurs*, and Native guides) set off from Fort Enterprise, the winter quarters they had built themselves close to the Coppermine River. Descending the river by two large birchbark canoes to its mouth, Franklin parted company with some of their Native allies, who agreed to leave supplies at the Fort to await their return, and turned east. From here on the journey, by any objective standard, was an accumulation of error, disaster, and tragedy. Franklin and his party were inadequately provisioned, were unable to live off the land, failed to make contact with local Inuit whose expertise and resources they might have drawn on, and continued their exploration far longer than was wise. On the return trek to Fort Enterprise the expedition, reduced to feeding on lichen, boiled bones, and shoe leather, divided into three groups under the pressure of starvation and fatigue. In the most macabre turn of events, in the hindmost group one of the *voyageurs*, already suspected of having murdered and cannibalized two of his comrades, was then also accused of killing one of the officers; fearing for their own lives, one of the remaining officers shot the *voyageur* in a pre-emptive strike. Reunited at Fort Enterprise, where no food was found on arrival, the expedition clung to life but suffered further fatalities before being rescued, and nursed back to health, by their Native allies. In total, eleven of the twenty men on the expedition died, either through starvation or more nefarious means. Given these circumstances, it is perhaps surprising that, when Franklin eventually made his way back home, arriving in London on 23 October 1822, he was greeted as a hero and rapidly promoted.

Even before the expedition's return, reports of its calamitous and sensational outcome had begun to appear in the press, and in November the *Literary Gazette* gave its readers a graphic account of the 'horrid repasts' composed of the 'mangled remains' of their comrades that the explorers had unwittingly accepted (303: 712). John Barrow, however, was evidently satisfied with the results of the expedition and with Franklin's performance as its leader, and strongly urged him to write a narrative; despite deep reservations about his own qualifications for authorship, Franklin duly set to work, and his *Narrative of a Journey to the Shores of the Polar Sea* was published the following spring.

Like Ross's and Parry's volumes, Franklin's narrative was cast in the plain, 'unvarnished,' workmanlike style required of official travel narratives; what sets his narrative apart is the unshakeable Christian faith he describes as having sustained the British explorers, and which sounds an insistent note in his writing. Even when forced to scrape lichen off rocks for a 'scanty supper,' Franklin looks 'with humble confidence to the great Author and Giver of all good, for a continuance of the support which had hitherto been always supplied to us in our greatest need' (Franklin 413), and when the 'Indians' finally relieve the emaciated remnant of the expedition at Fort Enterprise he welcomes their arrival as the 'seasonable interposition of Providence' (467). As Janice Cavell rightly says, 'in no other narrative was religious feeling so closely woven into the very texture of the book' (103).

The response to Franklin's narrative among professional readers was overwhelmingly positive. Once again, long reviews incorporating generous extracts or lengthy summaries provided readers unable to access the exorbitantly priced quarto (a cheaper, two-volume octavo appeared in 1824) with a more than adequate vicarious reading experience, and, in terms of their excerpting strategies, the reviews followed a pattern familiar from the reception of works such as Hearne's, Ross's, and Parry's. Apart from the obvious drama of the expedition's final weeks, and the harrowing descriptions of hunger, mental breakdown, and violence, reviewers showed a keen interest in matters relating to Franklin's interactions with indigenous peoples. The *British Review* pointed out that, despite the abundance of 'books of American travels,' serious studies of '"The Red Men"' were few and far between, and it therefore valued the account of the Cree furnished by Franklin's associate, John Richardson, along with other anecdotes illustrative of 'savage life' (22: 8). (Here, as so often in dealing with Native groups, the distinction between American and Canadian contexts, so sharp when politically sensitive issues such as emigration are to the fore, is blurred or treated as inconsequential.) In line with the journal's religious agenda, this reviewer deplored the picture provided of the employees of two large fur trading companies, who should have been helping to 'extend the faith of the cross' by their own example, instead fostering 'the most degrading sensualities, to which savage life is prone' (9).

The *Monthly Review* also took note of Richardson's observations on the Cree, finding in them a useful corrective to loose statements about 'the savage character' (102: 8); with its characteristic philosophical orientation, however, it valued the detailed account of the manners and customs of this nation because 'it is by viewing our species in all its phases of history and situation, that we may ultimately hope to generalize the principles of human society' (9). Descriptions of hunting reindeer, musk ox, and grizzly bears, and the Inuit method of constructing an igloo also proved popular with reviewers, reinforcing the impression of a reading public accustomed to ethnographic portraits in the form of enumerations of timeless, repeated rituals. However, in the face of Mary Louise Pratt's well-known critique of the 'normalizing, generalizing' ethnographic approach favoured by Romantic-era travel writing, it is worth noting that a journal like the *Monthly* was very alert to evidence provided by Franklin of how the 'peculiar usages' of the Cree had been modified by contact with Europeans, and even how their belief-systems had hybridized with those of their 'European neighbours.' Pratt's harsh evaluation itself seems misleadingly overgeneralized in light of such responses.

Of special note among contemporary reviews was the coverage given to Franklin's expedition by the *Mirror of Literature, Amusement, and Instruction*, a weekly magazine launched in November 1822 by John Limbird at the bargain price of two pence and regarded by book historians as a pioneering 'mass-audience periodical' (Altick 321). The *Mirror* not only offered a commentary on the expedition – 'One of the most arduous enterprises ever undertaken,' typifying Britons 'who, however difficult or dangerous may be the object in which they are engaged, sink all personal considerations in zeal for their duty to their country' (1: 412) – but also added several (admittedly crude) wood engravings of fine prints from the quarto: one showed a white wolf killed at Fort Enterprise, another was a copy of George Back's impressive drawing of the Wilberforce Falls (Figure 3.7). The latter illustration, depicting two explorers contemplating the majestic stepped Falls in a manner reminiscent of a de Loutherbourg Alpine landscape, presented the *Mirror*'s readers with a visual representation of the Canadian Arctic quite different to the icy desolation of the scenes in Ross or Parry. By reproducing a scene redolent of aesthetic calm, in which the natural environment gratifies rather than threatens the observer, the journal, wittingly or unwittingly, restored some dignity to Franklin's calamitous venture, and reaffirmed its editorial stance supporting state-sponsored exploration.[23]

Naturally enough, professional readers were unanimous in focusing their attention on the final stages of Franklin's desperate journey (all the horrors of which were concentrated in the long concluding chapter of his book), and most found rich material here for moral, religious, or political reflection. The *New Annual Register* chose to give a sentimental gloss to its selection of extracts ('It is hardly possible to read this unaffected and truly pathetic tale without being moved to tears. What is the poetical distress of tragedy to its melancholy details!' [44: 99]]), but this was not a typical approach. One aspect of the narrative that few reviewers could resist commenting on was the stark contrast between the resilience of the British explorers and the apparent spinelessness of the French-Canadians. John Barrow, in his long *Quarterly* review, compared the high mortality rate among the *voyageurs* to that of the Britons, of whom only one lost his life (murdered), in order to highlight the 'mental and moral energy' of his countrymen with their 'firm reliance on a merciful Providence' (28: 373). The *Monthly Review* and *British Review* were just two of many other periodicals to point up, in quiet self-congratulatory fashion, this contrast, the latter agreeing with the *Quarterly* in connecting the fortitude and self-possession of the Britons to the strength of their Protestant faith. For Barrow, the expedition, despite its appalling casualty toll, was a vindication of the national character as well as of the national religion; it was also exemplary of 'the fatal effects of insubordination and disobedience' (403) and

---

[23]   Far from having exhausted its interest in the region, in November 1823 the *Mirror* published a supplementary number devoted to a 'clear, connected, and intelligible narrative' (2: 429–30) of the search for a Northwest Passage, beginning with Henry Hudson in the early seventeenth century and concluding with Parry's abortive second voyage of 1821–23. Included in this brief history were a much more detailed summary of Franklin's expedition and a reproduction of his diagram of an igloo.

THE FALLS OF WILBERFORCE.

Estimated at 250 feet high.

Fig. 3.7   George Back, *The Falls of Wilberforce*; illustration for John
                Franklin, *Narrative of a Journey to the Shores of the Polar Sea*
                (1823). Library and Archives Canada, Acc. No. R9266–560 Peter
                Winkworth Collection of Canadiana.

a pointed message to the 'Hunts' and 'Hones' back home (an unusually explicit political reference) of the virtues of order and firm discipline on both a micro and macro scale. It was therefore a perfect dramatization of the values for which the *Quarterly* stood.

The *British Review*'s unidentified reader was very much on the same wavelength as John Barrow, albeit more ambivalent concerning the quest for the Northwest Passage, the continuation of which in the face of so many disappointments indicated a stubborn 'desire to establish a favourite hypothesis' (22: 4). The expedition had tested human beings to the limit and reflected well on the national character, demonstrating the renewal in peacetime of those energies that had successfully resisted an 'implacable enemy' (1) in the Napoleonic wars. It had also proved that a 'spirit of vital religion' was compatible with 'prowess and enterprise' (25). This reader, while glad to see the *Review*'s moral and religious principles underscored, also gave weight to the *Narrative*'s sheer imaginative power – 'hurrying us out of ourselves to hunger and freeze in the howling desert, until we start, as from a painful dream, and rejoice to find, that we have had no other participation in these calamities, than that produced by the influence of a rapt fancy' (24). The liberal *Monthly Review* surrendered its normal scepticism to the general tide of 'commiseration and applause,' confessing to 'lively and patriotic sensations' (102: 1) on reading Franklin's narrative. Despite its 'truly afflicting' denouement, the expedition was considered another 'illustrious example ... of what British valor, under the direction of education and religious dependence, can endure and achieve in the pursuit of knowledge and the discharge of professional duty' (167–8).

Criticism of Franklin was indeed hard to find. The *London Magazine* reported the 'multiplied calamities' of his voyage and suggested that some of his decisions were driven 'rather by zeal than prudence' (7: 576), but concluded that the expedition had given support to those who maintained 'the practicability of a North-west Passage' (578). In attending to his narrative's record 'of spirit and perseverance, of exertion and suffering' (573) on an unparalleled scale, the magazine joined the periodicals' ostensible campaign to build Franklin's reputation as the hero of a quest narrative, equal to his awful trials and ordeals, and a fitting representative of a country whose achievements in exploration were just one manifestation of her special place in the divine scheme. Perhaps the independent-minded *Eclectic*'s non-committal coverage conveyed rare, implicit criticism: its reader begins by commending Franklin's 'combination of prudence, courage, and ability' (19: 521), but then retells the story of the expedition from the time of its arrival at the mouth of the Coppermine in a way that brings home to readers the folly of the whole journey eastwards when the party was so poorly provisioned. In finishing the review somewhat abruptly with the scene of 'aggravated wretchedness' at Fort Enterprise, and offering nothing by way of summary comment on the mission, he or she perhaps invites readers to form their own, not entirely flattering, conclusions.

Nevertheless, overall the consensus among professional readers of Franklin's *Journey* was remarkable: a near-apocalyptic story of deprivation, derangement, and death was greeted with a mixture of ethnocentric pride and religious self-complacency. In the reception of this travel narrative, more than any other, exploration had become a matter of earnest, indeed obdurate, self-definition, on both individual and national levels. The search for the Northwest Passage would continue (merging eventually with the search for Franklin himself, following his fatal last voyage of 1845),[24] and the mysteries of the Canadian Arctic would slowly be revealed, but by this stage in the evolution of the travel genre Romantic readers were already well aware that there could be a lot more at stake in such literature than mere 'amusement' and occasional 'instruction.' In the years after Waterloo, with Britain's position in Europe strengthened and her global empire extended, professional and general readers alike seemed more inclined to place voyages and travels, and their personal 'journeys in the mind,' in the context of a larger story.

---

[24]   Thirty-two separate expeditions joined in the search for Franklin. It was John Rae who, in 1854, first gathered convincing evidence, from conversations with local Inuit, of the demise of Franklin's party somewhere in the vicinity of King William Island; but it was left to Leopold McClintock to discover the human and other remains of the expedition, in 1859. Franklin himself, it was revealed, had died in June 1847, but other men lingered on until at least 1851, and 'a handful almost made it out of the Arctic' (Delgado 163).

Chapter 4
'Of such books we cannot have too many': Romantic Poets as Travel Readers

In the previous three chapters I considered the evidence of how North American travels were received in the Romantic period, looking at both the formal, professional or semi-professional responses embodied in periodical reviews and the fugitive records of more private reading experiences. Celebrated authors of the period have so far been included in the discussion only insofar as they fitted into one of these categories – that is, either in the guise of part-time or occasional reviewers, or in their personal reactions and opinions as recorded in letters, diaries, and so on. In this chapter I shall examine a number of Romantic writers who engaged with the subject of America and drew on travel books relating to North America in tangible – in many cases self-documented – ways within literary texts, and determine whether these literary uses of travel literature are a special case or represent modalities of reading consistent with those studied so far.

It scarcely needs demonstrating that the poets and novelists of this era were just as enthralled as any other contemporary reader by voyages and travels in general, and by North American travels in particular. Alan Frost has argued that the clearest indication of the importance of new geographical perspectives – of radically different human scenes and physical landscapes – to Romantic literature is the centrality of the voyage metaphor ('Imaginatively, it is a progress from inherited and conventional views of reality to the perception of a new and very different reality' [12]), and that those writers who never ventured outside Europe in actuality were nevertheless mental travellers on a global scale and saw themselves 'in terms of the experience they gained vicariously through their readings' (8). Perhaps North America offered rich possibilities for such vicarious voyaging because, at this early stage in its development as an outpost of European colonialism, it was still capable of generating travel accounts that were so different from each other: Wayne Franklin, whose focus is more on seventeenth-century encounters with the New World, discriminates three main genres of 'discovery,' 'exploration,' and 'settlement' narrative, and it is worth pointing out that, as the continent was opened up to Europeans in ways covered in earlier chapters, the Romantic period threw up notable examples of all three types of North American travel experience. Serious critical interest in the indebtedness of major writers to this body of literature dates back to the early twentieth literature, and some of this work, as I shall have occasion to show, still holds value. More recently, Michael Wiley has surveyed the territory anew, with a particular focus on those Romantics who emigrated, planned to emigrate, or 'speculated imaginatively upon emigration' (56) to North America, in most cases as an alternative space in which to realize social and political ideals disappointed at home. Wiley's account usefully highlights the play between positive and negative representations in the Romantics' 'literary understanding of America' (58) and makes the case that, although America ultimately failed most of those who practised or contemplated emigration, the tensions of their imaginative preoccupation with the continent were a vital and productive feature of British Romantic art.

Examples of transatlantic influences and engagements are certainly not hard to find. As long ago as 1937, Robert Heilman presented the astonishing statistics that between 1760 and 1800 at least a third of new novels in every five-year bloc introduced the subject-matter of North America, if only peripherally, and that from the War of Independence onwards more than fifty per cent of novels made some reference to transatlantic affairs or employed America for elements of plot, character, or setting (56).[1] Most of these works, whether affirming or denying the American ideal, relied heavily on travel books for their authenticity: 'a whole coterie of novels,' Heilman claims, 'refurbishes travel accounts for a second consumption ... America was in the imagination again as it had not been since the days of Raleigh' (85). Heilman's language of consumption implies a very passive recycling of the source material. In his recent study of *Americans in British Literature, 1770–1832*, Christopher Flynn brings a more sophisticated critical palate to bear on the subject and offers a more nuanced and contextualized analysis of fictional representations of America, while traversing much of the same literary terrain: Robert Bage's *Mount Henneth* (1788) and *Hermsprong* (1796), Gilbert Imlay's *The Emigrants* (1793), Charlotte Lennox's *Euphemia* (1790), and the anonymous *Disobedience* (1797) are among the works under the spotlight.

Romantic poetry was no less shaped and informed by transatlantic perspectives, albeit this influence could sometimes be less conspicuous and more indirect than in the case of fiction. An especially intriguing case, from the heart of the Romantic canon, is that of Keats, whose brother George and sister-in-law Georgiana emigrated to the United States, inspired by Morris Birkbeck's enthusiastic account of the Prairie Albion settlement in Illinois. Fiona Robertson has argued convincingly that this was not an inconsequential byway of Keats's biography but, rather, an episode that throws valuable light on the entire curve of his poetic career: the evolution from early work such as the sonnet 'On Reading Chapman's Homer,' with its themes of westering movement and imaginative conquest, to later poems that invoke the heritage of European literary culture as benign counterweight to an 'afflicting, starving, unnatural nature' (35), mirror the course of George's financial difficulties and disillusionment with the American dream. Even an otherworldly ballad such as 'La Belle Dame Sans Merci,' Robertson says, is explicable in terms

---

[1]   Heilman's findings, which one is tempted to observe (enviously) must be the fruits of an era of more leisured scholarship, are based on the examination of 438 novels. It is hard to believe that modern archaeologies of the eighteenth-century novel could materially alter his figures.

of Keats's sympathy with his brother's disenchantment and his exasperation with the false romanticism of proselytes like Birkbeck.[2]

Another figure who deserves fresh scrutiny in this connection is Anna Barbauld, whose background in radical Dissent makes obvious sense of her lifelong interest in American affairs and open-minded endorsement of the republican project: while perusing a history of the American Revolution in May 1791, she told a correspondent that 'the old story of Greece and Rome' was of no moment 'when we have events of such importance passing before our eyes' (Oliver 194–5), and her enthusiasm was undimmed nearly thirty years later, when she declared that 'the whole field of ancient history' was insignificant compared to 'the vast continent of America, with its fresh and opening glories!' (303). In her best-known poem, *Eighteen Hundred and Eleven*, Barbauld envisions a post-apocalyptic future in which Europe lies in ruins, and American cultural tourists come 'From the Blue Mountains or Ontario's lake ... to press the sod / By statesmen, sages, poets, heroes trod' (lines 130–132). Among many 'heroes' cited by Barbauld is Joseph Priestley, a former colleague of her father's at the Warrington Academy who encouraged her poetic aspirations as a child and who emigrated to America in 1794. Too little is known about the books – including, presumably, works of travel – that fuelled Barbauld's admiration for the country that clearly embodied her political ideals.

For the purposes of this chapter, I shall focus on six poets with well-documented transatlantic interests: William Wordsworth, Samuel Taylor Coleridge, Robert Southey, Thomas Moore, Thomas Campbell, and Felicia Hemans. Of the six, only Moore actually visited North America, although, as is well known, Coleridge and Southey planned to emigrate to Pennsylvania in the mid-1790s to found their 'Pantisocratic' community. In all six cases, there are records of at least some of the books from which the authors gathered their knowledge of America, and in several notable examples this evidence is incorporated in their work in the form of discursive footnotes – a minor phenomenon of the period worthy of consideration in its own right. In all six cases, too, my focus is exclusively on the poet as a reader of 'factual' travel literature: more specifically, my concern is to explore how each poet read 'voyages and travels' as part of a process of acquiring and producing knowledge about America, and passing on those images and understandings to his or her own readers. Whether the poets' ulterior motives as literary end-users made their activity as readers significantly different from that of the reviewers and recreational readers studied in previous chapters is a point worth addressing.

William Wordsworth

In a letter probably written in spring 1812, William Wordsworth informed Francis Wrangham that he saw 'no new books except by the merest accident,' but added: 'The only *modern* Books that I read are those of travels, or such as relate to Matters

---

[2]   On the importance of his brother's emigration experience to Keats's self-fashioning as a poet, see also Chandler 469–77.

of fact; and the only modern books that I care for' (*Letters* 3: 9). Little had changed since he wrote to James Tobin in March 1798, urging his correspondent to collect 'books of travels' for him, 'as without much of such reading my present labours [by which he meant his projected philosophical masterwork, *The Recluse*] cannot be brought to a conclusion' (*Letters* 1: 212). Throughout his life Wordsworth, a restless spirit whose own travels in Britain and on the Continent provided him with raw materials for a series of unique 'memorials' or poem-sequences, was an avid consumer of travel literature. Thanks to Duncan Wu's meticulous research on *Wordsworth's Reading* between 1770 and 1815, and the two volumes of Mark Reed's Wordsworth *Chronology* covering the same period, in addition to the work of earlier scholars, we now possess more detail on what Wordsworth read, and when he read it, than we do for almost any other canonical author. While it is clear that his reading was more diverse than the remarks I have quoted from his letters might imply, it is undeniable that he read a lot of travel books, and the influence of these upon his poetry has long been of interest to Wordsworthians. Many such debts were first identified by William Knight in his pioneering edition of the *Poetical Works* of 1882–86, then republicized in de Selincourt's standard edition of 1940–49. Charles Norton Coe, in a book that is rarely, and never adequately, acknowledged in related modern studies, drew together existing knowledge on the subject in *Wordsworth and the Literature of Travel* in 1953, itemizing borrowings from travel books in forty-four poems and offering thoughtful commentary on certain trends revealed in these appropriations. That Wordsworth knew the genre well, and was familiar in particular with major works of North American travels, is not in question; what I would like to do here is not to try to establish new parallels but to highlight several notable examples of his leaning upon travel sources and to ask what these reveal as to *how* he read these much-prized narratives.

One well-known and transparent case in point is 'The Complaint of a Forsaken Indian Woman' from the 1798 *Lyrical Ballads*, which, as Wordsworth's long prefatory note makes clear, is based on a passage in Samuel Hearne's *Journey ... to the Northern Ocean*. Hearne describes how the wife of one of his Chipewyan companions becomes too weak to continue the journey and is left, 'without much ceremony ... to perish above-ground.' His published text[3] continues:

> Though this was the first instance of the kind I had seen, it is the common, and indeed the constant practice of those Indians; for when a grown person is so ill, especially in the Summer, as not to be able to walk, and too heavy to be carried, they say it is better to leave one who is past recovery, than for the whole family to sit down by them and starve to death; well knowing that they cannot be of any service to the afflicted. On those occasions, therefore, the friends or relations of the sick generally leave them some victuals and water; and, if the situation

---

[3]   It is worth noting that the entire passage concerning this woman was an addition to Hearne's journal in the published narrative, and may therefore owe something to editorial intervention. However, since the published version was the only version Wordsworth knew, the issue is not relevant to this discussion.

of the place will afford it, a little firing. When those articles are provided, the person to be left is acquainted with the road which the others intend to go; and then, after covering them well up with deer skins, &c. they take their leave, and walk away crying.

Sometimes persons thus left, recover; and come up with their friends, or wander about till they meet with other Indians, whom they accompany till they again join their relations. Instances of this kind are seldom known. The poor woman above mentioned, however, came up with us three several times, after having been left in the manner described. At length, poor creature! she dropt behind, and no one attempted to go back in search of her.

A custom apparently so unnatural is perhaps not to be found among any other of the human race: if properly considered, however, it may with justice be ascribed to necessity and self-preservation, rather than to the want of humanity and social feeling, which ought to be the characteristic of men, as the noblest part of the creation. Necessity, added to national custom, contributes principally to make scenes of this kind less shocking to those people, than they must appear to the more civilized part of mankind. (Hearne 131–2)

Hearne's text, as this long quotation should make plain, equivocates between sociological understanding and 'civilized' sensibility – between seeing the behaviour in question as a necessary product of harsh living conditions and either responding sympathetically to the woman's plight ('poor creature!') or anticipating outrage on the part of his readers ('A custom apparently so unnatural'). His ambivalence is reproduced and transformed in Wordsworth's poem.

Wordsworth's prefatory note, which begins by condensing and paraphrasing the main elements of the situation as described by Hearne, then states that 'It is unnecessary to add that the females are equally, or still more, exposed to the same fate.' Despite saying it is unnecessary, Wordsworth adds the comment nonetheless, thereby making an issue out of gender in precisely the way that Hearne does not. He thus promises to cast the Indian woman in a similar role to the numerous suffering, distressed, or abandoned lone women who populate his early poetry from *An Evening Walk* onwards. However, Wordsworth's most striking formal intervention in adapting Hearne's story is to put it into the first person, imagining the woman's predicament from her own point of view; by forgoing a (default) male narrator there is no man of feeling to invite the reader's participative sorrow – any decision to pity the Indian woman has to be the reader's own from within his or her own cultural framework. Instead, our initial impression of the woman's soliloquy is of a slightly unnerving, emotionally inert acceptance of her approaching demise:

My fire is dead: it knew no pain;
Yet is it dead, and I remain.
All stiff with ice the ashes lie;
And they are dead, and I will die.
When I was well, I wished to live,
For clothes, for warmth, for food, and fire;

But they to me no joy can give,
No pleasure now, and no desire.
Then here contented will I lie;
Alone I cannot fear to die. (lines 11–20)

As the poem progresses, however, the woman's utterance becomes more unstable: she accuses her own people ('Alas! You might have dragged me on / Another day, a single one!' [21–2]); she bitterly laments her temporary lack of fortitude ('For strong and without pain I lay, / My friends, when you were gone away' [29–30]); she is tormented by recollections of enforced separation from her child, who looked at her 'As if he strove to be a man / That he might pull the sledge for me' (37–8); she resolves to summon her energies and rejoin the group ('In spite of all my weary pain, / I'll look upon your tents again' [53–4]), then again stoically accepts the inevitable ('My journey will be shortly run, / I shall not see another sun' [61–2]. We are left uncertain quite how to 'read' her: as Tim Fulford puts it, 'Pitiable and awesome in turn' she remains 'an enigma' (175), both recognizable yet disconcertingly different; arguably, this suggests to us that people of diverse cultures cannot be reduced to a single standard without conceptual – and possibly material – violence.

Wordsworth's reading of Hearne is far from one-dimensional. At one level, he appears to go to Hearne's travels for 'Matters of fact,' just as his letter to Wrangham implies is his predilection. At another level, he reads constructively, with the grain of the original, resuming in his own terms a debate initiated in Hearne's text: just as Hearne gestures at sentimental portraiture but overlays this with a stern doctrine of necessity, so Wordsworth highlights female vulnerability but offsets this with equanimity in face of death. More challengingly still, Wordsworth reads Hearne creatively and interrogatively, using this short passage in the *Journey* as the occasion for a radical reimagining of a human situation from which Hearne, Wordsworth implies, remained too aloof, hiding behind token expressions of sympathy and philosophical platitudes. Wordsworth has learned something from Hearne, but Hearne takes on a second life in his writing, rustling and crackling like the Northern Lights on which Wordsworth comments in his prefatory note.

Hearne's *Journey* clearly made a strong impression on Wordsworth; it is quite possible that it lies behind another lyrical ballad featuring a forsaken woman, of indeterminate ethnicity but with strong suggestions of indigenous North American extraction,[4] namely the 'Mad Mother.' Given the larger context of response to Hearne's and similar travel works, as investigated in earlier chapters, it is no surprise that, from the diverse content of Hearne's narrative, it was episodes highlighting the treatment of Native women that stirred Wordsworth to poetry; here, his idiosyncratic literary preoccupations ran with the broader current of public interest. Hearne may also have made an impact on his later poetry. Charles

---

[4]   Wordsworth himself seemed to wish still to leave the question open in a letter of September 1836, indicating that the woman was 'either ... of these islands, or a North American' (*Letters* 6: 293).

Norton Coe puts the case that the *Journey* was the key influence on the well-known passage at the end of Book 3 of *The Excursion* in which the Solitary describes making a transatlantic crossing following his disillusionment with the French Revolution. Residing first in an unidentified city (presumably New York) on the eastern seaboard, he finds the young republic 'a motley spectacle ... of high pretensions – unreproved / But by the obstreperous voice of higher still' (lines 897–9). Disappointed that Europeans have not been morally regenerated by transplantation to an uncontaminated environment, he sets off in search of Native Americans in frontier regions of still 'unappropriated earth' (939), expecting to find in such people, though seemingly doomed to extinction, humanity's best hope, the epitome of manly independence and spiritual freedom:

> So, westward, tow'rd the unviolated woods
> I bent my way; and, roaming far and wide,
> Failed not to greet the merry Mocking-bird;
> And, while the melancholy Muccawiss
> (The sportive bird's companion in the grove)
> Repeated o'er and o'er his plaintive cry,
> I sympathised at leisure with the sound;
> But that pure archetype of human greatness,
> I found him not. There, in his stead, appeared
> A creature, squalid, vengeful, and impure;
> Remorseless, and submissive to no law
> But superstitious fear, and abject sloth. (944–55)

Coe picks out the various attributes of the Solitary's ignoble savage ('appearance, cruelty, slothfulness, and superstitious nature' [95]) and finds passages in Hearne that might have suggested each negative trait, but the evidence is far from conclusive: similar passages could be found in many other travel narratives that Wordsworth is known to have read in the late 1790s and early 1800s, including those books that Coe, following Knight, adduces as sources for the 'merry Mocking-bird' and 'melancholy Muccawiss' in the above quotation, namely Jonathan Carver's *Travels through the Interior Parts of North America* (1778) and Thomas Ashe's *Travels in America* (1808). If Wordsworth indeed had Hearne in mind when writing this section of his poem, it would represent a radical change in the way he was disposed to read the *Journey*; or, allowing for the fact that this is dramatized utterance, he would be attributing to the Solitary a simplified, reductive reading of Hearne very different to the one he took responsibility for at the time of *Lyrical Ballads* – a reading that reflected and reinforced the nuances and tensions in Hearne's treatment of the 'Northern Indians.'

Another popular travel book of the period with which Wordsworth has long been linked is William Bartram's *Travels through North and South Carolina, Georgia, East and West Florida* (1791). This is a rich, complex text, in which Bartram's scientific attention to the natural world (like his father, he was a trained botanist, whose expeditions were devoted to collecting plants and seeds for collectors in

England)[5] goes hand in hand with a romantic veneration of the divine principle that animates its every production, both animal and vegetable, and in which his sociological observations based on close association with indigenous peoples of the southern states are somehow compatible with outbreaks of primitivist fantasy. N. Bryllion Fagin, in his comprehensive study of Bartram, finds the *Travels* lurking behind a wide range of Wordsworth's poems, including works as thematically and chronologically diverse as *The Borderers*, *The Prelude*, 'The Blind Highland Boy,' 'The Kitten and Falling Leaves,' 'Hofer,' and 'Address to my Infant Daughter'; he even considers the possibility that the 'William' who is the first-person narrator of 'Expostulation and Reply' may be a stand-in for Bartram rather than a persona adopted by Wordsworth. Probably the most fascinating and critically productive of the connections, though, is between Bartram and 'Ruth,' first published in the 1800 *Lyrical Ballads*.

In this poem, Ruth is an English girl who, at the age of seven, becomes a foster-child of nature when her mother dies and she is slighted by her new stepmother. Having reached adulthood, she meets and falls for a 'Youth from Georgia's shore' (line 13), who wears a Cherokee headdress and has 'roam'd about with vagrant bands / Of Indians in the West' (113–4) but speaks 'the English tongue' (20) and appears to have fought in the American War. Seduced by his promise of an idyllic pastoral life in the New World, Ruth marries the silver-tongued 'Stripling' (110), but she is subsequently deserted by him just prior to embarkation. Ruth loses her mind and is imprisoned for a while; when she regains her freedom her mental health is restored by the natural surroundings of the 'Banks of Tone' (190) in Somerset, although she is reduced to begging by the roadside to satisfy her material needs.

With its transatlantic themes and 'Indian' content, 'Ruth' has proved fertile ground in recent years for critics such as Carol Bolton, Michael Wiley, and Tim Fulford, but the infrastructure of textual allusions to Bartram that provides the ground of their various arguments was brought to light by Lane Cooper ('Wordsworth's Sources') over a hundred years ago, and later revisited by Fagin and Coe. Cooper speculates that if Wordsworth 'did not carry Bartram's *Travels* in Georgia, Florida, etc. with him to Germany [where 'Ruth' was written in 1799], he must have had that entertaining journal almost by heart before he started' (*Methods* 110). Wordsworth's own footnote to lines 58–60, referencing Bartram for the American youth's intoxicating talk of 'flowers that with one scarlet gleam / Cover a hundred leagues and seem / To set the hills on fire,' is on closer inspection the merest tip of the intertextual iceberg. The landscape of 'green Savannahs' (61) and lakes with 'fairy crowds / Of islands' (63–4) is pure Bartram, while images of the majestic 'Magnolia, spread / High as a cloud' (55–6) and 'plants divine and strange / That ev'ry day their blossoms change' (49–50) have also been sourced to the *Travels*. The youth from Georgia's feathered 'Casque,' it is suggested, is modelled on the king of the Seminoles depicted on the frontispiece of Bartram's book, and a pastoral vision of a future in which Ruth will help 'drive the flying deer' (90) may draw on a fanciful hunting scene Bartram describes in the Alachua area.

---

[5]   For a useful overview of the careers of father and son, see Edelstein.

These well-documented allusions are examples of Wordsworth's plundering of Bartram for 'matters of fact,' or of a tactic of selecting and combining words and images from a travel source in order to add exotic texture to his poem. At a deeper level, early Wordsworthians were minded to notice the comparability of Wordsworth's attitude to nature with Bartram's dual perspective, which combines minute attention to form and function with a religious wonder at 'that which animates the inimitable machines, which gives them motion, impowers them to act, speak, and perform' (Bartram xvii). 'The truth is,' Fagin argues, 'that, in spite of an occasional implication of disapproval, Wordsworth found himself kin to the gentle Quaker, wandering in the woods, along rivers and lakes, untrodden ways, watching Indians and traders, picking plants, and loving and contemplating all nature' (175).

As Fagin's reference to 'disapproval' implies, it would be wrong to think of Wordsworth's reading of Bartram as merely utilitarian (extracting details of topography or natural history to provide the background to a poem) or wholly affirmative (predicated on a shared religion of nature). On the contrary, I would argue that ambivalence towards Bartram is integral to the moral and social argument of 'Ruth.' Part of the American youth's irresistible but 'perilous' talk of the transatlantic paradise concerns

> Girls, a happy rout,
> Who quit their fold with dance and shout
> Their pleasant Indian Town
> To gather strawberries all day long,
> Returning with a choral song
> When day-light is gone down. (43–8)

This recollects a well-known mock-Edenic scene in the *Travels* in which Bartram takes in a 'most enchanting view' of green meadows and a meandering river, with 'herds of deer ... bounding over the hills' and, most alluringly of all, 'companies of young, innocent Cherokee virgins' busily gathering wild strawberries. Bartram's narrative then toys with presenting himself as a serpent in this paradise:

> nature prevailing over reason, we wished at least to have a more active part in their delicious sports. Thus precipitately resolving, we cautiously made our approaches, yet undiscovered, almost to the joyous scene of action. Now, although we meant no other than an innocent frolic with this gay assembly of hamadryades, we shall leave it to the person of feeling and sensibility to form an idea to what lengths our passions might have hurried us, thus warmed and excited, had it not been for the vigilance and care of some envious matrons who lay in ambush, and espying us, gave the alarm, time enough for the nymphs to rally and assemble together. (355)

In the end, Bartram's (and his companion's) 'more active part' is limited to sharing a picnic of strawberries with the Cherokee 'nymphs' and agreeing terms of trade for future supplies, but the threat of sexual violence has been invoked at the same time as the neoclassical diction lends a roguish charm to the 'innocent frolic.' Insofar as Wordsworth's lines rehearse this episode in the *Travels*, the latter text anticipates the 'voluptuous thought[s]' (128) and 'low desires' (147) that wreck the young American's marriage to Ruth, and underscores the hopeless idealism of her proposed new life as a 'sylvan huntress' (90) on the green savannah.

It has been suggested that the 'Youth from Georgia's shore,' who is of indeterminate ethnicity, is based to some extent on a young man of mixed race who accompanies Bartram on one of his expeditions, and is credited with potent rhetorical skills:

> The young mustee, who came with me to the Mucclasses from Mobile, having Chactaw blood in his veins from his mother, was a sensible young fellow, and by his father had been instructed in reading, writing and arithmetic, and could speak English very well. He took it into his head to travel into the Chactaw country: his views were magnanimous, and his designs in the highest degree commendable, nothing less than to inform himself of every species of arts and sciences, that might be of use and advantage when introduced into his own country, but more particularly music and poetry. With these views he privately left the Nation, went to Mobile, and there entered into the service of the trading company to the Chactaws, as a white man; his easy, communicative, active and familiar disposition and manners, being agreeable to that people, procured him access every where, and favoured his subtilty and artifice ... at a great dance and festival in the Mucclasse, a day or two after our arrival, the youth pressed him to give out some of his new songs; he complied with their entreaties, and the songs and dance went round with harmony and eclat. There was a young Chactaw slave girl in the circle, who soon after discovered very affecting sensations of affliction and distress of mind ... (504–5)

This 'young Orpheus,' as Bartram dubs him, has a mesmerizing effect on those who listen to him, so that 'a stranger is for a moment lost to himself' (506); the comparison with Ruth, who hears the American speak 'In finest tones' (26) of a distant land, sheds a 'solitary tear' (93) but agrees to emigrate nonetheless, then loses her own mind upon being deserted, is far from exact but is certainly provocative. By invoking this master of 'subtilty and artifice,' Wordsworth strengthens the impression that there is trouble in paradise, and confirms the status of 'Ruth' as an anti-Pantisocratic or anti-emigration poem. The message is strengthened by a significant revision of Bartram's scenario: for whereas in Bartram it is the songs the young mustee has learned from white men that have sinister effects when imported into Native circles, in 'Ruth' the imposition is entirely a matter of the American youth feeding a vulnerable girl false dreams of an Elysium far removed from the 'civilized,' Christian country she grew up in.

These admonitory allusions to Bartram's text are symptomatic of a wider unease on Wordsworth's part concerning the world Bartram depicts – perhaps occasioned by the rebellious strains of romanticism and noble savagery in Bartram's coolly scientific prose, perhaps aroused by the very foreignness of the nature he represents. For Wordsworth – who is otherwise closely identified with a belief in the moral influence of natural objects – is at pains in 'Ruth' to emphasize that the climate and environment of the southern states is at least partially responsible for the American youth's degeneracy: the 'tumult of a tropic sky' was 'dangerous food' for him (116–7), the 'Irregular' properties of the climate gave a 'kindred impulse' to his own mind (122–4), the sensuous riches of 'Fair trees and lovely flowers' generate equally 'voluptuous' thoughts (128–30), and the 'lawless' (162) life of the Indians he consorts with encourages his own baser instincts. In Lane Cooper's phrase, he has 'accepted a dangerous education from nature' ('Wordsworth's Sources' 499); or, as Carol Bolton puts it, 'Wordsworth portrays America as a heady, exotic land that has disfigured the youth's "moral frame" and now has ruined Ruth's life with its seductive foreign images,' underlining the wisdom of 'accepting the limits of lived experience in one's own world, instead of desiring another existence' (107). I would go further than this. In beginning the series of autobiographical blank verse reflections that evolved into *The Prelude*, a project exactly contemporary with the composition of 'Ruth,' Wordsworth was in no doubt that the ministry of nature was benign in his own case, albeit sometimes severe in its operations. It seems, however, that reading Bartram convinced him that surroundings very different to those of his own childhood – the rugged contours, sparse vegetation, and challenging climate of the English Lake District – might exercise a less positive influence, and this reinforced his suspicion of the kind of utopian dreams of settling in America that had temporarily entranced Coleridge and Southey. Reading travel literature introduced Wordsworth to varieties of landscape shockingly dissimilar to the lakes and mountains of his homeland, and much less easily theorizable in terms of the tutelary power of natural objects. 'Ruth,' perhaps, marks the beginning of Wordsworth's long, elegiac retreat from his belief in the impossibility of nature's betrayal.

Over the course of his poetic career, Wordsworth undoubtedly at times made use of travel books in fairly superficial ways. In 'To H.C. Six Years Old,' for example, his description of Hartley Coleridge as a 'faery voyager' who 'dost float / In such clear water, that thy boat / May rather seem / To brood on air than on an earthly stream' (5–8) makes evocative use of Jonathan Carver's account of canoeing on Lake Superior, where the water 'was as pure and transparent as air; and my canoe seemed as if it hung suspended in that element' (*Travels* 133), but there is no meaningful connection with the content or context of Carver's narrative. Similarly, his self-reproving image, in 'Stanzas Written in my Pocket-Copy of Thomson's "Castle of Indolence,"' of a man who would sit in the shade of an apple tree and 'like a naked Indian, slept himself away' (27), and his memorable description, in *The Prelude*, of his five-year-old self as running wild like 'A naked savage' (1: 304), may possibly allude to Bartram's account of the 'naked red warrior' or 'wandering Siminole' who 'reclines, and reposes' in the shade after the toils of the hunt (Bartram 105);[6] but such casual figures would be guilty of reducing in-depth ethnographic studies in the source material to mere

---

[6]   As Cooper ('Wordsworth's Sources' 499) and Coe (77–8) respectively suggest.

stereotypes. At his most interesting, however, Wordsworth reads travel texts in a way that draws out their inherent tensions and complexities and allows him to work through his own attitudes to foreign peoples and places that explorers, travellers, and colonists were making better known in Britain through the medium of print culture. With ambitions to pronounce on man, on nature, and on human life in his unfinished lifework, *The Recluse*, Wordsworth realized that travel narratives challenged his assumptions about the intrinsic purity and grandeur of the natural environment, about what was universal in human nature and what was practicable and desirable in the organization of human communities; in his best poetry he adapted and subtly reinterpreted those narratives in ways that allowed him to rise to that challenge, becoming in the process one of the most creative and sceptical travel readers of the period.

Samuel Taylor Coleridge

The transition from Wordsworth to his friend, poetic collaborator, and fellow 'Laker,' Coleridge, seems natural enough in any circumstances; my focus upon Wordsworth's response to Bartram's *Travels* in the previous section makes it an even more logical progression, since Bartram has an important place in Coleridge's intellectual history too. Coleridge, like Wordsworth, was an avid reader of travel books: writing to Joseph Cottle in 1797 of the extensive preparation necessary for tackling an epic poem, he lists an impressive range of scientific disciplines in which he would want to become proficient, then adds that he would also want to know 'the *mind of man* – then the *minds of men* – in all Travels, Voyages and Histories' (*Letters* 1: 320–321). Here, the discrimination of 'the *minds of men*' in the explicit context of voyages and travels is a clear acknowledgement that part of the value of such works lay in questioning lazy assumptions about a universal human nature, shared mentalities, and the ease of intercultural communication. Coleridge consumed travel narratives relating to all parts of the globe, including North America, and was as interested in the accounts of older voyages (such as those collected in *Purchas His Pilgrimes* [1625]) as in reports of contemporary ventures. The special significance of North American travels in his literary life was, firstly, that they played a large part in shaping the Pantisocratic emigration scheme that he concocted with Robert Southey, and secondly, that they contributed notably to major poems such as 'The Rime of the Ancyent Marinere' and 'Kubla Khan.'

The story of Pantisocracy, the values of which continued to inform Coleridge's work long after it had passed into history as a viable life-choice, has been told many times, and only the briefest summary is required here. Twelve men and twelve women would settle on the banks of the Susquehanna in Pennsylvania, clearing and cultivating the land and building log cabins to live in, possibly with the assistance of hired labour. Having established their commune on the basis of 'an abolition of individual property' (Coleridge, *Letters* 1: 96), the Pantisocrats would also institute an 'equalization of labour' (Southey, *New Letters* 1: 90), estimating the required input (on a thousand-acre site) at a mere two hours a day. The rest of their time would be devoted to the life of the mind, to personal development, and to the education of their children; even the two hours' work need not be too onerous, for Southey imagined that 'when Coleridge & I are sawing down a tree we shall discuss metaphysics, criticise poetry when hunting a buffalo, & write sonnets whilst following the plough' (*New Letters* 1: 72). The role of women was a slightly tricky area, although it was clear from the start that, despite having disowned possessiveness with regard to property, monogamy was to be the rule. Reclusive and inward-looking as it might sound, Pantisocracy nevertheless had lofty ambitions: by 'removing all Motives to Evil' and making themselves '*necessarily* virtuous' (Coleridge, *Letters* 1: 114), the small band of settlers would begin the task of 'regenerating mankind' (Southey, *New Letters* 1: 71). This project was feasible only in America, Coleridge and Southey believed, sharing with Tom Paine the view that this was 'the only spot in the political world, where the principles of universal reformation could begin' (Paine 159).

Although Joseph Cottle, Coleridge's friend and publisher, later dismissed Pantisocracy as an 'epidemic delusion,' or one of those 'airy schemes of happiness ... projected in every age' that founder on the 'old and intractable leaven in human nature' (Cottle 5, 3), the practicability of the plan does not look quite so far-fetched when placed in its contemporary context, including the wider picture of transatlantic emigration outlined in Chapter 2. As Michael Wiley points out in his excellent overview of the project, the Pantisocrats carried out extensive research, and their ideas were based 'upon many of the perceived realities of the time' (64), not least the real-life example of the famous natural philosopher and radical Dissenter, Joseph Priestley. Although Priestley's grand ambitions for a 700,000-acre settlement, populated by political and religious refugees from Britain, at Northumberland, Pennsylvania (at the junction of two branches of the Susquehanna) were never fulfilled, he himself remained there for the rest of his life and, as an émigré friend of liberty, 'embodied the promise that American emigration held for people like the Pantisocrats' (Wiley 71).

The eminence of Priestley, a fellow Unitarian and the subject of one of Coleridge's early sonnets, would have made him an important influence on the young poet's thoughts about relocation, but there were numerous written accounts by travellers and emigrants that also helped shaped Pantisocracy. The talk of two hours' work a day being sufficient to keep the commune running almost certainly derived from Brissot de Warville's *Travels in the United States of America* (1794), which painted a reassuring picture of the settler way of life in the Ohio country:

> The facility of producing grain, rearing cattle, making whisky, beer, and cyder, with a thousand other advantages, attract to this country great numbers of emigrants from other parts of America. A man in that country works scarcely two hours in a day, for the support of himself and family; he passes most of his time in idleness, hunting, or drinking. (Brissot 1: 219)

As for the specific area of Pennsylvania that the Pantisocrats, following Priestley, favoured for their experiment, they depended on Thomas Cooper's *Some Information Respecting America*, which promoted the state as one in which 'emigrants easily find plenty of land, rich, cheap, well watered, within the reach of navigation, under a good government and in a favourable climate' (23), and described the 'delightful' situation of Northumberland, where the log houses were 'as comfortable, and as clean, and as convenient, as any brick or stone house,' and the soil was 'apparently excellent for almost any kind of vegetation' (105–6), in terms that resonated with the aspiring emigrants. Concerns about 'security from hostile Indians' (Coleridge, *Letters* 1: 99) were relieved on reading Crèvecoeur's account of life in the back country, 'in the bosom of that peace it has enjoyed ever since I have known it, connected with mild, hospitable people, strangers to *our* political disputes, and having none among themselves,' part of a 'little society, united in perfect harmony with the new-adoptive one in which we shall be incorporated' (214–5). Sister Eugenia, surveying the indebtedness of Pantisocracy to American travel literature, also gives special mention to the *Journal* of John Woolman,[7] itinerant Quaker preacher and anti-slavery campaigner, which conveyed the 'beneficial results of trading with the Indians; the opportunity for self-communion possible in the open spaces of America; the leisurely method of living; and the advantages for quiet in literary work' (Eugenia 1078). Woolman's steady conviction that God was 'graciously moving on the hearts of people, to draw them off from the desire of wealth, and bring them into such an humble, lowly way of living, that they may ... repair to the standard of true righteousness' (Woolman 182) would also have appealed to a young visionary possessed of the belief that Pantisocratic communitarianism would be the kernel of a wider social transformation.

These travel narratives, along with others known to have been familiar to Coleridge, such as Gilbert Imlay's *Topographical Description of the Western Territory of North America* (1792), had a key role in shaping and inspiring a small-scale emigration scheme which continued to influence his thought and work long after it ceased to be a going concern. As a letter of March 1801 shows, Coleridge still dreamt of an American idyll even when the interpersonal foundations of Pantisocracy had been recreated in the Lake District, and this entailed a highly selective processing of the relevant travel literature:

> It fills me with indignation to hear the *croaking* accounts, which the English Emigrants send home of America. The society is so bad – the manners so vulgar – the servants so insolent. – Why then do they not seek out one another, & make a society – ? It is arrant ingratitude to talk so of a Land in which there is no Poverty but as a consequence of absolute Idleness. (*Letters* 2: 709–10)

Coleridge provides a perfect digest of the negative reporting on American manners discussed in Chapter 2 – represented most recently for him, perhaps, by Isaac

---

7   Woolman's *Journal* was first published posthumously in 1774 and subsequently republished many times, including a Dublin edition that appeared in 1794.

Weld's *Travels*, published in 1799. Clearly he chose to turn a deaf ear to such prejudiced commentary and to put his faith instead in the eulogistic prose of people like Cooper and Crèvecoeur. Ostensibly, travel writing was of interest chiefly as a source of practical information and advice to would-be emigrants, but, in Coleridge's case, its trustworthiness was evaluated mainly in terms of its conformity to the predisposition of the reader.

This was not the only way Coleridge read travel books, however, and no consideration of him as a travel reader would be adequate without taking account of how such materials fed into his best poetry. Here one has to begin by absorbing the lessons of John Livingston Lowes's classic study, *The Road to Xanadu*, so much of which is concerned with reconstructing the conscious or unconscious influence of voyages and travels, old and new, on 'The Rime of the Ancyent Marinere' and 'Kubla Khan.' Travel narratives have always been of great interest to poets, Lowes argues, because they deal with the boundaries between the known and the unknown, and the imagination (of the quasi-magical workings of which *The Road to Xanadu* is a protracted celebration, in terms largely borrowed from Coleridge himself) is an 'assimilating energy' keen to practise its skills on the novelties and mysteries that lie beyond our current geographical horizons. Above all, Lowes says,

> the appearance of new visitants from beyond the confines of the familiar challenges the creative impulse of the poet to exert its power, and domiciliate the stranger. And the imagination has always leaped to seize, from the vivid and chaotic welter of fresh impressions which crowd the pages of the adventurers, matter which it may transmute into elements of whatever fabric it is shaping. (106)

Matter fit for transmutation was discovered in many kinds of books, as Lowes is keen to demonstrate with close reference to the Gutch Notebook (writing, as he does, well before Coburn's standard scholarly edition of the Notebooks appeared), but travel narratives were a particularly important genre. Reading such books threw up diverse materials that later found their way into poems like 'The Rime of the Ancyent Marinere,' and Lowes stresses that poetic potential could be found in the most unpromising places. He also makes the interesting observation that 'Coleridge not only read books with minute attention, *but he also habitually passed from any given book he read to the books to which that book referred*' (34). Not only did he not respect the integrity of single works in a way that might be more readily associated with the consumption of modern digital media but also his mind was constantly busy, at a largely preconscious level, in linking one set of words and images to others, selecting and combining in a seemingly unstoppable quest of similitude in difference. His was, Lowes asserts, 'one of the most extraordinary memories of which there is record, stored with the spoils of an omnivorous reading, and endowed into the bargain with an almost uncanny power of association' (40). Furthermore, the associative streams that fed into the 'Rime' and 'Kubla Khan' paid no regard to geographical fidelity: east and west could happily interchange, and north could just as easily substitute for south, in the manufacture of compelling poetic images.

This makes Coleridge a rather curious case as a travel reader. He read travel narratives avidly, but not with any discernible intent to furnish his poems with authentic settings or ethnographic content. Instead, his imagination worked promiscuously with travel books of any period, dealing with any part of the world, fashioning its 'ceaseless, vivid flow of ... linked images' (Lowes 377) without regard for topographical or chronological appropriateness. As such, North America, which occupied such a unique, dedicated place in Coleridge's intellectual and affective life in respect of the Pantisocracy scheme, featured only in random and unpredictable ways as a source of ideas and images for his poems. Tim Fulford, for example, has argued that the 'most profound literary response to what Britons wrote about Native Americans' (Fulford 156) was Coleridge's 'Rime of the Ancyent Marinere,' based as it was on his reading in Samuel Hearne, James Adair, and others about the influence of shamans or Indian 'conjurors' over members of their communities, which fuelled his interest in the power of superstition and the equivalent capacity (as he saw it) of his own countrymen for mental enslavement. However, as Fulford also points out, Coleridge also found aids to reflection on this subject in Bryan Edwards's account of the West Indies – indeed, it was the British people's uncanny similarity to 'American and African peoples' (165) more generally that he wanted his readers to think about – and the end product was 'a poem that was not set in America at all and whose hero was not a Romantic Indian but a British sailor' (156).

Although much the same could be said about Coleridge's poetic uses of other North American travel books, it is worth giving consideration to the book that plays such a prominent part in Lowes's study of his imagination – namely, William Bartram's *Travels*. Beginning with the obvious instance of Coleridge's own footnote to Bartram glossing the creaking flight of the 'last rook' in 'This Lime-Tree Bower My Prison,' N. Bryllion Fagin finds Bartram everywhere in his work – in *Osorio*, 'Lewti,' 'The Wanderings of Cain,' 'Christabel,' 'Frost at Midnight,' and elsewhere – to the extent that the English countryside begins to resemble the Georgian savannah. Fagin reminds us too, though, of Lowes's claim – a not inconsiderable claim given the six hundred pages the latter devoted to tracking Coleridge's sources for just two poems – that 'none of the books which Coleridge was reading during the gestation of "The Ancient Mariner" left more lively images in his memory than Bartram's *Travels*' (Lowes 43).

Lowes gives particular attention to a cluster of references in the Gutch Notebook that all derive from the same thirty-page section in the *Travels*. He also finds other passages in that section that seem to have made an impression on Coleridge, such as Bartram's rhapsody on the yellow bream:

> What a most beautiful creature is this fish before me! gliding to and fro, and figuring in the still clear waters, with his orient attendants and associates ... the whole fish is of a pale gold (or burnished brass) colour, darker on the back and upper sides ... the scales are of a proportionable size, regularly placed, and every

where variably powdered with red, russet, silver, blue, and green specks ... the
ultimate angle of the branchiostega terminates by a little spatula, the extreme
end of which represents a crescent of the finest ultramarine blue, encircled with
silver and velvet black. (Bartram 151–2)

The phrase 'velvet black' in particular, Lowes argues, no less than the shared
emotional response to natural beauty, betrays Bartram's influence on the revelatory
appearance of the water-snakes in Part 4 of the 'Rime':

> Within the shadow of the ship
> > I watch'd their rich attire:
> Blue, glossy green, and velvet black
> They coil'd and swam; and every track
> > Was a flash of living fire. (lines 269–73)

However, as Lowes's discussion clarifies, Coleridge's lines on the water-snakes
draw on numerous other sources, including Cook's *Voyage to the Pacific Ocean*,
Purchas's retelling of Richard Hawkins's *Voyage into the South Sea*, Dampier's
New Voyage round the World, Priestley's *Opticks*, and a letter in the *Philosophical
Transactions of the Royal Society*. As Lowes says, the cumulative effect is of 'a
series of passages which might have been devised by an ingenious psychologist
expressly to illustrate the association of ideas' (46): the water-snakes have no
regionally specific provenance, and their connection to the southeastern United
States is entirely adventitious.

Another 'reminiscence' of Bartram that Lowes comments on concerns the
lines in Part 7 of the 'Rime' in which the Hermit compares the sails of the returning
ship to

> The skeletons of leaves that lag
> > My forest brook along:
> When the Ivy-tod is heavy with snow,
> And the Owlet whoops to the wolf below
> > That eats the she-wolf's young. (566–70)

According to Lowes, Coleridge is here recalling a passage from that same part of
the *Travels* that he 'read most intently' (198), in this case an account of meeting a
company of wolves on the Alachua plains:

> we rode up towards them; they observing our approach, sat on their hinder parts
> until we came nearly within shot of them, when they trotted off towards the
> forests, but stopped again and looked at us, at about two hundred yards distance:
> we then whooped, and made a feint to pursue them; when they separated from
> each other, some stretching off into the plains, and others seeking covert in the
> groves on shore. (Bartram 197)

'Unless all signs fail,' Lowes remarks, 'the owlet's whoop to the wolf below
echoed in Coleridge's memory that whoop to the wolves in Florida' (199). While

this may very well be true (no one is in a position to disprove it), it is difficult to do much more with the allusion. Lowes himself argues that the preceding lines draw on Dorothy Wordsworth's journals, Coleridge's own observations of the countryside around Nether Stowey and Alfoxden in 1797–98, and a well-established proverbial phrase; the Bartram reference is thus grafted onto some very homely verbal stock. Coleridge's reading of Bartram serves here purely as a neutral conductor of images, perhaps even just a striking concurrence of sounds: it is neither the intention nor the effect to put Bartram's observations on the natural history of Florida to work in any way that respects their original context; it is merely the juxtaposition of wolves and whooping that seems to have caught the poet's attention and introduced a further element into his characteristic blending of associations.

Arguably, Bartram plays a more consequential role in Lowes's reading of 'Kubla Khan.' Among the group of allusions to Bartram in the notebook on which he lavishes so much attention is a teasing reference to 'Some wilderness-plot, green & fountainous & unviolated by Man' (entry 220). This, Lowes is certain, was inspired by Bartram's Isle of Palms on Lake George in Florida:

> What a beautiful retreat is here! blessed unviolated spot of earth, rising from the limpid waters of the lake: its fragrant groves and blooming lawns invested and protected by encircling ranks of the Yucca gloriosa. A fascinating atmosphere surrounds this blissful garden; the balmy Lantana, ambrosial Citra, perfumed Crinum, perspiring their mingled odours, wafted through Zanthoxylon groves. I at last broke away from the enchanting spot. (Bartram 155).

Impressions of the Isle of Palms, Lowes is equally confident, 'were among the sleeping images in Coleridge's unconscious memory at the time when "Kubla Khan" emerged from it' (333), and must take responsibility for the latter's 'gardens bright with sinuous rills, / Where blossom'd many an incense-bearing tree; / And ... forests ancient as the hills, / Enfolding sunny spots of greenery' (lines 8–11). Even allowing for the possibility that a 'thousand other impressions' (Lowes 333) coexisted in Coleridge's memory with the Bartram passage (most obviously the description of the Mongol emperor's 'stately Palace' in *Purchas his Pilgrimage*, as signposted by Coleridge's prefatory note to the published poem), this does appear a more semantically productive use of the travel-book source material: Bartram's 'enchanting spot' provides a surcharge of real-world charm to the poetic evocation of a legendary earthly paradise, even though this melds the material and imaginative geographies of East and West.

The key additional component of the pleasure dome in Coleridge's poem is, of course, the 'mighty fountain' (19), and Lowes discovers its progenitors in Bartram too. In fact, he uncovers an embarrassment of fountains in the *Travels* that allegedly lent their waters to 'Kubla Khan.' Just a few pages further on from the Isle of Palms passage Bartram writes of an

> amazing crystal fountain, which incessantly threw up, from dark, rocky caverns below, tons of water every minute, forming a bason, capacious enough for large

shallops to ride in, and a creek ... which meanders six miles through green meadows, pouring its limpid waters into the great Lake George ... About twenty yards from the upper edge of the bason, and directly opposite to the mouth or outlet of the creek, is a continual and amazing ebullition, where the waters are thrown up in such abundance and amazing force, as to jet and swell up two or three feet above the common surface. (163–4)

It is easy to see why Lowes links this with Coleridge's mighty fountain that 'flung up' from subterranean sources, through 'ceaseless turmoil,' a river that then 'meander[ed]' for miles through 'wood and dale' before debouching into a larger body of water. However, as Lowes says, Bartram was 'inordinately fond' (336) of ebullient fountains, and later in his expedition the Manatee Springs disclose another 'astonishing' eruption, 'throwing up small particles or pieces of white shells, which subside with the waters at the moment of intermission ... yet, before the surface becomes quite even, the fountain vomits up the waters again, and so on perpetually' (229). Here, it seems, Coleridge derived the image of vaulting 'fragments' and the 'half-intermitted Burst[s]' of activity. Another eight pages on, and Bartram recounts the story, told by an eye-witness, of the last eruption of an 'incomparable fountain' which produced what came to be known as the Alligator Hole:

> looking round, he saw the earth overflowed by torrents of water, which came, wave after wave, rushing down a vale or plain very near him, which it filled with water ... attended with a terrific noise and tremor of the earth ... It continued to jet and flow in this manner for several days, forming a large, rapid creek or river, descending and following the various courses and windings of the valley, for the distance of seven or eight miles, emptying itself into a vast savanna, where was a lake and sink which received and gave vent to its waters ... at places, where ridges or a swelling bank crossed and opposed its course and fury, are vast heaps of fragments of rocks ... which were collected and thrown into the lateral vallies. (237–8)

This passage, Lowes rightly comments, conveys a violent spectacle more akin to Coleridge's 'savage place,' its 'noise and tremor of the earth' reminiscent of the 'fast thick pants' of the land in 'Kubla Khan,' its 'vast heaps of fragments' anticipating the 'Huge fragments' dancing above the pleasure-dome's fountain, and its 'lake and sink' paralleling the 'caverns' and 'lifeless ocean' into which the sacred Alph eventually falls. Taken together, the three passages represent a 'concourse of ... hooked atoms,' or 'confluence of images from ... separate yet closely linked reports of actual fountains' (Lowes 337), that seemingly renders indisputable the proximity of Xanadu to Bartram's Florida.

Once again, though, the picture is more complicated than this, in that an array of other sources potentially contributed to the topography of Coleridge's dream-vision: Lowes cites Bruce's *Travels* in Abyssinia as the origin of the sacred river, and woven in too were elements of the mythical geography of the Nile which Coleridge could have imbibed from various books. America evidently had no more of a monopoly on his imagination where this poem was concerned than it had with regard to the 'Rime.' The depth of allusion to Bartram does give 'Kubla Khan' a particularly strong American connection, however, and in the wake of the Pantisocracy debacle the Elysian strain in Bartram makes his a fertile pre-text for the poem's yearning to recapture the 'deep delight' of its vision of earthly paradise. It is also worth mentioning the links critics have perceived between 'Kubla Khan' and Mary Wollstonecraft's Scandinavian *Letters*: Lowes points out the striking similarities between the 'mighty fountain' and the Trollhätten falls described in Wollstonecraft's Letter 17, while Richard Holmes develops the association by suggesting that Coleridge's 'woman wailing for her demon-lover' may be a figuration of the heart-troubled Wollstonecraft herself (Holmes 41). Recalling Wollstonecraft's own plans, early in her relationship with Gilbert Imlay, to relocate to the United States, and arguing that she came to 'associate the failure of their plans for emigration with the failure of their relationship' (64), Tilar Mazzeo contends that Coleridge 'understood Wollstonecraft's travels as a response to the failure of utopian faith in the transatlantic context' (66) and that 'Kubla Khan' can be interpreted as a response to their shared experience as emigrants *manqués.*

This line of criticism presents 'Kubla Khan,' refreshingly perhaps, as a relatively coherent expression of personal and communal feelings of disorientation and loss, rather than the psychedelic patterns of an opium-fuelled reverie. It also shows Coleridge's reading of travel literature being put to work in his poetry in an earnest and focused way, just as it was in framing his plans for a Pennsylvanian version of pastoral. However, the lesson of Lowes's and others' researches into Coleridge's sources is that he was a very unusual, and very inconsistent, travel reader. With a pet project like Pantisocracy uppermost in his mind, he read travel books with an extraordinarily partial eye, receptive only towards those elements of texts that nourished and endorsed his utopian imaginings. By contrast, in many of his poems, including 'The Rime of the Ancyent Marinere,' memories of travel books, North American travel books among them, were just one branch of a vast reservoir on which he drew in producing a richly overdetermined flow of images, more or less shaped to artistic ends as the individual interpreter decides. His appropriation of fragments of travel narrative or travel description often seems extreme in its disregard of the prior text's own *raison d'être*: he decontextualizes words and phrases, free-associates, and re-engineers meaning with complete abandon; he is the implied reader's demonic alter-ego.

Robert Scholes states that reading has 'two faces,' one looking 'toward the source and original context of the signs we are deciphering,' the other looking 'forward, based on the textual situation of the person doing the reading' (7). Although this is offered as a more general proposition about the interaction between writer and reader, it could also be taken as a fair account of the practice of allusion among writers who engage in constructive, tangible ways with prior texts. As we have seen, however, Coleridge typically pays scant attention to his rear-view mirror; his usual *modus operandi* is the smash-and-grab raid on another writer's most memorable and recombinable utterances. It is strange that the one poem that does seem, in the acts of reading it performs, to look in two directions, both honouring original intent and asserting its own creative role, is the one that has traditionally been viewed as having the 'utter inconsequence' (Lowes 373) of a dream.

Robert Southey

Coleridge's aspiring co-Pantisocrat, Robert Southey, was another enthusiastic reader of travel literature, only too happy to do the job professionally in numerous reviews for the *Annual Review*, *Quarterly Review*, and other periodicals. His commonplace books provide ample evidence of his keen interest in both contemporary and historical travels in all parts of the world, not least (unsurprisingly) in North America, and of his methodical approach to note-taking in respect of travel-related material that might prove serviceable in his poetry. One commonplace book contains a large section headed 'American Tribes,' assembling material from diverse sources, and including dozens of extracts from Jonathan Carver's *Travels* that constitute a potpourri of 'Indian' culture as well as curiosities of natural history; another contains a heterogeneous collection of excerpts from travel books as old as Dampier's *New Voyage* (1697) and as recent as George Vancouver's *Voyage of Discovery to the North Pacific Ocean* (1798) and Thomas Ashe's *Travels in America* (1808). Southey's colloquist in the late *Sir Thomas More* (1829), who describes the revival of exploration and associated multiplication of travel books under George III and declares that 'of such books we cannot have too many' (2: 273), appears to mouth his own lifelong opinion.

One poem in which Southey put to use the miscellaneous information about North America that he had gathered from travel books was his 45-book epic, *Madoc* (1805), where the extent of his dependence is revealed in voluminous prose footnotes that offer revealing insights into his activity as a travel reader. Southey's poem tells the story of the legendary twelfth-century Welsh prince, one of a bewildering number of brothers whose fierce rivalry plunges the nation into civil war upon the death of their father, Owain Gwynedd. Escaping the war-torn country, Madoc goes to sea with a small band of followers and discovers America three hundred years before Columbus. After returning to Wales to recruit as many settlers as he can, he sails west again, never to return. On his first visit, Madoc had formed good relations with the indigenous Hoamen people and liberated them from their Aztec rulers, but declined to occupy the latter's capital city or prohibit their religion, believing that peaceful coexistence was possible provided that they abandon the practice of human blood sacrifice. On his return to America, however, Madoc finds that the Hoamen have been persuaded by scheming Aztec priests into joining a plot against the Welsh settlers; his colonial policy thereupon becomes more aggressive, first putting down the Hoamen rebellion and imposing full Christian conversion upon them, then renewing battle with the Aztecs, his final triumph achieved with the timely assistance of a massive volcanic eruption.

As even this brief plot summary must indicate, *Madoc* represents a later stage on a complicated journey by the erstwhile English Jacobin who had dreamed of a small-scale, peaceful, communitarian settlement on the banks of the Susquehanna. In fact, scholars have shown that the poem has a complex textual history – begun in the summer of 1794, revised in 1797–99, and revised again for eventual publication in 1805) – and therefore shadowed the poet's metamorphosis from 'incendiary young radical to older belligerent Tory apostate' (Pratt 152), or from staunch republican, Unitarian, and cultural relativist to ideologue of 'Christian imperialism' (Leask, 'Southey's *Madoc*' 143). To some extent, the contradictions embodied in this development are preserved in the published text: Carol Bolton argues that the early books of the poem still communicate Southey's 'clear Pantisocratic vision of America,' but that as the narrative progresses this 'becomes muddied by colonial politics and racial anxiety' (80); while Nigel Leask maintains that Madoc's hasty costume-change from medieval peace-loving Pantiscocrat to all-conquering Welsh Cortes who slaughters the Native people and imposes his own religion by force is undermotivated, and that if the Welsh 'are the poem's ultimate victors, it is not always clear that they deserve to be' (148).

Given that virtually everything Southey knew about America came from books, it would not be unreasonable to relate these tensions and ambiguities to his reading of travel narratives. In the heyday of Pantisocracy, Southey, like Coleridge, was inspired by the glowing accounts of salesmen-travellers like Gilbert Imlay and Thomas Cooper, the reassuring reports of Jonathan Carver (made an honorary chief by the Naudowessies), and the Edenic vistas of William Bartram to dream of settling in the United States as a pastoral retreat and political asylum, secure from all the contaminating influences of the Old World. Something of the joyous, prospective mentality of this early phase is still present in the 1805 text, especially in the revelatory moment of first arriving on the coast of Florida in Part 1, Book 4, when 'like a cloud, the distant land arose / Grey from the ocean, . . when we left the ship ... And stood triumphant on another world' (lines 230–233). Southey could have drawn on various travel narratives and other writings[8] to convey the elation of discovery; in fact, to confirm Madoc's detection (before land is sighted) of 'gentle airs, that breathed, / Or seemed to breathe, fresh fragrance from the shore' (224–5), he footnotes Daniel McKinnen's *Tour through the British West Indies* (1804), which states that the 'first notice of the approach of land was the fragrant and aromatic smell of the continent of South America' (Southey, *Works* 2: 282).

In its later stages, Madoc's story becomes more and more embroiled in colonial politics – a world away from the alluring picture painted by land-jobbers like Cooper. Since Southey's own views on international affairs shifted significantly over the years that he was working on the poem, it seems fair to assume that, in a corresponding way, he had started to extract different messages from the travel

---

[8]   In 1795 Southey borrowed John Williams's *Farther Observations on the Discovery of America* (1792) from the Bristol Library (Whalley 119).

literature on which he continued to rely, or had begun to read with a different focus. Carol Bolton usefully highlights the way Madoc rehearses the familiar colonial act of taking linguistic possession of territory by obliterating indigenous names and replacing them with names resonant of the colonizers' homeland (the settlement in Florida is dubbed 'Caermadoc'); Madoc also compares his new surroundings to the remembered landscapes of Wales and insists that the Hoamen learn Welsh. Through such measures, as Bolton suggests, he domesticates the foreign, superimposing 'the outlines of a familiar knowledge system onto one that is alien' (86). Southey would have found such strategies exemplified in much contemporary exploration literature: in Alexander Mackenzie's *Voyages from Montreal* (which he reviewed for the *Annual Review*), for example, or Samuel Hearne's *Journey*. (Ironically, Southey would later ridicule this tendency in his review of the first published account of the Lewis and Clark expedition in the *Quarterly*.)

There is also little doubt that, as he progressed his epic in later years, Southey began to pay more attention to reports in travel narratives and emigrant literature of the dangers and insecurities of colonial life, especially on the frontier. His commonplace book contains a twenty-page excerpt from William Hubbard's *Narrative of the Troubles with the Indians* (1677), which, as its title suggests, provides a graphic account of violent encounters with Native groups. Although this was historical material, it clearly made an impression on Southey. Samuel Hearne's *Journey*, which he called 'one of the most interesting books I have ever seen' (Southey, *Selections* 1: 92), contained many positive and sympathetic representations of the author's close working relationship with the Chipewyan First Nation, but, as we have seen in Chapter 3, the sensationalized report of the Bloody Falls massacre was the part of the book that gripped most readers' imaginations. Jonathan Carver's *Travels*, which Southey comprehensively filleted in his commonplace book and referenced several times in the notes to *Madoc*, provided, on the one hand, a gratifying account of the trader's acceptance by the Naudowessies during a residence of five months and the valuable role he played as a mediator in their conflict with the Chipeways; on the other, it contained a long chapter describing the Indians' 'Manner of Making War' and their sadistic treatment of prisoners which was guaranteed to reinforce dominant negative stereotypes. Troy Bickham has shown how the 'gore of Indian warfare' (67), and the fearsome qualities of Indian warriors who did not 'differentiate between combatants and non-combatants' (80), became a staple newspaper topic during the Seven Years' War, in which Native Americans fought on both sides. Indian cruelty and cunning was again in the headlines during the War of Independence, when the British government had to deal with public unease over employing 'savages' against their own compatriots. With more recent travel books adding fuel to these established perceptions of how nasty, brutish, and short life in the New World could be, it is not impossible to understand how 'the peaceful philosophical precepts of Pantisocracy' gave way to 'the instability and anxiety of the colonial frontier in *Madoc*' (Bolton 95). Travel literature played a large part in shaping both perspectives: it was either a case of Southey reading different travel books, or, perhaps, of American travel books being read by a different Southey at different times.

The fierce and vengeful character of Native Americans, along with their martial pride and reverence for the warlike deeds of their ancestors, are also to the fore in Southey's 'Songs of the American Indians,' written in 1799 and collected in his *Metrical Tales* (1805).[9] Although these poems purport to be the dramatized utterances of members of specific nations (Huron, Araucana, Chickasaw), they present a familiar composite portrait of 'Indian' psychology and society. 'The Huron's Address to the Dead' is a funeral lament for a once great warrior ('Unhappy man was he / For whom thou hadst sharpened the tomahawk's edge!' [83]), who is laid to rest in a 'coffin of bark' with his bow and arrows and despatched to the 'Country of the Dead' (85). 'Song of the Araucans during a Thunderstorm' imagines the commotion in the heavens as a ghostly re-enactment of their ancestors' successful resistance against the Spanish invaders ('Pursue them! pursue them! remember your wrongs, / Let your lances be drunk with their wounds' [91]). In 'Song of the Chikkasah Widow' the singer looks forward to avenging her dead husband by torturing and killing prisoners of war:

> The stake is made ready, the captives shall die;
> To-morrow the song of their death shalt thou hear;
>   To-morrow thy widow shall wield
>   The knife and the fire; . . be at rest! (92)

Themes of combat, revenge, and honouring fallen warriors again provide the kernel of 'The Old Chikkasah to his Grandson,' in which a young Indian is urged to fulfil his destiny by killing his father's conquerors:

> Go now and revenge him my Boy!
> That his Spirit no longer may hover by day
>   O'er the hut where his bones are at rest,
>   Nor trouble our dreams in the night. (97)

The use in these latter two poems of a female speaker and a juvenile addressee reinforces the impression of an entire population indoctrinated in a culture of violence, moderated only by family honour and a penchant for ritual and ceremony.

In composing these songs, Southey may well be drawing on a variety of sources, some of them undoubtedly containing more precisely informed ethnographies, but the cumulative effect of the 'Songs' is one-dimensional and stereotypical. Carver's *Travels*, for instance, includes material on the merciless treatment of prisoners, and the need to prepare the dead for an afterlife very similar to the life they have just departed ('They ... bury with them their bows, their arrows, and all the other

---

[9]   Quotations from these poems, not all of which are included in the new scholarly edition of Southey's *Poetical Works*, are cited by page number in *Metrical Tales*.

weapons used either in hunting or war' [402]), which certainly parallels aspects of the 'Songs.' On the other hand, Carver also describes Indian hunting methods, feasts and dances, recreations, and forms of government – none of which seems to make much impression on Southey. Southey is fixated on the Indians' 'Manner of Making War' and oblivious to their 'Manner of Making Peace' (both chapter titles in Carver's book). He appears to have swallowed Carver's verdict (substantially qualified in context) that Indians are 'guided by passions and appetites, which they hold in common with the fiercest beasts that inhabit their woods' (408), and to have had no appetite for any contrary, humanizing elements in his account.

The extensive footnotes to *Madoc* do, however, show Southey incorporating other aspects of his travel reading in the poem in addition to the Indian propensity for violence. On the one hand, he shows a keen interest – reflected in his commonplace book – in matters of natural history: from John Atkins's *Voyage to Guinea, Brasil, and the West Indies* (1735), for example, he takes evidence of the beautiful appearance of dolphins; from John Davis's *Travels ... in the United States of America* (1803) he glosses his allusion to the mockingbird; and from Bartram's *Travels* he substantiates a description of the wild turkey-cock's loud dawn chorus. In these cases, referencing of travel books indicates a desire to create a realistic backdrop to the improbable events of the poem, or to give the legend of Madoc (which Southey knew by 1805 to be a fabrication) a foothold in the territory of empirical truth. On the other hand, he also draws on travel literature to provide a scholarly subtext to his representation of the customs and beliefs of indigenous peoples. However, this apparently scrupulous regard for authenticity largely dissolves on closer inspection, given the fearless way in which Southey mixes such heterogeneous materials. In sections of the poem dealing with the Hoamen on matters such as the pretensions of Indian conjurors, the design of Indian council-halls, and beliefs regarding the afterlife and the restless spirits of those who have died without equal loss of enemy blood, he cites the authority of David Brainerd's *Journal* (1748), Henry Timberlake's *Memoirs* (1765), Carver's *Travels* (1778), and Adair's *History of the American Indians* (1775). Any distinctions arising from the fact that Brainerd's dealings were with the Delaware nation, Timberlake was writing of the Cherokees, Carver resided with the Dakota Sioux, and Adair's remarks were inspired by the Creeks are entirely obliterated in Southey's generalizing treatment.

In similar fashion, when describing the Aztecs Southey sees fit to draw on such diverse sources as Thomas Jefferson (speaking of the Delawares) and George Heriot (writing of the Natchez). It seems that information from just about any ethnographical source can be taken out of context and gratefully spooned into a general repository of what H. N. Fairchild called 'savage lore.' Southey, of course, was not alone in the period in adopting such an approach (nor were some of the travellers just cited averse to making sweeping statements about 'Indians,' at least some of the time), but he does practise this idealizing and homogenizing technique to an extraordinary degree for a scholar so well read in the primary literature. It is, finally, striking that so many of Southey's learned references concern issues of superstition, ritual, and folk medicine, where the pay-off in terms of British readers' self-satisfaction is assured – rather than focusing, for instance, on travellers' (plentiful) observations of Native peoples' resourcefulness and adaptability. Astrid Wind correctly remarks that Southey gathers 'information about the Indians from sources that span three centuries' and condenses this 'vast and varied material into a single picture of Indian society,' depicting Indians as 'a static people' whose 'cultures make no significant progress until they come in contact with their European discoverers' (49). It was essential to the argument of *Madoc* that he constructed such a picture, and he put his formidable knowledge as a travel reader in the service of that thesis, construing texts with or against the grain as required. Quite unlike Coleridge's freewheeling misappropriation of phrases and images from a multitude of sources, Southey read travel books carefully, methodically, yet very single-mindedly: he knew what he wanted to find in such books and was adept at filtering out anything that did not match his predetermined criteria.

Thomas Moore

Thomas Moore (1779–1852) was a young man when he toured the United States and Upper and Lower Canada in 1803–04 and recorded his impressions in a series of poems that appeared piecemeal in his *Epistles, Odes, and Other Poems* (1806), and were later grouped together more coherently as 'Poems Relating to America.'[10] Moore's adolescence had been influenced by the euphoria of the early years of the French Revolution and the subsequent disillusionment of its perceived descent into anarchy. Unlike the slightly older Wordsworth and Coleridge who also rode this emotional rollercoaster, Moore was in Ireland, where he supported the Irish Rebellion, engaged in radical student politics at Trinity College, Dublin, and was close friends with leading United Irish activist Robert Emmet, who was later to be publicly hanged, drawn, and quartered. Jeffery Vail concludes that Moore was therefore 'well situated among the prominent writers of the time to appreciate not only the horrors of violent revolution, but also the barbarity and injustice of which the English government and the Protestant Ascendancy in Ireland were all too capable,' and was less likely than most to be 'pushed to the Right' (43).

Having learned in growing up to think of America as a terrestrial paradise, Moore visited the United States as a friend to liberty, predisposed to be favourably impressed, and so his subsequent disenchantment, which mirrored that of so many other British and Irish travellers who could not come to terms with cultural difference, was all the more severe. He travelled initially to take up the post of Admiralty registrar in Bermuda, where he arrived in January 1804 after a two-month stay in Norfolk, Virginia; finding his income derisory, he immediately started planning his escape, and after making the most of the island's social scene

---

10   For a factual account of the tour, see Jones, *The Harp*, ch. 4.

he left for New York on 25 April. His route then took him back to Norfolk, and onward to Richmond, Fredericksburg, Washington, and Philadelphia (where he was befriended and entertained by Joseph Dennie and his literary circle), before returning to New York. He then headed north to the tourist honeypot of Niagara, where he enthused in conventional terms over the sublime spectacle, crossed into Upper Canada, and descended the St Lawrence by boat before leaving for England from Halifax, Nova Scotia, sometime in October. The eventual publication of *Epistles, Odes*, with its fierce anti-American flavour, produced a long-lasting estrangement between Moore and his American audience; ten years later he regretted having published his 'crude and boyish tirades' and was prepared to acknowledge once more 'the bright promise which America affords of a better and happier order of things than the World has ... ever yet witnessed' (*Letters* 1: 397).

Moore tried to explain or excuse his hostile reaction to the United States by declaring that he had judged the 'abuse' rather than the 'use' of 'democratic principles,' and that the 'little information' he had taken the trouble to seek out had come to him 'through twisted and tainted channels' (*Letters* 1: 458). Although the latter phrase could be interpreted in different ways, it could well refer to the travel narratives in which Moore was clearly well versed by the time of his visit, since the footnotes to *Epistles, Odes* conduct a dialogue with some of the best-known British and French authors on transatlantic themes. It would have been disingenuous of Moore to blame written sources entirely for his pejorative opinion of the United States, however, because the notes show that he was conversant with both flattering and unflattering accounts.

The bulk of the opprobrium that Moore heaped on Jeffersonian America is contained in four verse epistles. Herbert Eldridge neatly summarizes his 'satirical target' in these poems as 'the familiar difference between man's foolish hopes and ideals and his actual moral and political performance'; Moore, he adds, 'depicts himself as representative of the youthful hope and idealism of his generation back home, undergoing maturation as the realities of the New World unfold during his travels' (55). In 'To Miss Moore, from Norfolk, in Virginia' he laments the disappointment of his 'glorious dreams' (18)[11] of 'man's new world of liberty' (17), a refuge for all those fleeing 'From the dark ills of other skies, / From scorn, or want's unnerving woes' (16). The poem itself does not explain the causes of this disappointment, but a long footnote blames Imlay, Crèvecoeur, and other unidentified 'French travellers' for disseminating seductive views of the United States and saying nothing of its 'vulgarity of vice' (17), which Moore sees as a symptom of the toxic spread of French Jacobinism. He acknowledges that Norfolk is a particularly 'unfavourable specimen of America' (18) and refers readers to Isaac Weld and La Rochefoucauld-Liancourt (author of the rapidly translated *Travels through the United States of North America* [1799]) for further information on this point. This long note handily encapsulates Moore's strategy of continuing in prose a defamation begun in verse, by the complementary means

[11]   References are to page numbers in *Epistles, Odes*.

of scorning the misrepresentations of pro-American ideologues and quoting with approval the negative impressions of less sympathetic travellers. More focused in its assault is 'To Lord Viscount Forbes, from Washington,' which adduces the flagrant contradiction of institutionalized slavery in a free state ('slaving blacks and democratic whites, / And all the pye-bald polity that reigns / In free confusion o'er Columbia's plains' [160–161]), along with the 'love of gold' and corruption in public office, as proof of the premature decay of political ideals in the New World. Moore cites Jedediah Morse's *American Geography* (1789) as illustration of the irrational yet persistent desire to 'stamp perfection on this world at last' (155).[12]

'To Thomas Hume, Esq. M. D. from the City of Washington,' perhaps the most controversial of the epistles in that it repeats a popular libel that Jefferson had a black mistress, draws extensively on Weld's *Travels* in a series of footnotes to fortify its satirical portrait of the federal city as a second Rome. (It is worth noting that although there is light irony in Weld's allusion to the naming of 'the spot of ground on which the capitol now stands' as 'Rome' [Weld 83], he also predicts straight-facedly that Washington 'will become the grand emporium of the west, and rival in magnitude and splendour the cities of the old world' [80]. Moore, that is, presents Weld as much more derogatory towards the United States than he actually was.) This poem takes the course of contrasting the sublime natural scenery of America with both the 'half-organiz'd, half-minded race / Of weak barbarians' who are its original inhabitants and the European settlers, the 'motley dregs of every distant clime' (190), who are taking their place. Moore again attempts to consolidate his position in a lengthy footnote: alluding to the environmental and climatic determinism espoused by Buffon and Cornelius De Pauw, who insisted on the degeneracy of American nature (in which they included Native Americans), Moore states that the picture 'drawn of the American Indian, though very humiliating, is, as far as I can judge, much more correct than the flattering representations which Mr Jefferson has given us' (190). Moore's qualifying clause seems appropriate: his tour was, after all, a limited one, and his only first-hand experience of Native Americans seems to have been a brief encounter with the Oneida at Niagara, who 'received the little man courteously' (H. M. Jones 83); Jefferson, whose *Notes on the State of Virginia* set out to refute Buffon's and De Pauw's theories, had a greater claim to authority. Neither of the latter philosophers had ever set foot on American soil, and they based their ideas solely on travellers' reports; Moore's 'evidence' for his hostile representation therefore consists of third-hand subjective impressions.

There is a similar contrast of the mighty world of American nature and the poverty of mind and spirit that exists alongside it in 'To the Honourable W. R. Spencer, from Buffalo, upon Lake Erie.' 'Christians, Mohawks, democrats and all / From the rude wigwam to the congress-hall' are condemned alike for their moral

---

[12]   In the same passage of the *Geography*, but not quoted by Moore in his footnote, Morse declares that it is 'well known that empire has been travelling from east to west,' and suggests that 'her last and broadest feat will be America' (469).

and intellectual torpidity; the speaker is apparently alone in heeding the 'muse of inspiration' (239). Here, Moore cites travel writing – Charlevoix's *Journal of a Voyage to North America* (1761) – to underpin his description of the 'grand and lovely' natural scenery (238), but declines any secondary authority for his indictment of the human population. Instead he merely adds a long note to identify (as 'Mr Dennie and his friends') the 'sacred few' (240) who provided him with civilized companionship in Philadelphia, and who offer hope that the future of the country will not be doomed forever to 'mob-mania' (241).

In many of his aspersions on the United States, Moore seems to have followed the lead of Isaac Weld's *Travels*: Weld, for instance, complains repeatedly that Americans are 'totally dead to the beauties of nature' (2: 328), a tendentious claim that Moore seems intent on publicizing in his epistles. And like Weld before him, who felt more at home once he had crossed the border into Canada, and urged potential emigrants to settle there rather than in the States, Moore's spirits, on the evidence of his poems, lifted considerably on entering British North America.[13] His 'Ballad Stanzas,' though they make no explicit reference to travel books, are of particular interest in this connection. D. M. R. Bentley makes the important point that this poem, by virtue of its position in the (loose) sequence of *Epistles, Odes*, is a kind of 'homecoming poem, a poem whose positive and reposeful tone reflects its author's "relief" at being back on "British ground"' ('Construction'). The tone is certainly different to the bad-tempered, declamatory style of the American tour poems:

> I knew by the smoke, that so gracefully curl'd
>   Above the green elms, that a cottage was near,
> And I said, 'If there's peace to be found in the world,
>   A heart that was humble might hope for it here!'
>
> It was noon, and on flowers that languish'd around
>   In silence repos'd the voluptuous bee;
> Every leaf was at rest, and I heard not a sound
>   But the wood-pecker tapping the hollow beech-tree. (257)

Bentley argues convincingly that the second stanza here alludes to a passage in Weld describing a journey through a wood, where 'the most solemn silence imaginable reigned throughout, except where a woodpecker was heard now and then tapping with its bill against a hollow tree' (Weld 2: 320). If so, the poem may well invoke the general context of Weld's discouragement of American emigration and counterbalancing praise of Canadian settlers and their way of life. With its elaboration (in the third and fourth stanzas) of a patriarchal idyll of sharing the

---

[13]   Moore's principal tourist destination in visiting Canada was, of course, Niagara Falls, and, although he made the usual noises about the inadequacies of language to convey the experience, he wrote to his mother that Weld's account was 'the most accurate I have seen' (*Letters* 1: 77).

lonely cottage with a blushing maid who will play Eve to the speaker's Adam, 'Ballad Stanzas' would thereby give rhetorical force to Weld's politically inflected travelogue, constructing Upper Canada as (in Bentley's words) 'a refuge from the post-lapsarian world, a green and shady garden to one side of the United States.'

This more romanticized approach to Canada continues in Moore's celebrated 'Canadian Boat-Song,' loosely adapted, according to his elaborate note, from a song supposedly sung by *voyageurs* as they set out on their annual journey from Montreal to Grand Portage on the Utawas River. The poem begins:

> Faintly as tolls the evening chime,
> Our voices keep tune, and our oars keep time.
> Soon as the woods on shore look dim,
> We'll sing at St Ann's our parting hymn.
> Row, brothers, row, the stream runs fast,
> The Rapids are near and the daylight's past! (275–6)

It is quite possible that this poem, too, owes an unacknowledged debt to Moore's fellow countryman, Weld, who describes in his own journey down the St Lawrence how the French-Canadian oarsmen keep up a musical accompaniment with singing and have one 'favourite duet ... which as they sing they mark time to, with each stroke of the oar' (Weld 2: 51). Moore's acknowledged debt, though, is to Alexander Mackenzie and his account of the *voyageurs'* annual journey into the interior. In a separate note to line 4 of the poem, he quotes Mackenzie's observation that it is at the rapids at St Ann's 'that the Canadians consider they take their departure, as it possesses the last church on the island [of Montreal], which is dedicated to the tutelar saint of the voyagers' (Mackenzie 85). One effect of this citation is to flesh out the geographical specificity implied by the presence of place-names in the 'Boat-Song' and to root its beguiling lyricism in recorded experience. At the same time, however, the effect is to incorporate more compellingly that feeling of imaginative 'expansion' to which Francis Jeffery, in his review in the *Edinburgh* (see Chapter 3), responded in the scale and difficulty of Mackenzie's undertaking. Bentley modifies this by suggesting that the 'tranquil and wistful mood' of the poem 'lends psychological complexity to the *voyageurs* and ... constructs or construes them as sensitive and introspective Romantics whose piety marks them as part of a culture that has escaped the *bouleversement* of the French Revolution' ('Near the Rapids' 362). Whatever the precise inflection, it remains the case that Moore's travel sources work in an entirely different way – supply an inspirational, affirming gloss – in the Canadian, as opposed to the American, part of *Epistles, Odes*. Moore, in fact, presents a striking case of a poet who makes thoroughly tendentious use of travel literature, alternately to vilify the United States and to romanticize British possessions, and he does this almost exclusively via the paratextual means of the discursive footnote.

In the last of his epistolary tour poems, 'To the Lady Charlotte Rawdon, from the Banks of the St Lawrence,' Moore cites a plethora of British and French travellers in North America – Thomas Anburey, Charlevoix, Mackenzie, Carver, the Baron de Lahontan, Morse, Jean Bossu, Imlay, Joseph-François Lafitau – to authenticate details of the nature description he supplies either *in propria persona* or in the embedded chant of a departed 'Indian Spirit.' In the poem's concluding verse paragraphs, Moore declares that, despite the manifold attractions of 'this blooming maze / Of lovely nature' (he alludes to Niagara Falls, Lake Ontario, and the Thousand Islands area of the St Lawrence River), he is happiest when some object or sensation reminds him of home ('Trent's inspiring stream ... Donington's green lawns') and of pleasures he shared with the female addressee (286). The poem thus highlights the importance of human and cultural associations in mediating one's experience of nature: 'landscape is the work of the mind,' in Simon Schama's neat formulation, its scenery 'built up as much from strata of memory as from layers of rock' (7). Perhaps this helps explain the very proliferation of documented travel sources in the apparatus of *Epistles, Odes*: in a colonial situation, travel writers prepare the ground for the poet, providing a set of reference points or rudimentary pre-knowledge of an area, which aesthetic travellers, following the paths they have broken, then develop, adapt, and interpret. Faced with a landscape largely bereft of the 'strata' of accumulated historical significance, Moore cluttered his poems with references to recent travel books in order to give them an emergency injection of cultural capital. To put it another way, poems are often said to be built out of other poems, but in a colonial context, writing poems about places and landscapes that had yet to acquire an Anglophone poetic tradition, Moore draws on travel writing as the next best thing to a heritage in verse.

It is, finally, a nice irony that Moore, having felt the want of literary associations in his passage down the St Lawrence – he is forced to invoke the Bible and Dante's *Purgatorio* by way of a more elite intertext – should then himself have provided rich layers of associations for later visitors and writers. His 'Canadian Boat-Song' quickly became the best-known poem about Canada, and by the 1830s it seems that renditions of it had already become part of the 'tourist experience' on the St Lawrence, while the location of the 'cottage' and 'sumach' tree mentioned in 'Ballad Stanzas' were soon as eagerly debated as the precise location of the dark sycamore where Wordsworth allegedly composed 'Tintern Abbey.' In an emigration tract published in 1831, 'literary resonances' generated by Moore 'were held to add to the appeal of North American locales for prospective emigrants' (Bentley, 'Construction') a somewhat bizarre outcome, it has to be said, given the attitudes held by many of the travel writers whom he was fond of citing.

Thomas Campbell

'If I were not a Scotsman, declared Thomas Campbell late in life, 'I should like to be an American' (*Life* 3: 420). Campbell (1777–1844), author of *The Pleasures of Hope* (1799) and, more relevantly to this discussion, *Gertrude of Wyoming* (1809), never visited the United States, although he had strong family connections with the country: his father spent the early part of his life in Virginia, establishing himself in the tobacco business, while his uncle and two of his brothers also adopted America as their home (Duffy 346–7). As a young man struggling to make a living after graduating from Glasgow University, he was on the verge of emigrating himself before his eldest brother intervened and instructed him not to 'quit Britain' until he had 'acquired more useful knowledge.' Thus, despite the fact that his political sympathies drew him in that direction (in the same letter, written in March 1798, he states that 'Ever since I knew what America was, I have loved and respected her government and state of society' [*Life* 1: 225]), he never made it across the Atlantic, and his travels were restricted to Europe. Unlike Thomas Moore, his knowledge of America was derived almost exclusively from books, including many of the same travel writers who have already figured prominently in this chapter. This did not prevent Washington Irving from crediting Campbell with having performed an important service in taking a part of the American landscape (the Wyoming valley on the Susquehanna) and colouring it with literary associations, imbuing a locality with 'a charm that dignifies it in the eyes of the stranger, and endears it to the heart of the native' (qtd in Duffy 351).

Gertrude of Wyoming deals with a notorious episode in the War of Independence in which Loyalist forces, assisted by Iroquois allies, killed more than three hundred American settlers at Forty Fort in the Wyoming Valley in Pennsylvania. Alleged atrocities committed against non-combatants, prisoners, and fleeing soldiers made the incident controversial in Britain and intensified unease – present since the French and Indian War of 1757–63, in which Native groups also fought on both sides – over British or Loyalist troops fighting side by side with Indian 'savages' against white settlers who were still, essentially, their compatriots. Campbell's poem simplifies what was in actuality a very messy colonial situation. His 'Advertisement' states that 'the testimonies of historians and travellers concur in describing the infant colony as one of the happiest spots of human existence, for the hospitable and innocent manners of its inhabitants, the beauty of the country, and luxuriant fertility of the soil and climate,' but that in 'an evil hour, the junction of European and Indian arms, converted this terrestrial paradise into a frightful waste' (3). In fact, as Tim Fulford informs us, the Wyoming settler community had been 'wracked by strife between Pennsylvania and Connecticut colonists competing for the same land since it was first sold by the Indians in 1755'; by the start of the War of Independence, 'old feuds between the settlers were entrenched,' and the War 'allowed their renewal, with the aid of the British and of Indians who resented settlers' attempts to expand into their territory' (186–7).

Campbell's alternative rendering of events pits virtuous Patriots against the British and their Mohawk allies, 'unearthly fiends' (part 3, stanza 19)[14] led by the 'Monster Brandt' (3: 16).[15] In the first part, an Oneida chief called Outalissi rescues a young boy, Henry Waldegrave, from a Huron assault on a British

---

[14]   Subsequent parenthetical references to the poem cite part and stanza number only, to facilitate reference to different editions. References to the notes cite page numbers in the fifth edition (1814).

[15]   In fact, as Campbell later had to acknowledge when confronted by Brandt's son, Brandt and his Mohawk followers played no part in the massacre; it was Seneca warriors who assisted the British.

settlement and, at the request of his dying mother, delivers him into the care of Albert, Gertrude's widowed father. In the intervening period, Outalissi has taken a paternal interest in Henry, and he sings him a parting song in which he promises, should the occasion arise, to teach him 'in the battle's-shock, / To pay with Huron blood thy father's scars' (1: 26). In part 2, Henry, who has apparently been away in England for a number of years, returns, initially in disguise, and claims the love of Gertrude. Part 3 narrates the outbreak of the War of Independence – 'When Transatlantic Liberty arose ... wrapt in whirlwinds, and begirt with woes' (3: 6) – and Henry's determination to join the Patriot army. Before the massacre itself, in which Albert and Gertrude are killed, an elderly Outalissi returns, now the last of his tribe following a battle with Brandt's Mohawks, and the poem ends with his death-song, in which he urges his 'Christian boy' (3: 35) to avenge the slaughter of his loved ones.

Like Southey and Moore, Campbell supplies his poem with extensive prose notes, drawing mainly on contemporary travel literature, and added to these in later editions to make use of more recently published material. Isaac Weld's *Travels* seem to have been a principal reference point for Campbell, as they were for Moore, his Advertisement citing Weld's observation that 'the ruins of many of the villages' in Wyoming, 'perforated with balls, and bearing marks of conflagration, were still preserved by the recent inhabitants' (3) when he passed through in 1796. This sets the tone for the pro-American bias of the poem that follows, since Weld, who was unsympathetic to so many features of republican America, was nevertheless under no illusions about the 'dreadful massacre,' which he asserted would 'forever remain a blot on the English annals' (Weld 2: 351). Campbell, however, chooses to ignore Weld's more complex portrait of Joseph Brandt, which takes full measure of his propensity for violence and indiscipline but also acknowledges that he has 'managed the affairs of his own people with great ability' [2:282], endeavouring to strengthen their position by not getting sucked into the internal disputes of white colonists. By reading Weld selectively in this way, Campbell facilitates his strategy of setting stereotypical 'good Indians' and 'bad Indians' in opposition to each other, so that he can 'play down the guilt of the British and of the American settlers' (Fulford 192).

Campbell's notes, heavily concentrated in the first part of the poem, fall into two broad categories: a small number of notes concerning facts of natural history, and a much larger number that deal with the 'manners and customs' of the 'Indians' – subject-matter that was, as we have seen, a standard constituent of North American travel narratives. In the first category are a quotation from Thomas Ashe's detailed description of the mockingbird, to gloss the poem's reference to the 'merry mock-bird's song' (1: 3), which provides a delightful accompaniment to life in pre-war Wyoming; and a passage from Bartram on the terrifying appearance of the alligator, used to heighten the impact of the farewell speech at the end of part 1 in which Outalissi offers to teach Henry to sport with such creatures, as preparation for his revenge on the Huron. Campbell concludes the latter note with Bartram's comment that an 'old champion' alligator 'acts his part like an Indian chief, when rehearsing his feats of war' (*Gertrude* 111), thus cementing its relevance to the role of Outalissi. However, the fact that an Oneida chief would have been highly unlikely ever to have seen an alligator, a resident of the southeastern United States, indicates that strict factual accuracy was less important in this context than a general sense of exotic American-ness.

In the second category of footnote, Campbell displays boundless zeal in marshalling evidence from reputable travel writers to authenticate aspects of his presentation of Outalissi – who, to modern readers, conversely appears a stereotypical noble savage. In the first edition of 1809, Campbell drew on Cadwallader Colden's *History of the Five Indian Nations of Canada* (1747) to validate Outalissi's offer of a wampum belt as a token of friendship, as well as his 'metaphorical manner' of speaking; Ashe's *Travels* for a humorous gloss on the use of the calumet or pipe of peace; Jefferson's *Notes on Virginia* for a real-life parallel to phrases from Outalissi's death-song; and, once again, the ubiquitous Isaac Weld to enlighten readers on aspects of Indian childcare and – at great length – the highly developed pathfinding skills that Outalissi apparently possesses in common with 'North American Indians' in general. By the time the fifth edition of *Gertrude of Wyoming* appeared in 1814, Campbell had evidently furthered his research on Indian ethnography and acquainted himself with early reports of the Lewis and Clark transcontinental expedition.[16] From the latter, he pulled additional material to support his description of Outalissi's 'swarthy lineament' (1: 13) and 'Impassive' temperament (1: 23) and bolster unnecessarily his praise of the 'trained eye' with which the Oneida warrior found his way through the wilderness. From older accounts, such as Robert Rogers's *Concise Account of North America* (1765) and Adair's *History of the American Indians* (1775), he extracted further information on wampum belts, the pipe of peace, and the 'active as well as passive fortitude of the Indian character' (*Gertrude* 97), while from Charlevoix's *Journal* he was able to corroborate the seriousness with which Outalissi treated dreams, as 'the most ordinary way in which the gods make known their will to men' (108).

These long and varied footnotes – of which the above summary is by no means a complete rendering – comprise a melting-pot of discrete items of information which, in their original context, often relate to specific Native groups or 'tribes' but which, in Campbell's redaction, lose their identity as part of a rich stew of 'authentic' knowledge about American Indians in the round. Campbell, a self-professed lover of the United States, was an enthusiastic reader of North American travels who kept pace with this lively area of literary production. What seem to have interested him most are 'facts' relating to the indigenes of that continent, which he proceeded to deploy eagerly and indiscriminately in constructing his poetically appealing portrait of a heroic Indian combining manly virtues with an intuitive understanding of the natural environment. Like Southey and Moore, he applied a simplifying lens to his reading, concerned more with what he could integrate into his overall poetic design (which had an opposite tendency to those other poets' projects) than with enriching his geographical or ethnographical

---

[16]   In fact, Campbell's knowledge seems to be limited to one of several bastardized compilations, masquerading as the authentic *Travels* of Lewis and Clark, which appeared from 1807 onwards; see Coues 1: cviii–cxvii for details.

knowledge. If all his efforts at documentary verisimilitude nonetheless resulted in a figure who, to modern eyes, epitomizes a stale eighteenth-century brand, it may just go to show how little our notions of characterization now have to do with surface realism and generic traits – a wampum belt here, an emotionless exterior there – as opposed to novelistic forms of interiority and individual psychology.

Felicia Hemans

As a final example of a Romantic-period travel reader with a strong interest in North America, we can take Felicia Hemans (1793–1835). Like Thomas Campbell, Hemans never visited the United States (despite the internationalism of her work, she seems never to have ventured outside Britain and Ireland), although her father deserted the family for Canada while she was still a child, her third brother became deputy assistant commissary-general in Upper Canada, and two of her sons later went to America, one in the capacity of British consul at Buffalo, New York (Sweet). Her poetry was hugely popular in the United States, where it was republished frequently during the nineteenth century; at the height of her fame she was offered (but declined) a lucrative sinecure as editor of a magazine, with no requirement to perform any editorial duties. On the evidence of her poetry, which makes copious use of prose headnotes and footnotes, Hemans was an avid consumer of travel literature, and in some respects she filters and interprets her sources more aggressively than any of the male contemporaries I have discussed above.

Several of Hemans's poems perform variations on the popular genre of the Indian death-song, which in its classic form was the utterance of a proud warrior enduring excruciating tortures and confronting inevitable death with perfect equanimity, often continuing to hurl abuse at his enemies while they took sadistic pleasure in his degradation. 'Edith, a Tale of the Woods' is based, according to Hemans's note, on incidents narrated in Lydia Sigourney's *Sketches of Connecticut* (1824). Edith is an Englishwoman whose husband dies in battle; she is then looked after by an elderly Native American couple who have lost their own daughter. Through the influence of her own piety Edith succeeds in converting the couple to Christianity before she herself wastes away. The 'ancient warrior of the waste' (Hemans 5: 175) then sings a kind of death song for her, turning the conventions of the genre upside-down with its sentimental evocation of weeping nature and heavenly pastures:

> The mossy grave thy tears have wet,
>   And the wind's wild moanings by,
> Thou with thy kindred shalt forget,
>   'Midst flowers – not such as die.

> The shadow from thy brow shall melt
>   The sorrow from thy strain,
> But where thine earthly smile hath dwelt
>   Our hearts shall thirst in vain. (5: 179)

Throughout, American forest scenery – boundless woods emphasizing the burdensome solitude – provide a suitably awe-ful setting for the story. In the 'Indian Woman's Death-Song,' based (Hemans informs us) on an episode in William Keating's *Narrative of an Expedition to the Source of St Peter's River* (1824), a blank-verse opening paragraph sets the scene of the eponymous woman in a canoe, her baby asleep at her breast, heading 'dauntlessly' towards a waterfall and inevitable self-destruction (5: 192). She seeks oblivion in response to her husband having 'look'd upon another's face,' and, in taking responsibility for rescuing her little girl from the possibility of a similar fate, she generalizes the pain of her own abandonment:

> And thou, my babe! though born, like me, for woman's weary lot,
> Smile! – to that wasting of the heart, my own! I leave thee not;
> Too bright a thing art *thou* to pine in aching love away,
> Thy mother bears thee far, young Fawn! from sorrow and decay. (5: 194)

The poem thus somewhat ambiguously feminizes the death song, evoking female courage of an order conventionally assigned to male warriors, yet implying that there is no other valid response by a woman to desertion by her partner than self-annihilation.

A third example of the genre, which does not name a specific source in Hemans's reading, is 'The Aged Indian.' This features the more traditional male speaker, in this case an elderly Indian close to death who longs to join 'the brethren of his prime' (2: 268), but he strikes a curiously enfeebled pose: in place of the display of defiant machismo that was the hallmark of the death song, this aged Indian seems capable only of imploring his younger companions to put him out of his misery. He 'shrinks not from the friendly dart' (2: 269) but is preoccupied with his own physical decline and isolation within the tribe, and with the fact that his 'kindred-chiefs in days of yore' are now, for reasons that are never very clear, 'unremember'd' by all but himself (2: 268). A final variation on the death song, 'The Indian with his Dead Child,' is inspired, according to Hemans's note, by Henry Tudor's *Narrative of a Tour in North America* (1834), which tells the story of 'An Indian, who had established himself in a township of Maine' and felt 'indignantly the want of sympathy evinced towards him by the white inhabitants,' who then 'dug up the body of his child, and carried it with him two hundred miles through the forests to join the Canadian Indians' (Hemans 6: 27). The paternal speaker of the poem wishes to take his son back to 'rest by sounding waters / That yet untamed may roll' (6: 28). This vicarious death song enunciates passive resistance to, rather than defiance of, the 'pale race' that let down the speaker's son, implying that untamed nature offers a better resting-place than the soulless demesne of European settlers.

In her experiments with the Indian death song, Hemans takes a genre that first came to public notice via the narratives of travellers and traders in North America, and which in its Anglicized poetic form expressed fierce energies and a heroic self-possession that were clearly fascinating to culturally repressed, genteel readers, and opens it to a wider range of experience and emotions, tilting it towards her preferred territory of female subjectivity and the domestic affections. Similar priorities are evident in other poems that draw on Hemans's well-thumbed collection of American travel books. In 'The American Forest Girl' a 'fair-hair'd youth of England' is bound at the stake preparing to be burned to death, a situation that promises the opportunity to compare a white man's final utterance under extreme physical torment with the death songs of 'red warriors' with which the literary marketplace was already saturated. This, however, is not the route Hemans takes; instead, she explores the 'secret heart' of the Englishman in what are purportedly his last moments – thoughts of his 'far home,' his 'young sisters' gathered around the hearth, the prayer learned at his mother's knee – before sending in a young Indian girl to rescue him, convincing the 'fierce throng' that she speaks with the authority of the Great Spirit in demanding his release (5: 206–9). Hemans does not reference any particular source in this poem, but the scenery – the green savannahs, the cypresses, the lianas – recall Bartram more than anyone.

No doubts about provenance exist in the case of 'The Exile's Dirge,' since Hemans's long headnote provides the passage from Timothy Flint's *Recollections of the Last Ten Years Passed in ... the Valley of the Mississippi* (1826) on which it is based. The exile in question is a German settler, whose compatriots mourn his passing with much invocation of the 'immortal Fatherland' (6: 52) where he now resides (Flint had spoken of how often the word '*Vaterland*' had occurred in the funeral hymn that he would 'long remember'). Hemans's familiar themes are nostalgia for home, the sadness of bereavement, and the consolations of religion, and the American setting, conjured up with the compulsory allusions to gloomy forests and a clichéd image of Indian arrows flying around the exile's wilderness home, gives these themes picturesque expression.

The Christianizing approach to Indian material illustrated by 'The Exile's Dirge' is present again in 'The Indian's Revenge.' Hemans is, in fact, a kind of missionary in verse, descending on (literary representations of) Indians whose own rituals and beliefs (as purveyed by travellers) were an integral part of their interest for many readers and bringing them into line with her own core beliefs. This is more obviously so in 'The Indian's Revenge,' which presents an encounter, in dialogue form, between a missionary called Herrmann and an Indian called Enonio who is on his way to take revenge on the man who killed his brother. Herrmann eventually persuades Enonio that the voices he hears in the (deep, gloomy) forest, and the other signs he thinks he has observed in nature of his brother calling for vengeance, are merely the projection of his own emotions; he claims that Enonio's brother was himself a convert to Christianity and died with forgiveness on his lips. Enonio puts down his weapons and stays for further instruction. 'The Indian's Revenge' has an epigraph from *Gertrude of Wyoming*,[17] which means that Hemans is, in effect, poetically 'converting' Campbell's Outalissi.

---

[17]   Hemans states in a note that the poem was inspired by circumstances recorded in 'Carne's Narrative of the Moravian Missions in Greenland' – presumably a reference to David Crantz's *History of Greenland Including an Account of the Mission Carried on by the United Brethren in that Country* (1820).

Hemans's obsession with gloomy forest scenery, which her 'American' poems collectively suggest is virtually synonymous with the country, reaches its apogee in 'The Forest Sanctuary,' a long narrative poem written in a variant of the Spenserian stanza. The poem is spoken by a former Spanish conquistador who undergoes a Protestant conversion experience after witnessing an auto-da-fé in which an old friend and the latter's two sisters are executed for heresy. Imprisoned for the same crime, he escapes and flees to South America with his wife and son. His wife, who remains staunchly Catholic and believes her husband is doomed to eternal damnation, dies while they are waiting to land; subsequently he wanders with his son in the Andes, but feels oppressed by the equatorial climate and migrates to the North American frontier, where they now inhabit the forest sanctuary of the title. The poem is accompanied by a sizeable prose apparatus acknowledging some of Hemans's debts, which include Alexander von Humboldt for the South American settings. It is noteworthy that all three documented allusions to works with North American themes – one to Anne Grant's *Memoirs of an American Lady* (1808), and two to Adam Hodgson's *Letters from North America* (1824) – have to do with forest scenery. However, these are not just a matter of calling on written authorities to lend credence to Hemans's landscape descriptions. It is fundamental to the poem's symbolic structure to contrast the forest sanctuary as natural temple, a 'lonely world ... But for His presence felt, whom here my soul hath sought' (4: 67), with the 'mighty minster, dim, and proud, and vast' (4: 31) in Spain where the protagonist underwent spiritual enlightenment – an edifice that embodies the ancient faith 'Whose weight had grown a mountain's on my heart' (4: 32).

For this reason, the borrowings take on greater significance, the most interesting being Hemans's second allusion to Hodgson. Part 1 of the poem concludes with the narrator-protagonist addressing his son in their wilderness home:

> Thou hast a rich world round thee: – Mighty shades
> Weaving their gorgeous tracery o'er thy head,
> With the light melting through their high arcades,
> As through a pillar'd cloister's: but the dead
> Sleep not beneath; nor doth the sunbeam pass
> To marble shrines through rainbow-tinted glass;
> Yet thou, by fount and forest-murmur led
> To worship, thou art blest! – to thee is shown
> Earth in her holy pomp, deck'd for her God alone. (4: 37)

Hemans's note quotes a passage from Hodgson's *Letters*, in which Hodgson in turn quotes from Daniel Webster's Plymouth Rock oration. In his famous bicentenary speech, Webster recalled the first settlers of New England and their 'teachers and leaders' – men 'bred in the antique cloisters of Oxford and Cambridge' who sailed to 'another world,' took up residence in 'solitary villages, hardly indenting the vast forest that overshadowed the continent,' and there 'exhorted their fellow-pilgrims to constancy' (Hodgson 2: 304). Then followed the sentences quoted by Hemans:

Sometimes, their discourse was held in the deep shades of moss-grown forests, whose gloom and interlaced boughs first suggested that Gothic architecture, beneath whose pointed arches, where they had studied and prayed, the particoloured windows shed a tinged light; scenes, which the gleams of sunshine, penetrating the deep foliage, and flickering on the variegated turf below, might have recalled to their memory. (Hodgson 2: 304–5)

As should be clear, this quotation goes to the narrative and thematic heart of Hemans's poem, which similarly concerns a pious man escaping from religious persecution, who sets up home in the American wilderness and finds in the vast forest, where there are no institutional boundaries to a personal communion with God (but where his surroundings nevertheless have the capacity to evoke memories of his former existence), a more fulfilling context for his spiritual life. The deep and gloomy forests, which in other Hemans poems are no more than shorthand for the American landscape, are here pregnant with historical and contemporary meaning;[18] her reading of American travels has in this case yielded not merely arboreal furniture for her excursions into Indian subject-matter but a rich and informing context of prior discovery and settlement.

As a final example of Hemans's engagement with American themes through the medium of travel writing, it seems fitting to close with a poem that draws on one of the Romantics' favourite travel books. Hemans, like Wordsworth, Coleridge, and others, knew William Bartram's *Travels* very well. 'The Isle of Founts: An Indian Tradition' is prefaced by a long, abridged quotation from Bartram. Bartram describes a 'vast accumulation of waters' containing 'some large islands or knolls,' one of which is the focus of a Creek legend:

they say it is inhabited by a peculiar race of Indians, whose women are incomparably beautiful; they also tell you that this terrestrial paradise has been seen by some of their enterprising hunters, when in pursuit of game, who being lost in inextricable swamps and bogs ... were unexpectedly relieved by a company of beautiful women, whom they call daughters of the sun ... they further say, that these hunters had a view of their settlements, situated on the elevated banks of an island, or promontory, in a beautiful lake; but that in their endeavours to approach it, they were involved in perpetual labyrinths, and, like enchanted land, still as they imagined they had just gained it, it seemed to fly before them, alternately appearing and disappearing ... When they reported their adventures to their countrymen, their young warriors were enflamed with an irresistible desire to invade, and make a conquest of, so charming a country; but all their attempts hitherto have proved abortive, never having been able again to find that enchanting spot. (Bartram 25–6)

---

18   Hemans's 'Song of Emigration,' a contrapuntal lyric expressing the conflicted feelings of male and female Scottish emigrants, shows her awareness of the economic, as opposed to religious, motives of recent waves of settlers.

Hemans's poem, addressed by an anonymous Indian speaker to a 'Son of the stranger' who might be tempted to go in search of the 'Fountain Isle' (4: 101), dramatizes and embroiders upon Bartram's account, but with one significant difference. Whereas the young warriors in the legend Bartram reports are frustrated in their 'irresistible desire' to locate and invade the enchanted island, their equivalents in Hemans's poem suffer a still worse fate, their 'fever's agony' apparently proving mortal:

> E'en thus our hunters came of yore
>   Back from their long and weary quest; –
> Had they not seen th'untrodden shore,
>   And could they 'midst our wilds find rest?
> The lightning of their glance was fled,
> They dwelt amongst us as the dead!
> ....
>   They bent no more the forest-bow,
>   They armed not with the warrior-band,
> The moons waned o'er them dim and slow –
>   They left us for the spirits' land!
> Beneath our pines yon greensward heap
> Shows where the restless found their sleep. (4: 104)

Here, the failure of the 'long and weary quest' leaves the hunters dissatisfied with their homeland, socially incapacitated, and liable to a wasting illness that is as much mental as physical. It would have been better, the poem implies, not to have set out at all, to have remained an active and contented member of the community to which one naturally belonged. In the spirit of Wordsworth's Ruth, who listens to her American youth's talk of an 'endless lake / With all its fairy crowds / Of islands' (lines 62–4) but has her 'dream and vision' (103) of a new life dashed, Hemans seems to be warning against 'vain dreams' (Hemans 4: 104) of any 'terrestrial paradise' – such as America represented for the young Coleridge, Southey, and others of their generation, and perhaps for some who joined the post-war surge in transatlantic emigration.

In this, Hemans is faithful to her travel-writer source, for Bartram, although he presents the reader with many Elysian scenes, also writes of nature in proto-Darwinian terms as a site of perpetual warfare, and writes of conflict between Native peoples as well as between 'Indians' and settlers. Indeed, immediately after the passage quoted by Hemans in her preface to the 'Isle of Founts,' he tells another story regarding the inhabitants of the enchanted island, namely that they are 'the posterity of a fugitive remnant of the ancient Yamases, who escaped massacre after a bloody and decisive conflict between them and the Creek nation ... and here found an asylum, remote and secure from the fury of their proud conquerors' (26). Bartram, despite his occasional rhetorical exuberance, knew this was no paradise; Hemans, who read her travel writers carefully, was evidently under no illusions either.

As a travel reader, therefore, Hemans illustrates some of the same tendencies that we have witnessed, to varying degrees, in other poets discussed in this chapter: she is drawn to North American travels as a repository of 'authentic' Indian material; she distils from their varied landscape descriptions a limited yet powerful repertoire of images that provides the scenic backdrop to her verse; while occasionally she engages with travel texts in more intellectually rigorous ways that are productive of real semantic complexity in the resulting poems. These modes of reading have clear affinities with the activities of professional and private readers explored in earlier chapters. At the same time, as a literary end-user or more intentional, goal-oriented reader, Hemans, like Wordsworth, Coleridge, and the other poets I have looked at, brings her own personality, beliefs, and cultural biases to bear on the process. In her case, a coalescence of interests in female psychology, domestic affections, and Christian morality ensure that her take on transatlantic subject-matter is quite unlike any other poet's. This underlines one of the key lessons of the research outcomes presented in this book: that, however much they share a discursive environment or acquire shape and direction from a particular interpretive community, readers, and reading experiences, are always unique.

Conclusion

Felicia Hemans, with whom I concluded my study of Romantic poets as travel readers in the previous chapter, emerged as a particularly strong and purposeful reader of North American travels. Although in some poems she appears to reduce her source material to descriptive formulae or stock images in the interests of picturesque scene-setting, in other cases, as in her reworkings of the Indian death song or her use of Adam Hodgson's *Letters* in 'The Forest Sanctuary,' she develops a thoughtful and sometimes assertive dialogue with her host text. In her range of poetic responses to American travel books she was not unique, as the foregoing studies of Wordsworth, Coleridge, and others made clear. While it was not uncommon for poets to draw on travel narratives in superficial and opportunistic ways, for example as a store of ready-made images or of anecdotal ingredients for narrative verse, there were also many instances of poets putting travel writers to work in the service of highly partisan agendas (as with Thomas Moore's selective referencing of Isaac Weld and other travellers to shore up his anti-American and pro-Canadian position) or establishing more complex relationships with the original travel source (as with Wordsworth's assimilation and transformation of Hearne in his 'Complaint of a Forsaken Indian Woman'). In broad terms, the heavy indebtedness of Romantic poets to the literature of travel and exploration might be explained as serving purposes either of *authentication* (claiming 'real-world' authority for what might otherwise be taken as workings of the imagination) or *enrichment* (adding depth or complexity by incorporating specific elements of the travel source, sometimes in ways that disturb the new context). In both cases, by contrast with the better-known phenomena of intrapoetic allusion, the seeming imperative that readers be aware of the source material explains the popularity of the prose footnote providing references and, frequently, quoted extracts. These observations are not, of course, unique to writers dealing with North American subjects: authentication and enrichment arguably cover most explicit uses of travel literature by creative writers in the Romantic period.

Although the literary terrain surveyed in Chapter 4 presents what is, for obvious reasons, a more transitive form of engagement with travel narratives than that represented by the periodical reviews or the records of private reading experiences discussed in earlier chapters, in other ways the poets are not radically different, as travel readers, to any other reader discussed in this book. Their particular concern, for example, as literary end-users, to employ excerpts from travellers' accounts accepted for their veracity to authenticate what might appear far-fetched elements of poetic invention, simply mirrors the importance placed by periodical reviewers on distinguishing fact from fiction in works of travel and exploration and condemning those authors suspected of having strayed from the norms of careful observation and accurate reportage in the interests of mere 'book-making.' It remains, then, to draw some conclusions regarding the reception of North American travels, on the basis of this study of diverse Romantic readers.

1.   The overwhelming impression made by all records of reading experiences of travel books on North America – whether in the public or private realm, by professional or recreational readers, and regardless of class or gender – is that the reading of travel literature was curiosity-driven. While such curiosity sometimes took less wholesome or intellectually respectable forms, the genuine thirst for knowledge about distant, unfamiliar parts of the world, not least North America with its ever-moving frontier, cannot be understated. In fact, North America, owing to the combination of a continuously high volume of published travels and continually shifting boundaries of exploration and settlement – offering perpetual novelty on the one hand, the potential for corroboration or correction on the other – was particularly well placed to satisfy the curious travel reader.

2.   While all aspects of foreign countries, including their topography, natural history, trade and industry, and cultural development were of interest to readers in this period, the appetite for information and anecdotes relating to the indigenous peoples of North America was inexhaustible. Ethnographical and anthropological material concerning Native Americans was the mainstay of reviews and a principal talking point for private readers, but, as the United States continued its bewilderingly rapid growth and development, the separate identity of European Americans – and their relative capacities and status vis-à-vis the British – also became a major preoccupation for readers.

3.   There was very little interest in the individual persona of the traveller, or in the kinds of interior or spiritual journeys that have come to be equated with the notion of Romantic travel. It is, of course, a critical commonplace to assert the opposite – to identify a 'shift towards the travelling subject' in travel writing from the second half of the eighteenth century onwards, as Barbara Korte puts it in her excellent survey of the genre (53). However, the literary preeminence of a few major authors, such as Byron (who popularized the persona of a brooding, melancholy young man travelling to assuage his tortured spirit, but was not a travel writer in the conventional sense), has arguably distorted our perception of voyages and travels in general. A related point is that the development Korte describes is usually illustrated with respect to travels in Continental Europe, where the familiarity of the terrain lessened the importance of the travel narrative's 'object orientation' (Korte's phrase) and hollowed out a void that subjective experience and strong sensibility conveniently came to fill. Where travel writing was concerned with newly 'discovered' or relatively little-known parts of the world, readers were likely to be far more interested in its authentic, empirical content, and all the evidence presented in this book suggests that this was the case with regard to North America. It is worth recalling my reference to Anna Larpent's diary entry for 4 December 1829, in which she wrote of Augustus Granville's *St Petersburgh* (1828) that 'when a person is so inflated with Vanity & Egotism I dare say much represented is falsely coloured'; complaining that there was 'no strength of observation' or 'firm principle of discrimination' in the work, she

dismissed it as 'a sort of <u>twaddle</u> emanating from one point <u>self</u> & what <u>self</u> does = & what is <u>done to self</u>.' The severe piety of the ageing Larpent probably made her an especially intolerant critic of such solipsistic excesses, but her belligerent disapproval is just an extreme expression of an attitude that many readers shared towards the nonfiction travel book. Unless the entire historical record of public and private reception is misleading in this regard, in the transatlantic context the travelling self was of slender significance to Romantic readers compared to the vast 'continent of information' that travellers in North America were opening up.

4.   The periodical press played a vital role in disseminating travel knowledge at a time when travel works themselves were prohibitively expensive for all but the most affluent readers (albeit more widely accessible through libraries and reading societies). The much-derided convention of constructing reviews out of lengthy excerpts was arguably of great value in providing economically disadvantaged readers with a vicarious experience of the latest voyages and travels. Reviewers, though inevitably constrained on some matters of opinion by the ideological bias of particular journals, were more independent-minded in their responses to travel books than in reviewing literary genres that bore more closely on matters of politics and morality, and generally were keen to find original content to transmit to their readers. Reviews of North American travels became conspicuously politicized when diplomatic relations between Britain and the United States were strained; at other times, reviewers kept the interests of the general reader in mind and were, in the main, more liberal and internationalist than the travellers whose books they were evaluating.

5.   Private or informal responses to North American travels, as represented by letters, diaries, marginalia, and other forms of evidence, do not reveal a radically different reading culture to that embodied in periodical reviews. There is the same hunger for new knowledge, the same desire for instruction and (in moderation) amusement, the same suspicion of rhetorical imposition, the same impatience with authorial self-promotion: essentially, the ideal or implied reader projected by reviews of travel books *is* the reader one finds in conversation or correspondence with friends, or in moments of self-communion.

6.   Nevertheless, records of private reading experiences do more characteristically express an individuality that is often obscured by the corporate voice to which contributions to the magazines and reviews were subtly assimilated. It is only in such accounts, for example, that one registers the delight in imaginative transport – in being taken on journeys in the mind to unfamiliar or newly discovered lands – that was evidently a key benefit of travel literature in a period when expanding geographical horizons coexisted (for the majority) with circumscribed lives, and when printed books enjoyed a near-monopoly in providing a curious public with their window on the world. In testimonies of this nature the 'scent of vanished humanity' (to recall Robert Darnton's evocative phrase) is particularly strong.

7.   Of course, readings of travel works, whether in the impersonal medium of an anonymous review or the intimacy of a diary entry, took place in a wider

cultural and political context and were inevitably shaped by such factors. The travel writers featured in this book, few of whom were professional authors and many of whom were reluctant conscripts to the literary marketplace, were or had been part of a messy, unstable, and sometimes violent world of transatlantic relations, and their readers were necessarily caught up in the debates and controversies that were a part of that world. The discourse on emigration, so tightly threaded through writings on North America, offers the most conspicuous example of a hot political issue on which neither writers nor readers could remain neutral. Readers' responses to travels in the United States and Canada were often coloured by attitudes to emigration even when this was not a major or explicit theme in the work itself. Narratives of Arctic exploration, owing to the perceived high stakes of this long-running enterprise, offer another scenario in which readers seemed to abandon their finer judgement and get swept up in a tidal surge of patriotic sentiment.

8.   Finally, it is the nature of the case that travel literature from earlier periods such as the Romantic routinely confronts one with values and beliefs that are politically or morally offensive. Merely denouncing such defects wherever they appear, with perfect twenty-first-century hindsight, becomes tedious and repetitive, however necessary it is to recognize sexist, racist, and imperialist attitudes for what they were and incorporate them within a properly historicized understanding of travel texts. The same goes for the historical readers of such texts, few of whom would make natural pen friends for their modern counterparts. However, we also need to beware of the receptive fallacy, and not lazily assume that readers were constructed in the image of the most ignorant and objectionable colonial travellers. As this study has shown, readers were quite capable of questioning or dissenting from attitudes expressed by travel writers, and of taking out of books what they found instructive while leaving in what they did not like. (They were, of course, just as capable of shared sympathies and antipathies that we now find distasteful, but that conformed to the dominant ideology of the day.) A diligent reception study cannot help but inspire one with respect for Romantic readers: in a society saturated with print culture, they read travel books, as they doubtless read other genres, with an enthusiasm, sustained attention, and intellectual appetite that their modern descendants would do well to emulate, and rarely deserve the ritual condescension of posterity. One of the guiding lights of this study has been Robert Darnton's observation that 'As our ancestors lived in different mental worlds, they must have read differently' (*Kiss* 187). With respect to transatlantic voyages and travels, it has been a challenge to try to recover some of those differences; it is a still greater challenge consistently to respect them.

Bibliography

Primary Texts

NB: Items in this section marked with an asterisk (*) are individual copies of works consulted for the manuscript notes they contain. Except where explicitly indicated, parenthetical references in the text are to the unmarked copy.

Ashe, Thomas. *Travels in America, Performed in 1806, for the Purpose of Exploring the Rivers Alleghany, Monongahela, Ohio, and Mississippi.* 3 vols. London: R. Phillips, 1808.

*Ashe, Thomas. *Travels in America ...* 3 vols. London: R. Phillips, 1808. Beinecke Library, Beckford 143.

Bartram, William. *Travels through North & South Carolina, Georgia, East & West Florida, the Cherokee Country, the Extensive Territories of the Muscogulges, or Creek Confederacy, and the Country of the Choctaws.* Philadelphia: James and Johnson, 1791; London: rpt. for J. Johnson, 1792.

*Bartram, William. *Travels through North & South Carolina ...* Philadelphia: James and Johnson, 1791; London: rpt. for J. Johnson, 1792. Beinecke Library, Beckford 153.

Beckford, William. Commonplace book. 1793–1811. Bodleian MS Eng. misc.e.1236.

———. Reading notes. Bodleian MSS Beckford c.55–57.

Bennett, E. T. *The Gardens and Menagerie of the Zoological Society Delineated.* Vol. 1. London: Thomas Tegg, 1830.

Berry, Mary. *Extracts of the Journals and Correspondence of Miss Berry from the Year 1783 to 1852.* Ed. Maria Theresa Lister. 3 vols. London: Longmans, 1866.

Binns, John. *Recollections of the Life of John Binns: Twenty-Nine Years in Europe and Fifty-Three in the United States.* Philadelphia: Printed by the Author, 1854.

Birkbeck, Morris. *Notes on a Journey in America, from the Coast of Virginia to the Territory of Illinois.* 4th ed. London: James Ridgway, 1818.

Brissot de Warville, J. P. *New Travels in the United States of America: Including the Commerce of America with Europe; Particularly with France and Great Britain.* 2nd ed. 2 vols. London: J. S. Jordan, 1794.

Buffon, Count De. *Natural History, General and Particular.* 3rd ed. 9 vols. Trans. and ed. William Smellie. London: A. Strahan and T. Cadell, 1791. Vol. 5.

Campbell, Thomas. *Gertrude of Wyoming; a Pennsylvanian Tale. And Other Poems.* 5th ed. London: Longman et al., 1814.

———. *Life and Letters of Thomas Campbell.* Ed. William Beattie. 3 vols. London: E. Moxon, 1849.

Carter, Thomas. *Memoirs of a Working Man.* London: Charles Knight, 1845.

Carver, Jonathan. *Travels through the Interior Parts of North America, in the Years 1766, 1767, and 1768.* London: Printed for the Author, 1778.

Clairmont, Claire. *The Journals of Claire Clairmont.* Ed. Marion Kingston Stocking. Cambridge: Harvard UP, 1968.

Coleridge, Samuel Taylor. *Collected Letters of Samuel Taylor Coleridge.* Ed. E. L. Griggs. 6 vols. Oxford: Clarendon P, 1956–71.

———. *Marginalia.* Ed. George Whalley and H. J. Jackson. 6 vols. Princeton: Princeton UP, 1980–2001.

———. *The Notebooks of Samuel Taylor Coleridge.* Ed. Kathleen Coburn. Vol. 1. London: Routledge & Kegan Paul, 1957.

———. *Poetical Works.* Ed. J. C. C. Mays. 3 double vols. Princeton: Princeton UP, 2001.

A Companion to the London Museum and Pantherion, Containing a Brief Description of Fifteen Thousand Natural and Foreign Curiosities, Antiquities, and Productions of the Fine Arts. 15th ed. London: Printed for the Proprietor, 1812.

A Companion to the Museum, (Late Sir Ashton Lever's) Removed to Albion Street, the Surry End of Black Friars Bridge. London, 1790.

Cooper, Thomas (1805–92). *The Life of Thomas Cooper. Written by Himself.* 1872. Intro. John Saville. Leicester: Leicester UP, 1971.

Cooper, Thomas (1759–1839). *Some Information Respecting America.* Dublin: P. Wogan et al., 1794.

*Cooper, Thomas (1759–1839). *Some Information Respecting America.* 2nd ed. London: J. Johnson, 1795. British Library 10410.bbb.28.

Cottle, Joseph. *Reminiscences of Samuel Taylor Coleridge and Robert Southey.* London, 1847. Facsimile ed. Highgate: Lime Tree Bower P, 1970.

Crèvecoeur, J. Hector St John. *Letters from an American Farmer.* 1783. Ed. Susan Manning. Oxford: Oxford UP, 1997.

Dawson, Warren R. Commonplace book. 1823. British Library, Add. 45268.

Edgeworth, Maria. *The Life and Letters of Maria Edgeworth.* Ed. A. J. C. Hare. Vol. 1. Boston: Houghton, Mifflin & Co., 1895.

Franklin, John. *Narrative of a Journey to the Shores of the Polar Sea, in the Years 1819, 20, 21, and 22.* London: John Murray, 1823.

Hearne, Samuel. *A Journey from Prince of Wales's Fort in Hudson Bay to the Northern Ocean.* 1795. Ed. Richard Glover. Toronto: Macmillan, 1958.

*Hearne, Samuel. *A Journey from Prince of Wales's Fort in Hudson Bay to the Northern Ocean.* London: A. Strahan and T. Cadell, 1795. National Library of Scotland K.188.a.

*Hearne, Samuel. *A Journey from Prince of Wales's Fort in Hudson Bay to the Northern Ocean.* London: A. Strahan and T. Cadell, 1795. Rhodes House Library 400.111.s.6.

Hemans, Felicia. *The Works of Mrs Hemans; with a Memoir of her Life, by her Sister.* 7 vols. Edinburgh: Blackwood, 1839.

Henry, Alexander. *Travels and Adventures in Canada and the Indian Territories, between the Years 1760 and 1776.* New York: I. Riley, 1809.

Heriot, George. *Travels through the Canadas, Containing a Description of the Picturesque Scenery on Some of the Rivers and Lakes.* London: R. Phillips, 1807.

Hodgson, Adam. *Letters from North America, Written during a Tour in the United States and Canada.* 2 vols. London: Hurst, Robinson, 1824.

Howison, John. *Sketches of Upper Canada, Domestic, Local, and Characteristic: To which Are Added, Practical Details for the Information of Emigrants of Every Class.* Edinburgh: Oliver & Boyd, 1821.

Irving, Washington. *The Sketch-Book of Geoffrey Crayon, Gent.* 1820. Ed. Susan Manning. Oxford: Oxford UP, 1996.

Jeffrey, Francis. *Contributions to the Edinburgh Review.* 4 vols. London: Longman et al., 1844.

Jewitt, John R. *The Adventures and Sufferings of John R. Jewitt, Only Survivor of the Ship Boston, during a Captivity of Nearly Three Years among the Savages of Nootka Sound.* Edinburgh: Constable, 1824.

Lamb, Charles and Mary Anne. *The Letters of Charles and Mary Anne Lamb.* Ed. Edwin W. Marrs. 3 vols. Ithaca: Cornell UP, 1975–78.

Larpent, Anna Margaretta. *A Woman's View of Drama, 1790–1830: The Diaries of Anna Margaretta Larpent from the Huntington Library.* 9 reels. Marlborough: Adam Matthew, 1995. Microform.

Le Breton, Anna Letitia. *Correspondence of William Ellery Channing, D.D. and Lucy Aikin, from 1826–1842.* London: Williams & Norgate, 1874.

L'Estrange, Alfred Guy, ed. *The Life of Mary Russell Mitford, Related in a Selection from her Letters to her Friends.* 2 vols. London: Richard Bentley, 1870.

Mackenzie, Alexander. *The Journals and Letters of Sir Alexander Mackenzie.* Ed. W. Kaye Lamb. Cambridge: Cambridge UP, 1970.

Mitford, Mary Russell. *Letters of Mary Russell Mitford. Second Series.* Ed. Henry Chorley. 2 vols. London: Richard Bentley, 1872.

Moore, Thomas. *Epistles, Odes, and Other Poems.* Philadelphia: John Watts, 1806.
———. *The Letters of Thomas Moore.* Ed. Wilfred S. Dowden. 2 vols. Oxford: Clarendon P, 1964.

More, Hannah. *Hints Towards Forming the Character of a Young Princess.* 2 vols. London: Cadell and Davies, 1805.

Moritz, Carl. *Travels of Carl Philipp Moritz in England in 1782.* 1795. Ed. P. E. Matheson. London: Humphrey Milford, 1924.

Morse, Jedediah. *The American Geography; or, a View of the Present Situation of the United States of America.* 3rd ed. Dublin: John Jones, 1792.

Nicol, John. *The Life and Adventures of John Nicol, Mariner.* Ed. Tim Flannery. Edinburgh: Canongate, 2000.

Oliver, Grace A. *The Story of the Life of Anna Letitia Barbauld, with Many of her Letters.* Boston: Cupples, Upham and Co., 1886.

Paine, Thomas. *Rights of Man.* Ed. Eric Foner. Harmondsworth: Penguin, 1984.

Parkinson, Richard. *A Tour in America, in 1798, 1799, and 1800. Exhibiting Sketches of Society and Manners, and a Particular Account of the American*

System of Agriculture, with its Recent Improvements. 2 vols. London: J. Harding and J. Murray, 1805.

Parry, William Edward. *Journal of a Voyage for the Discovery of a North-West Passage from the Atlantic to the Pacific, Performed in the Years 1819–20, in His Majesty's Ships Hecla and Griper.* London: John Murray, 1821.

Piozzi, Hester Lynch. *The Piozzi Letters: Correspondence of Hester Lynch Piozzi, 1784–1821. Vol. 6: 1817–1821.* Ed. Edward A. Bloom and Lillian D. Bloom. Newark: U of Delaware P, 2002.

Robinson, Henry Crabb. *Henry Crabb Robinson on Books and their Writers.* Ed. E. J. Morley. 3 vols. London: Dent, 1938.

Ross, John. *A Voyage of Discovery, Made under the Orders of the Admiralty, in his Majesty's Ships Isabella and Alexander.* 2nd ed. 2 vols. London: Longman, 1819.

Seward, Anna. *Letters of Anna Seward: Written Between the Years 1784 and 1807.* Vol. 2. Edinburgh: A. Constable, 1811.

Smiles, Samuel. *Memoirs and Correspondence of the Late John Murray, with an Account of the Origin and Progress of the House, 1768–1843.* 2 vols. London: John Murray, 1891.

Somerville, Alexander. *The Autobiography of a Working Man.* 1848. London: Turnstile P, 1951.

Southey, Robert. *Metrical Tales and Other Poems.* London: Longman et al., 1805.

———. *New Letters of Robert Southey.* Ed. Kenneth Curry. 2 vols. New York: Columbia UP, 1965.

———. *Poetical Works 1793–1810.* Gen. ed. Lynda Pratt. 5 vols. London: Pickering and Chatto, 2004.

———. *Selections from the Letters of Robert Southey.* Ed. John Wood Warter. 4 vols. London: Longman et al., 1856.

———. *Sir Thomas More: or, Colloquies of the Progress and Prospects of Society.* 2 vols. London: John Murray, 1831.

———. *Southey's Common-Place Book.* 1st and 2nd series. Ed. John Wood Warter. London: Longman et al., 1849–50.

Stansbury, Philip. *A Pedestrian Tour of Two Thousand Three Hundred Miles, in North America. To the Lakes, –The Canadas, – and the New England States. Performed in the Autumn of 1821.* New York: J. D. Myers and W. Smith, 1822.

Sterne, Laurence. *A Sentimental Journey.* 1768. Ed. Graham Petrie. Harmondsworth: Penguin, 1967.

*Talbot, Edward. *Five Years' Residence in the Canadas.* 2 vols. London: Longman et al., 1824. Bodleian Arch H.e.9/1–2.

Trollope, Frances. *Domestic Manners of the Americans.* London: Whittaker, Treacher, and Co., 1832.

Walsh, Robert, Jr. *An Appeal from the Judgments of Great Britain Respecting the United States of America.* Philadelphia: Mitchell, Ames, and White, 1819.

Weld, Isaac. *Travels through the States of North America and the Provinces of Upper and Lower Canada during the Years 1795, 1796 & 1797.* 1799. 4th ed. 2 vols. London: John Stockdale, 1807.

Wollstonecraft, Mary. *A Short Residence in Sweden, Norway and Denmark.* 1796. Ed. Richard Holmes. Harmondsworth: Penguin, 1987.

The Wonders of Nature and Art: Being an Account of Whatever is Most Curious and Remarkable Throughout the World. 4 vols. Reading, 1750.

Woolman, John. *A Journal of the Life, Gospel Labours, and Christian Experiences of that Faithful Minister of Jesus Christ, John Woolman.* Dublin, 1794.

Wordsworth, Dorothy. *Journals of Dorothy Wordsworth.* Ed. E. de Selincourt. 2 vols. London: Macmillan, 1952.

Wordsworth, William. *The Poetical Works of William Wordsworth.* Ed. E de Selincourt and Helen Darbishire. 5 vols. Oxford: Clarendon P, 1940–49.

Wordsworth, William, and Dorothy Wordsworth. *The Letters of William and Dorothy Wordsworth.* Ed. Ernest de Selincourt et al. 2nd ed. 8 vols. Oxford: Clarendon P, 1967–90.

Wordsworth, William, and Samuel Taylor Coleridge. *Lyrical Ballads: The Text of the 1798 Edition with the Additional 1800 Poems and the Prefaces.* Ed. R. L. Brett and A. R. Jones. Rev. ed. London: Methuen, 1965.

Periodicals

NB: Parenthetical references in the text to periodical articles supply volume and page number(s), and, where necessary, the series number.

Analytical Review, 1788–98, 1st ser. Monthly.

Annual Review, 1803–09.

Anti-Jacobin Review, 1798–1821. Monthly.

La Belle Assemblée, 1806–09, 1st ser.; 1810–24, ns. Monthly.

Blackwood's Edinburgh Magazine, 1817–1980. Monthly.

Bristol Mercury. Daily.

British Critic, 1793–1813, 1st ser.; 1814–25, 2nd ser. Monthly.

British Review, 1811–25. Quarterly.

Caledonian Mercury. Daily.

Cobbett's Weekly Political Register.

Critical Review, 1756–90, 1st ser.; 1791–1803, 2nd ser.; 1804–11, 3rd ser.; 1812–14, 4th ser.; 1815–17, 5th ser. Monthly.

Eclectic Review, 1805–13, 1st ser.; 1814–28, 2nd ser.; 1829–36, 3rd ser. Monthly.

Edinburgh Magazine, 1785–92, 1st ser.; 1793–1803, ns. Monthly.

Edinburgh Review, 1802–1929. Quarterly.

English Review, 1783–96. Monthly.

European Magazine, and London Review, 1782–1825, 1st ser. Monthly.

Examiner, 1808–81. Weekly.

Gentleman's Magazine, 1731–1833, 1st ser. Monthly.

Literary Chronicle, and Weekly Review, 1819–28, 1st ser. Weekly.

Literary Gazette, 1817–58, 1st ser. Weekly.

Literary Journal, or Universal Review of Literature, 1803–06. Weekly; Twice-monthly; Monthly.

Literary Magazine, or Monthly Epitome of British Literature, Jan.-June 1797, 1ˢᵗ
  ser.; 1798–1801, ns; 1802–04, 3ʳᵈ ser.; 1805–06, 4ᵗʰ ser.
London Chronicle. Tri-weekly.
London Magazine, 1820–24, 1ˢᵗ ser. Monthly.
Mirror of Literature, Amusement, and Instruction, 1822–41, 1ˢᵗ ser. Weekly.
Monthly Magazine, 1796–1826, 1ˢᵗ ser.
Monthly Review, 1790–1825, 2ⁿᵈ ser.
New Annual Register, 1780–1825. Annual.
New London Review, or Monthly Report of Authors and Books, 1799–1800.
  Monthly.
The Times. Daily.
Universal Magazine, 1804–14, ns. Monthly.
Weekly Entertainer, or Agreeable and Instructive Repository, 1783–1819, 1ˢᵗ ser.;
  1820–25, ns.

Secondary Texts

Adams, Percy G. *Travelers and Travel Liars 1660–800*. New York: Dover, 1980.
Allan, David. *Commonplace Books and Reading in Georgian England.* Cambridge:
  Cambridge UP, 2010.
———. *Making British Culture: English Readers and the Scottish Enlightenment,
  1740–1830*. New York: Routledge, 2008.
Allen, H. C. *Great Britain and the United States: A History of Anglo-American
  Relations 1783–1952*. London: Odhams P, 1954.
Altick, Richard D. *The English Common Reader: A Social History of the Mass
  Reading Public, 1800–1900*. 1957. 2ⁿᵈ ed. Columbus: Ohio UP, 1998.
Atwood, Margaret. *Survival: A Thematic Guide to Canadian Literature*. 1972.
  New ed. Toronto: McClelland and Stewart, 2004.
Bailyn, Bernard. *The Peopling of British North America: An Introduction.* New
  York: Knopf, 1986.
Batten, Charles L., Jr. *Pleasurable Instruction: Form and Convention in
  Eighteenth-Century Travel Literature*. Berkeley: U of California P, 1978.
Beetham, Margaret. 'Open and Closed: The Periodical as a Publishing Genre.'
  Victorian Periodicals Review 22.3 (1989): 96–100.
———. 'Women and the Consumption of Print.' *Women and Literature in Britain
  1800–1900*. Cambridge: Cambridge UP, 2001. 55–77.
Benchimol, Alex. *Intellectual Politics and Cultural Conflict in the Romantic
  Period: Scottish Whigs, English Radicals and the Making of the British Public
  Sphere*. Burlington: Ashgate, 2010.
Benedict, Barbara. *Curiosity: A Cultural History of Early Modern Inquiry.*
  Chicago: U of Chicago P, 2001.
Bentley, D. M. R. 'Near the Rapids: Thomas Moore in Canada.' *Romantic Poetry.*
  Ed. Angela Esterhammer. Amsterdam: John Benjamins, 2002. 355–71.

———. 'Thomas Moore's Construction of Upper Canada in "Ballad Stanzas."' *Canadian Poetry* 35 (1994). Web.

Bickham, Troy. *Savages within the Empire: Representations of American Indians in Eighteenth-Century Britain*. Oxford: Clarendon P, 2005.

Bitterli, Urs. *Cultures in Conflict: Encounters between European and Non-European Cultures, 1492–1800*. Trans. Ritchie Robertson. Cambridge: Polity, 1989.

Blanton, Casey. *Travel Writing: The Self and the World*. New York: Twayne, 1997.

Bolton, Carol. *Writing the Empire: Robert Southey and Romantic Colonialism*. London: Pickering & Chatto, 2007.

Borm, Jan. 'Defining Travel: On the Travel Book, Travel Writing and Terminology.' *Perspectives on Travel Writing*. Ed. Glenn Hooper and Tim Youngs. Aldershot: Ashgate, 2004. 13–26.

Brewer, John. *The Pleasures of the Imagination: English Culture in the Eighteenth Century*. Chicago: U of Chicago P, 1997.

———. 'Reconstructing the Reader: Prescriptions, Texts and Strategies in Anna Larpent's Reading.' *The Practice and Representation of Reading in England*. Cambridge: Cambridge UP, 1996. 226–45.

Bridges, Roy. 'Exploration and Travel outside Europe.' *The Cambridge Companion to Travel Writing*. Ed. Peter Hulme and Tim Youngs. Cambridge: Cambridge UP, 2002. 53–69.

Brownell, Morris R. 'Hester Lynch Piozzi's Marginalia.' *Eighteenth-Century Life* 3 (1977): 97–100.

Burnett, John, David Vincent, and David Mayall. *The Autobiography of the Working Class*. 3 vols. Brighton: Harvester, 1984–89.

Butler, Marilyn. 'Culture's Medium: The Role of the Review.' *The Cambridge Companion to British Romanticism*. Ed. Stuart Curran. Cambridge: Cambridge UP, 1993. 120–147.

Buzard, James. *The Beaten Track: European Tourism, Literature, and the Ways to Culture, 1800–1918*. Oxford: Clarendon P, 1993.

Cameron, J. M. R. 'John Barrow, the *Quarterly Review*'s Imperial Reviewer.' *Conservatism and the* Quarterly Review*: A Critical Analysis*. Ed. Jonathan Cutmore. London: Pickering and Chatto, 2007. 133–49.

Cardinal, Roger. 'Romantic Travel.' *Rewriting the Self: Histories from the Renaissance to the Present*. Ed. Roy Porter. London: Routledge, 1997. 135–55.

Cavell, Janice. *Tracing the Connected Narrative: Arctic Exploration in British Print Culture, 1818–1860*. Toronto: U of Toronto P, 2008.

Caygill, Marjorie. *The Story of the British Museum*. 3rd ed. London: British Museum P, 2002.

Chandler, James. *England in 1819: The Politics of Literary Culture and the Case of Romantic Historicism*. Chicago: U of Chicago P, 1998.

Chard, Chloe. *Pleasure and Guilt on the Grand Tour: Travel Writing and Imaginative Geography*. Manchester: Manchester UP, 1999.

Chartier, Roger. *The Order of Books: Readers, Authors, and Libraries in Europe between the Fourteenth and Eighteenth Centuries*. Trans. Lydia G. Cochrane. Cambridge: Polity, 1994.

Christie, William. *The Edinburgh Review in the Literary Culture of Romantic Britain*. London: Pickering and Chatto, 2009.

Clark, Steve. 'Introduction.' *Travel Writing and Empire: Postcolonial Theory in Transit*. London: Zed Books, 1999. 1–28.

Clive, John. *Scotch Reviewers: The* Edinburgh Review, *1802–1815*. Cambridge: Harvard UP, 1957.

Cockburn, Lord. *Life of Lord Jeffrey, with a Selection from his Correspondence*. 2nd ed. 2 vols. Edinburgh: Adam and Charles Black, 1852.

Coe, Charles Norton. *Wordsworth and the Literature of Travel*. New York: Bookman Associates, 1953.

Colclough, Stephen. *Consuming Texts: Readers and Reading Communities 1695–1870*. Basingstoke: Palgrave Macmillan, 2007.

Colley, Linda. *Britons: Forging the Nation 1707–1837*. London: Yale UP, 1992.

Colombo, Claire Miller. '"This Pen of Mine Will Say Too Much": Public Performance in the Journal of Anna Larpent.' *Texas Studies in Literature and Language* 38.3/4 (1996): 285–301.

Conrad, Margaret, Alvin Finkel, and Cornelius Jaenen. *History of the Canadian Peoples. Vol. 1: Beginnings to 1867*. Toronto: Copp Clark Pitman, 1993.

Conway, Stephen. 'Britain and the Revolutionary Crisis, 1763–1791.' *The Oxford History of the British Empire, Vol. 2: The Eighteenth Century*. Oxford: Oxford UP, 1998. 325–46.

Cooper, Lane. *Methods and Aims in the Study of Literature*. Boston: Ginn, 1915.

———. 'Wordsworth's Sources.' *Athanaeum* 4043 (1905): 498–500.

Corner, David. 'The Tyranny of Fashion: The Case of the Felt-Hatting Trade in the Late Seventeenth and Eighteenth Centuries.' *Textile History* 22.2 (1991): 153–78.

Coues, Elliott, ed. *History of the Expedition under the Command of Lewis and Clark ... Performed during the Years 1804–5-6, by Order of the Government of the United States*. 4 vols. London: Henry Stevens, 1893.

Cowan, Helen I. *British Emigration to British North America: The First Hundred Years*. Rev. and enlarged ed. Toronto: U of Toronto P, 1961.

Crean, J. F. 'Hats and the Fur Trade.' *Canadian Journal of Economics and Political Science* 28.3 (1962): 373–86.

Crone, G. R., and R. A. Skelton. 'English Collections of Voyages and Travels 1625–1846.' *Richard Hakluyt and his Successors*. Ed. Edward Lynam. London: Hakluyt Society, 1946. 65–140.

Cruse, Amy. *The Englishman and his Books in the Early Nineteenth Century*. London: George G. Harrap, 1930.

Cutmore, Jonathan, ed. *Conservatism and the* Quarterly Review: *A Critical Analysis*. London: Pickering and Chatto, 2007.

———. *Contributors to the* Quarterly Review. London: Pickering and Chatto, 2008.

Daniells, Roy. *Alexander Mackenzie and the North West*. London: Faber, 1969.

Darnton, Robert. *The Great Cat Massacre and Other Episodes in French Cultural History*. Harmondsworth: Penguin, 1991.

———. *The Kiss of Lamourette: Reflections in Cultural History*. London: Faber, 1990.

———. 'Seven Bad Reasons Not to Study Manuscripts.' *Harvard Library Bulletin* 4.4 (1993): 37–42.

De Certeau, Michel. *The Practice of Everyday Life*. Trans. Steven Rendall. Berkeley: U of California P, 1984.

Delgado, James P. *Across the Top of the World: The Quest for the Northwest Passage*. London: British Museum, 1999.

Demata, Massimiliano. 'Prejudiced Knowledge: Travel Literature in the *Edinburgh Review*.' *British Romanticism and the* Edinburgh Review*: Bicentenary Essays*. Ed. Massimiliano Demata and Duncan Wu. Basingstoke: Algarve Macmillan, 2002. 82–101.

Demata, Massimiliano, and Duncan Wu, eds. *British Romanticism and the* Edinburgh Review*: Bicentenary Essays*. Basingstoke: Palgrave Macmillan, 2002.

Duchemin, Parker. '"A Parcel of Whelps": Alexander Mackenzie among the Indians.' *Canadian Literature* 124–5 (1990): 49–74.

Duffy, Charles. 'Thomas Campbell and America.' *American Literature* 13.4 (1942): 346–55.

Dugmore, A. Radclyffe. *The Romance of the Beaver: Being the History of the Beaver in the Western Hemisphere*. London: William Heinemann, 1914.

Edelstein, J. M. 'America's First Native Botanists.' *Quarterly Journal of Current Acquisitions* 15 (1958): 51–9.

Eldridge, Herbert G. 'Anacreon Moore and America.' *PMLA* 83.1 (1968): 54–62.

Eugenia, Sister. 'Coleridge's Scheme of Pantisocracy and American Travel Accounts.' *PMLA* 45.4 (1930): 1069–84.

Evans, Eric J. *The Forging of the Modern State: Early Industrial Britain 1783–1870*. Harlow: Longman, 1983.

Fagin, N. Bryllion. *William Bartram: Interpreter of the American Landscape*. Baltimore: Johns Hopkins UP, 1933.

Fang, Karen. *Romantic Writing and the Empire of Signs: Periodical Culture and Post-Napoleonic Authorship*. Charlottesville: U of Virginia P, 2010.

Fender, Stephen. *Sea Changes: British Emigration and American Literature*. Cambridge: Cambridge UP, 1992.

Ferris, Ina. 'Mobile Words: Romantic Travel Writing and Print Anxiety.' *Modern Language Quarterly* 60.4 (1999): 451–68.

Finkelstein, David, and Alistair McCleery. *An Introduction to Book History*. New York: Routledge, 2005.

Fish, Stanley. 'Literature in the Reader: Affective Stylistics.' 1970. *Is There a Text in This Class? The Authority of Interpretive Communities*. Cambridge: Harvard UP, 1980. 21–67.

Flynn, Christopher. *Americans in British Literature, 1770–1832: A Breed Apart*. Aldershot: Ashgate, 2008.

Fothergill, Brian. *Beckford of Fonthill*. Stroud: Nonsuch, 1979.

Franklin, Wayne. *Discoverers, Explorers, Settlers: The Diligent Writers of Early America*. Chicago: U of Chicago P, 1989.

Franta, Andrew. *Romanticism and the Rise of the Mass Public*. Cambridge: Cambridge UP, 2009.

Frost, Alan. 'New Geographical Perspectives and the Emergence of the Romantic Imagination.' *Captain James Cook and his Times*. Ed. Robin Fisher and Hugh Johnston. Vancouver: Douglas and McIntyre, 1979. 5–19.

Fulford, Tim. *Romantic Indians: Native Americans, British Literature, and Transatlantic Culture 1756–1830*. Oxford: Oxford UP, 2006.

Garrett, Martin. 'Mitford, Mary Russell (1787–1855).' *Oxford Dictionary of National Biography*, Oxford UP, 2004. 6 Jan. 2010. <http://www.oxforddnb.com/view/article/18859>.

The General Contents of the British Museum: With Remarks Serving as a Directory in Viewing that Noble Cabinet. 2nd ed. London: R. and J. Dodsley, 1762.

Gough, Barry. *First across the Continent: Sir Alexander Mackenzie*. Norman: U of Oklahoma P, 1997.

Grace, Sherrill E. *Canada and the Idea of North*. Montreal: McGill-Queen's UP, 2001.

Greenfield, Bruce. *Narrating Discovery: The Romantic Explorer in American Literature*. New York: Columbia UP, 1992.

———. 'The Rhetoric of British and American Narratives of Exploration.' *Dalhousie Review* 65.1 (1986): 56–65.

Gundy, H. Pearson. 'Literary Publishing.' *Literary History of Canada: Canadian Literature in English*. 2nd ed. Vol. 1. Toronto and Buffalo: U of Toronto P, 1976. 188–202.

Heilman, Robert Bechtold. *America in English Fiction 1760–1800: The Influence of the American Revolution*. Baton Rouge: Louisiana State UP, 1937.

Henderson, T. F. 'Thomas Ashe (1770–1835).' Rev. Rebecca Mills. *Oxford Dictionary of National Biography*. Oxford UP, 2004. 23 Sept. 2009. <http://www.oxforddnb.com/view/article/753>.

Herrick, Francis H. 'Thomas Ashe and the Authenticity of his Travels in America.' *Mississippi Valley Historical Review* 13.1 (1926): 50–57.

Hickey, Donald R. *The War of 1812: A Forgotten Conflict*. Urbana: U of Illinois P, 1989.

Higgins, David. *Romantic Genius and the Literary Magazine: Biography, Celebrity, Politics*. London: Routledge, 2005.

Holmes, Richard. Introduction. *A Short Residence in Sweden, Norway and Denmark*. By Mary Wollstonecraft. 1796. Harmondsworth: Penguin, 1987.

Hopwood, Victor G. 'Explorers by Land to 1867.' *Literary History of Canada: Canadian Literature in English*. 2nd ed. Vol. 1. Toronto: U of Toronto P, 1976. 19–53.

———. 'Explorers by Sea: The West Coast.' *Literary History of Canada: Canadian Literature in English*. 2nd ed. Vol. 1. Toronto: U of Toronto P, 1976. 54–65.

Horn, James. 'British Diaspora: Emigration from Britain, 1680–1815.' *The Oxford History of the British Empire, Vol. 2: The Eighteenth Century*. Oxford: Oxford UP, 1998. 28–52.

Houghton, Walter E., ed. *Wellesley Index to Victorian Periodicals 1824–1900*. Vol. 1. Toronto: Toronto UP, 1966.

Hutchings, Kevin. 'Writing Commerce and Cultural Progress in Samuel Hearne's *A Journey ... to the Northern Ocean*.' *Ariel* 28.2 (1997): 49–78.

Innis, Harold A. *The Fur Trade in Canada*. 1930. Rev. ed. Toronto: U of Toronto P, 1956.

Iser, Wolfgang. *The Act of Reading: A Theory of Aesthetic Response*. London: Routledge & Kegan Paul, 1978.

Jackson, Donald, ed. *Letters of the Lewis and Clark Expedition, with Related Documents, 1783–1854*. Urbana: U of Illinois P, 1962.

Jackson, Heather. *Romantic Readers: The Evidence of Marginalia*. New Haven: Yale UP, 2005.

Jarvis, Robin. 'Contesting the "Secret Grudge": The Image of America in the *Edinburgh Review*, 1803–1829.' *Symbiosis* 13.1 (2009): 45–60.

———. 'Curious Fame: The Literary Relevance of Alexander Mackenzie Reconsidered.' *Canadian Literature* 193 (Summer 2007): 54–73.

Jauss, Hans Robert. *Question and Answer: Forms of Dialogic Understanding*. Ed. and trans. Michael Hays. Minneapolis: U of Minnesota P, 1989.

———. *Towards an Aesthetic of Reception*. Trans. Timothy Bahti. Brighton: Harvester, 1982.

Johnson, Paul. *The Birth of the Modern: World Society 1815–1830*. New York: HarperCollins, 1991.

Johnston, H. J. M. *British Emigration Policy 1815–1830: 'Shovelling out Paupers.'* Oxford: Clarendon P, 1972.

Jones, Howard Mumford. *The Harp that Once – . A Chronicle of the Life of Thomas Moore*. New York: Henry Holt, 1937.

Jones, Maldwyn Allen. *American Immigration*. 2nd ed. Chicago: U of Chicago P, 1992.

Kaufman, Paul. 'Glimpses of Reading in Some West Country Book Clubs.' *Libraries and their Users: Collected Papers in Library History*. London: Library Association, 1969. 65–75.

———. 'Some Reading Trends in Bristol 1773–84.' *Libraries and their Users: Collected Papers in Library History*. London: Library Association, 1969. 28–35.

King, J. C. H. 'North American Ethnography in the Collection of Sir Hans Sloane.' *The Origins of Museums: The Cabinet of Curiosities in Sixteenth-*

and Seventeenth-Century Europe. Ed. Oliver Impey and Arthur MacGregor. Oxford: Clarendon P, 1985. 232–6.

Klancher, Jon. *The Making of English Reading Audiences, 1790–1832.* Madison: U of Wisconsin P, 1987.

Korte, Barbara. *English Travel Writing from Pilgrimages to Postcolonial Explorations.* Trans. Catherine Matthias. Basingstoke: Palgrave, 2000.

Lamb, W. Kaye. Introduction. *The Journals and Letters of Alexander Mackenzie.* Cambridge: Cambridge UP, 1970. 1–53.

Leask, Nigel. *Curiosity and the Aesthetics of Travel Writing, 1770–1840.* Oxford: Oxford UP, 2002.

———. 'Southey's *Madoc*: Reimagining the Conquest of America.' *Robert Southey and the Contexts of English Romanticism.* Ed. Lynda Pratt. Aldershot: Ashgate, 2006. 133–50.

Leed, Eric J. *The Mind of the Traveler: From Gilgamesh to Global Tourism.* New York: Basic Books, 1991.

Lowes, John Livingston. *The Road to Xanadu: A Study in the Ways of the Imagination.* 1927. London: Picador-Pan, 1978.

Machor, James L. 'Introduction: Readers/Texts/Contexts.' *Readers in History: Nineteenth-Century American Literature and the Contexts of Response.* Ed. James L. Machor. Baltimore: Johns Hopkins UP, 1993. vii–xxix.

MacLaren, I. S. 'Exploration/Travel Literature and the Evolution of the Author.' *International Journal of Canadian Studies* 5 (Spring 1992): 39–68.

———. 'Notes on Samuel Hearne's *Journey* from a Bibliographical Perspective.' *Papers of the Bibliographical Society of Canada* 31.2 (1993): 21–45.

———. 'Samuel Hearne's Accounts of the Massacre at Bloody Fall, 17 July 1771.' *Ariel* 22.1 (1991): 25–51.

MacLulich, T. D. 'The Explorer as Hero: Mackenzie and Fraser.' *Canadian Literature* 75 (1978): 61–73.

Marshall, Peter. 'British North America, 1760–1815.' *The Oxford History of the British Empire, Vol. 2: The Eighteenth Century.* Oxford: Oxford UP, 1998. 372–93.

Mazzeo, Tilar J. 'The Impossibility of Being Anglo-American: The Rhetoric of Emigration and Transatlanticism in British Romantic Culture, 1791–1833.' *European Romantic Review* 16.1 (2005): 59–78.

McGann, Jerome. *The Textual Condition.* Princeton: Princeton UP, 1991.

McGrath, Robin. 'Samuel Hearne and the Inuit Oral Tradition.' *Studies in Canadian Literature* 18.2 (1993): 94–109.

McKendrick, Neil. 'The Commercialization of Fashion.' *The Birth of a Consumer Society: The Commercialization of Eighteenth-Century England.* Ed. Neil McKendrick, John Brewer, and J. H. Plumb. London: Hutchinson, 1983. 34–99.

McKenzie, D. F. 'The Book as an Expressive Form.' *The Book History Reader.* Ed. David Finkelstein and Alistair McCleery. London: Routledge, 2002. 27–38.

Mears, Ray. *Northern Wilderness.* London: Hodder & Stoughton, 2009.

Meek, Ronald L. *Social Science and the Ignoble Savage.* Cambridge: Cambridge UP, 1976.

Mesick, Jane Louise. *The English Traveller in America, 1785–1835*. New York: Columbia UP, 1922.

Miller, Edward. *That Noble Cabinet: A History of the British Museum*. London: Andre Deutsch, 1973.

Moss, Carolyn J. 'Wordsworth's Marginalia in John Davis's *Travels ... in the United States.*' *Papers of the Bibliographical Society of America* 79.4 (1985): 539–41.

Nevins, Allan, and Henry Steele Commager. *America: The Story of a Free People*. 4ᵗʰ ed. London: Oxford UP, 1976.

Newman, Lance, Joel Pace, and Chris Koenig-Woodyard, eds. *Transatlantic Romanticism*. New York: Pearson, 2006.

Pace, Joel. 'Towards a Taxonomy of Transatlantic Romanticism(s).' *Literature Compass* 5.2 (2008): 228–91.

Parker, Mark. *Literary Magazines and British Romanticism*. Cambridge: Cambridge UP, 2000.

Pearson, Jacqueline. *Women's Reading in Britain 1750–1835: A Dangerous Recreation*. Cambridge: Cambridge UP, 1999.

Pottinger, George. *Heirs of the Enlightenment: Edinburgh Reviewers and Writers 1800–1830*. Edinburgh: Scottish Academic P, 1992.

Pratt, Lynda. 'Revising the National Epic: Coleridge, Southey and *Madoc.*' *Romanticism* 2.2 (1996): 149–64.

Pratt, Mary Louise. *Imperial Eyes: Travel Writing and Transculturation*. London: Routledge, 1992.

Raven, James, Helen Small, and Naomi Tadmor. 'Introduction: The Practice and Representation of Reading in England.' *The Practice and Representation of Reading in England*. Ed. James Raven, Helen Small, and Naomi Tadmor. Cambridge: Cambridge UP, 1996. 1–21.

The Reading Experience Database. The Open University. <http://www.open. ac.uk/Arts/RED/>.

Richardson, David. 'The British Empire and the Atlantic Slave Trade, 1660–1807.' *The Oxford History of the British Empire, Vol. 2: The Eighteenth Century*. Oxford: Oxford UP, 1998. 440–464.

Richter, Daniel K. 'Native Peoples of North America and the Eighteenth-Century British Empire.' *The Oxford History of the British Empire, Vol. 2: The Eighteenth Century*. Oxford: Oxford UP, 1998. 347–71.

Robertson, Fiona. 'Keats's New World: An Emigrant Poetry.' *Keats: Bicentenary Readings*. Ed. Michael O'Neill. Edinburgh: Edinburgh UP, 1997. 27–47.

Rodgers, Betsy. *Georgian Chronicle: Mrs Barbauld and her Family*. London: Methuen, 1958.

Rogers, Shef. 'Enlarging the Prospects of Happiness: Travel Reading and Travel Writing.' *The Cambridge History of the Book in Britain. Vol. 5: 1695–1830*. Ed. Michael F. Suarez, s.j., and Michael L. Turner. Cambridge: Cambridge UP, 2009. 781–90.

Roper, Derek. *Reviewing before the* Edinburgh*, 1788–1802*. London: Methuen, 1978.

Rose, Jonathan. 'How Historians Study Reader Response: Or, What did Jo Think of *Bleak House*?' *Literature in the Marketplace: Nineteenth-Century British Publishing and Reading Practices*. Ed. John O. Jordan and Robert L. Patten. Cambridge: Cambridge UP, 1995. 195–212.

———. *The Intellectual Life of the British Working Classes*. New Haven: Yale UP, 2001.

Ross, M. J. *Polar Pioneers: John Ross and James Clark Ross*. Montreal: McGill-Queen's UP, 1994.

Said, Edward. *Orientalism*. London: Routledge & Kegan Paul, 1978.

Sayre, Gordon. 'The Beaver as Native and Colonist.' *Canadian Review of Comparative Literature* 22.3–4 (1995): 659–82.

Schama, Simon. *Landscape and Memory*. London: HarperCollins, 1995.

Schoenfeld, Mark. *British Periodicals and Romantic Identity: The 'Literary Lower Empire.'* Basingstoke: Palgrave Macmillan, 2009.

Scholes, Robert. *Protocols of Reading*. New Haven: Yale UP, 1989.

Smith, James K. *Alexander Mackenzie, Explorer: The Hero Who Failed*. Toronto: McGraw-Hill Ryerson, 1973.

Speck, W. A. 'Robert Southey's Contribution to the *Quarterly Review.*' *Conservatism and the* Quarterly Review*: A Critical Analysis*. Ed. Jonathan Cutmore. London: Pickering and Chatto, 2007. 165–77.

St Clair, William. *The Reading Nation in the Romantic Period*. Cambridge: Cambridge UP, 2004.

Stewart, David. *Romantic Magazines and Metropolitan Literary Culture*. Basingstoke: Palgrave Macmillan, 2011.

Sullivan, Alvin. *British Literary Magazines: The Romantic Age, 1789–1836*. Westport: Greenwood P, 1983.

Sweet, Nanora. 'Hemans, Felicia Dorothea (1793–1835).' *Oxford Dictionary of National Biography*. Oxford UP, 2004. Accessed 13 July 2010. <http://www.oxforddnb.com/view/article/12888>.

Temperley, Howard. *Britain and America since Independence*. Basingstoke: Palgrave, 2002.

Todorov, Tzvetan. 'The Journey and its Narratives.' Trans. Alyson Waters. *Transports: Travel, Pleasure, and Imaginative Geography, 1600–1830*. Ed. Chloe Chard and Helen Langdon. New Haven: Yale UP, 1996. 287–96.

Tompkins, Jane, ed. *Reader-Response Criticism: From Formalism to Post-Structuralism*. Baltimore: Johns Hopkins UP, 1980.

Towner, John. *An Historical Geography of Recreation and Tourism in the Western World 1540–1940*. Chichester: John Wiley, 1996.

Vail, Jeffery. 'Thomas Moore in Ireland and America: The Growth of a Poet's Mind.' *Romanticism* 10.1 (2004): 41–62.

Verhoeven, W. M. 'Land-jobbing in the Western Territories: Radicalism, Transatlantic Emigration, and the 1790s American Travel Narrative.' *Romantic Geographies: Discourses of Travel 1775–1844*. Manchester: Manchester UP, 2000. 185–203.

Vincent, David. *Literacy and Popular Culture: England 1750–1914*. Cambridge: Cambridge UP, 1989.

———. *The Rise of Mass Literacy: Reading and Writing in Modern Europe*. Cambridge: Polity, 2000.

Whalley, George. 'The Bristol Library Borrowings of Southey and Coleridge, 1793-8.' *The Library* 4 (1949): 114-32.

Wheatley, Kim. 'The Arctic in the *Quarterly Review*.' *European Romantic Review* 20.4 (2009): 465–90.

———. 'Plotting the Success of the *Quarterly Review*.' *Conservatism and the Quarterly Review: A Critical Analysis*. Ed. Jonathan Cutmore. London: Pickering and Chatto, 2007. 19–39.

———, ed. *Romantic Periodicals and Print Culture*. London: Frank Cass, 2003.

Wiley, Michael. *Romantic Migrations: Local, National, and Transnational Dispositions*. Basingstoke: Palgrave Macmillan, 2008.

Williams, Glyndwr. 'The Pacific: Exploration and Exploitation.' *The Oxford History of the British Empire, Vol. 2: The Eighteenth Century*. Oxford: Oxford UP, 1998. 552–75.

Wind, Astrid. '"Adieu to all": The Death of the American Indian at the Turn of the Eighteenth Century.' *Symbiosis* 2.1 (1998): 39–55.

Wittmann. Reinhard. 'Was There a Reading Revolution at the End of the Eighteenth Century?' *A History of Reading in the West*. Ed. Guglielmo Cavallo and Roger Chartier. Trans. Lydia G. Cochrane. Cambridge: Polity, 1999. 284–312.

Wolf, Eric R. *Europe and the People without History*. Berkeley: U of California P, 1982.

Wu, Duncan. *Wordsworth's Reading 1770–1799*. Cambridge: Cambridge UP, 1993.

———. *Wordsworth's Reading 1800–1815*. Cambridge: Cambridge UP, 1995.

Index